Interpreting Ely Cathedral

INTERPRETING ELY CATHEDRAL

LYNNE BROUGHTON

Ely Cathedral Publications

This book is dedicated to Dorothy Denyer,
Mother-in-Law *extraordinaire*

Published in the United Kingdom by Ely Cathedral Publications

© Lynne Broughton 2008, 2011

First published 2008
Reprinted with corrections 2011

Designed and typeset by Peter Ducker MISTD
Printed in United Kingdom by Decent Print

A catalogue record for this book is available from the British Library

ISBN 978-1-873027-11-0 paperback

The author and publisher gratefully acknowledge the financial support of
the Friends of Ely Cathedral towards the cost of publication.

Contents

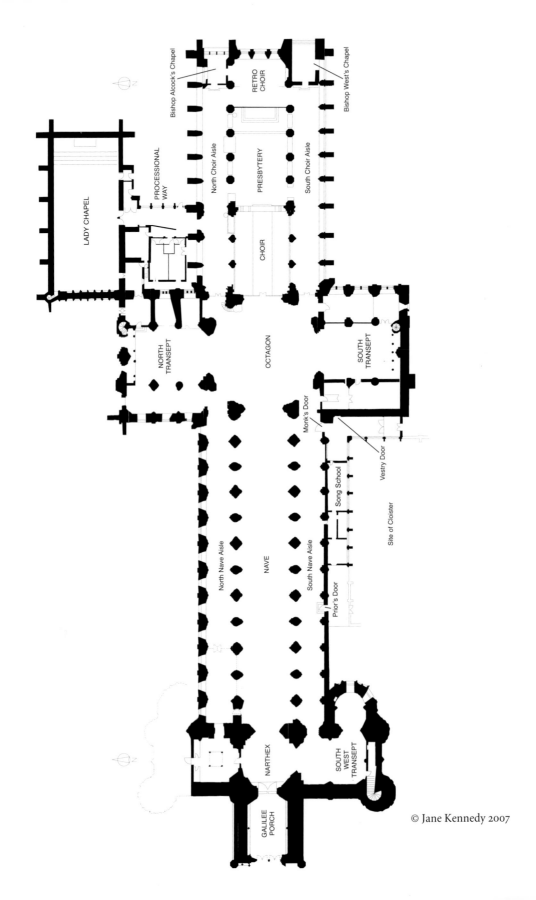

LADY CHAPEL

PROCESSIONAL WAY

Bishop Alcock's Chapel

RETRO CHOIR

North Choir Aisle

PRESBYTERY

South Choir Aisle

Bishop West's Chapel

CHOIR

NORTH TRANSEPT

OCTAGON

SOUTH TRANSEPT

Monk's Door

Vestry Door

Song School

Site of Cloister

North Nave Aisle

NAVE

South Nave Aisle

Prior's Door

NARTHEX

SOUTH WEST TRANSEPT

GALILEE PORCH

© Jane Kennedy 2007

Foreword

The depth of meaning and attractive power of one of the world's great cathedrals pose a massive challenge to the interpreter. Dr Broughton meets it brilliantly, imaginatively and with authority. Even her outstanding work on Lincoln Cathedral is surpassed by this vivid account of Ely. She not only has the necessary breadth of learning in architecture, scripture, worship, theology, history, art, music and literature; she also has that far rarer quality of sensitive spiritual wisdom. Leading us through Ely Cathedral she shows in detail how it unites beauty, meaning and history, and she brings readers into the heart of its open secret, the Christian faith that continues to energise it. She succeeds in drawing us into her own appreciation of this amazing building and of the people who have shaped it, worshipped in it and been part of its history. This is likely to be the classic portrayal of Ely for many years to come and is a model for what other cathedrals need.

David F. Ford
Regius Professor of Divinity, University of Cambridge

Preface

An interpretation of Ely Cathedral requires the resources of more than one scholarly discipline. In this book I have ranged over theology, history, art history, literature and music. Since the cathedral was the mother church of the diocese and had a message for everyone, I have attempted to write compactly for a wide audience. This has meant avoiding technical terms as far as possible and explaining arguments and evidence as simply as could be done without falsifying either. At the same time I have tried to base the argument on sound scholarship, using interpretations already available in print; in some cases my interpretation has differed from those of other scholars. I have also provided my own interpretations of some of the imagery, for instance of the Choirstalls and the Lady Chapel. References and arguments are provided in endnotes.

Non-expert readers who would like to know more about particular topics raised in this book can find pointers to further reading in the Notes and the Bibliography. A Glossary has also been provided as an aid to understanding the few necessary technical terms. One technical point needs to be dealt with here. Some words, such as 'church' and 'octagon', have dual meanings. I have followed the standard convention of distinguishing these meanings by the use of capitals or lower case initial letters. Thus church refers to the building and Church to the institution and/or its members; octagon refers to the shape and Octagon to the part of the cathedral which has this shape; choir refers to the group of singers, Choir to that area of the cathedral in which they generally sing.

This book aims to be complementary to the three other major books that have been recently published by the Cathedral Chapter: Dr John Maddison's account of the architectural history of the building[1]; the volume of essays on the history of the cathedral[2]; and the translation of the *Liber Eliensis* by Dr Janet Fairweather[3].

The approach taken in this book is synthetic and integrative. I have followed themes through the medieval centuries and, in some cases, up to the

opposite: Woodwose (wild man) guarding the 'Porta' gate

ix

present. The advantage of such an approach is that it demonstrates how the major beliefs and practices of Christianity have, although subject to change in their modes of expression, formed the basis of the cathedral's message from the time when it was first built to the present. The disadvantage is that it smooths away great differences over time. The twelfth century cathedral looked very different from that of the late fourteenth century; a late-fifteenth-century person transposed into the eighteenth-century cathedral would have had difficulty in recognising the building, let alone have been able to appreciate that the Communion service was similar to the Mass that he or she knew. Both the continuities and the discontinuities need to be acknowledged. But I have found, in talking even to those who have known and loved the cathedral for years, that the building and its decorations are generally perceived in discrete portions rather than as a whole: the nave and transepts are twelfth-century, the Octagon and Lady Chapel are fourteenth-century and the various modern sculptures may, or may not, be approved. What is lacking is a sense that, and how, it all fits together. This book is an attempt to show the integrity of the building and its message.

The structure of this book follows a route which might be taken by the visitor. First around the exterior, then to the West Front and entrance. Moving within, it halts in the narthex (vestibule) before traversing nave, transepts, Octagon, Choir and shrine area, then moves into the Lady Chapel. After this it steps outside again to consider the monastery and the entrances from the cloister to the cathedral. The tour is completed back inside, with a look at some of the monuments and the multitude of creatures carved in various places around the interior.

I share the Christian beliefs of those who, over the centuries have built and maintained this cathedral, and in it expressed their beliefs. And this no doubt made it easier for me to grasp what the cathedral means. But even those who do not share those beliefs might still find things of interest here. For on anybody's account the cathedral is extraordinarily impressive, and anybody might therefore wish to know what the building is intended to mean and what is therefore the explanation.

There is a fashion for discussing church art and architecture from an entirely secular modern viewpoint, using sociological and anthropological insights to gain a different perspective on the subject. This is supposed to be more 'objective' than a Christian approach. The secular ways of looking at churches have provided interesting sidelights on the multiplicity of motivations for the production of these structures. But they do only provide a view of incidentals. It is not more objective to research church buildings making entirely secular, materialistic assumptions than it is to approach them with an insider's understanding of the life of Christian worship, theology and spirituality. The latter was, after all, the explicit, central purpose for which they were built. Those who commissioned and paid for churches were steeped in the Bible and understood the art of building in biblical terms. Moreover, these are buildings whose function was to facilitate the various prayer services of the Church; it is impossible to appreciate them fully without an insight into, and respect for, this function.

I cannot hope to have entirely succeeded in such a complex task, given the dangers of oversimplification and overstatement in a wide-ranging but brief study, together with inevitable gaps in my knowledge and possible errors in understanding. Nevertheless I hope that it contains matter of interest to scholars and clergy, as well as enhancing the enjoyment of visitors to the cathedral.

Gargoyle on the cloister wall (probably re-set from elsewhere)

Acknowledgements

My foremost thanks must go to the cathedral itself. My ordination as deacon and later as priest took place here. Implicit in the chapter on the Octagon is something of the inner significance of these events in such a context.

The cathedral Chapter have graciously agreed to publish this book and have enthusiastically encouraged it. My thanks go particularly to Bishop John Inge and to the Vice-Dean, the Revd. Dr Peter Sills. The Friends of Ely Cathedral have most generously agreed to pay for publication costs.

Early drafts of the text were facilitated by a two week scholarship at St Deiniol's Library. For this I am grateful to the Warden Peter Francis. The librarians Patsy Williams and Sarah Moffat, and the administrator, Gregory Morris, very kindly helped me find elusive references.

Especial thanks are due to those who made time to read and comment on part or all of the manuscript: Christopher and Mary Barber, Pamela Blakeman, Christopher Brooke, Janet Fairweather, David Ford, Anna-Lisa Garvie, Robert Gribben, Susan Hilken, Clive Hillman, John Maddison, Louise Pirouet, Richard Rex, David Stazicker, Pamela Tudor-Craig.

As with any work of scholarship, I am greatly indebted to the various libraries in which I have worked and to the assistance provided by research staff. Mention must be made particularly of: the library and librarians of Trinity College Melbourne, The Baillieu Library in the University of Melbourne and Cambridge University Library. The British Library and the library of Trinity College Cambridge dealt efficiently and helpfully with my requests for illustrations from their manuscripts.

Sallyann Ford and Richard Clover of Ely cathedral staff kindly provided help in obtaining illustrations from the cathedral archives.

Margaret Bristan most generously sent copies of her translations of extracts from the Peterborough Consuetudinal and Pauline Thompson provided a copy of one of her articles on Etheldreda while pointing me toward another.

Philip Dixon and Jane Kennedy have allowed me to make use of their plans of, respectively, the monastery and the cathedral.

Credits for photographs are given in a separate list but I must register particular thanks to Philip Dixon, Richard Halsey, John Crook, Martin Fleet and Nigel Luckhurst for responding generously to, sometimes urgent, requests for particular shots.

Peter Ducker has coped patiently with my software-incompetence, has dealt uncomplainingly with numerous last-minute revisions and produced a magnificent design. It is largely due to his skill and generosity that this book has been completed and in such beautiful form.

My husband Nicholas Denyer has been a tower of strength: cook, translator of Latin texts, proof-reader, searcher-out of lost references, emender and stern critic of prose style. Without his help and support this book would not have been possible.

The book is dedicated to Dorothy Denyer with gratitude for her unwavering enthusiasm and encouragement.

Considering all the help I have been given by so many people, the book's faults must be entirely my own responsibility.

Note to the 2011 Reprint

I am most grateful to The Friends of the cathedral for covering the cost of a further print-run of my book. In it, I have taken the opportunity to correct some minor misprints. The major difference is in the Lady Chapel. In June 2011 the Bishop dedicated the new reredos and altar which had been designed by John Maddison and paid for by The Friends. These are shown in the replacement photograph on pages 134 and 151, kindly provided by John Hunting, who also provided the replacement photograph of the pulpit on page 76.

Photo credits

Nigel Luckhurst: 10, 11, 33, 54, 55, 56 top and bottom, 58, 67, 68, 69, 70 top, 73, 74 bottom, 76, 77, 84/3, 86 top, 87 top two, 88, 89 top two, 90, 91, 93, 100, 102, 103 top and bottom, 104 top, 123, 125, 127, 128, 130, 135 bottom, 137, 142, 143 top, 147, bottom, 179, 180, 181, 182, 184, 186, 187, 188, 189, 190, 192, 200, 202 top left, 203 middle, 204 top, 205 top, 207 top; **Martin Fleet:** 104 bottom, 105, 106, 107 top three, 108, 109, 110 bottom, 111, 170 top; **The late Ken Hitch:** 1, 4, 5, 6, 13, 14 top, 17 top, 28, 64, 86/2&4, 94, 101, 103 middle, 113, 120, 147 top, 151, 166 bottom, 197; **Philip Dixon:** 47, 49, 50, 65, 84/4, 107 bottom, 124 right, 194, 208; **Richard Halsey:** 163 top; **John Crook:** 2 right; © John Crook (www.john-crook.com); **The British Library:** 35 top; Harley MS 7026, f.13 © The British Library Board. All Rights Reserved; **Trinity College Library:** 20; The Trinity Apocalypse, R.16.2 f25b.68 © The Master and Fellows of Trinity College Cambridge. All Rights Reserved; **Stephen Byde and The Dean and Chapter of Canterbury cathedral:** 148; **The Dean and Chapter of Carlisle cathedral:** 83; **The Dean and Chapter of St Albans cathedral:** 115, 121 top; **Handbook:** 38, 79, 126; **Millers:** 165.

All other photographs were taken by the author.

Introduction

'Then one wintry evening I walked into the cathedral as they sang evensong. I was transported to a different plane. Footsore and tired, I was refreshed and restored in a way which I cannot adequately describe. This was the point at which I realized that Christianity is not just about fellowship here on earth but is about the transcendent and the breaking in of the eternal and infinite into our world...'[1]

SPIRITUAL tourism has a long and honourable history within Christianity. It began in the early days of persecution, when visits were made to the tombs of the martyrs on the anniversary of their death, their 'birthday into heaven'. It was given a boost by the Emperor Constantine's interest in the places where Jesus himself had walked, taught, died and risen again to life. Further destinations were added as newly converted peoples began to seek out the resting places of their own saintly heroes. By the late Middle Ages many thousands of people were taking to the roads to visit shrines, far and near, in search of spiritual or physical benefits. Undoubtedly many went along simply for the holiday or in a pretence of devotion. But there is ample evidence of griefs assuaged, ailments healed and lives transformed by what became known as pilgrimages. Ely is one of the places to which they came, and still come. This book is an attempt to show what draws people to this place and what the building signifies.

Ely cathedral has its own special character. No two cathedrals are the same, though they have much in common. All medieval churches are both functional

above: the cathedral from the river

left: Nave interior looking east

1

and symbolic. They were designed to provide an appropriate setting for communal worship, for all those services which make up the Christian Liturgy. They were also intended, by their shape and decoration, to teach and to inspire. Every medieval church was designed as an image of the Heavenly Jerusalem; yet each one portrays this in its own distinct way, for heaven is a place of infinite variety. This book sets out to explain the way in which Ely cathedral inspires with its own portrayal of heaven.

The Norman church and associated monastery was built to honour a group of local saints, and one in particular – St Etheldreda.[2] Daughter of Anna, king of the East Angles, she was married twice; first to Tondbert and then on his death, about 655, to Egfrith, king of Northumbria. Both marriages were unconsummated. After twelve years she left Egfrith to become a nun in the community at Coldingham. She then moved to Ely where she founded a double monastery of men and women. She died in 679 and was succeeded as abbess by her sister Sexburga[3] and then by the latter's daughter Eormenhild. Another sister, Withburga,[4] presided over a monastery at East Dereham in Norfolk where a holy well still marks the site of her burial.[5]

below left: the north transept

Etheldreda's monastery was overrun in 870 by Danish invaders who killed most of the monks and nuns and destroyed their buildings. Although a few survived and returned, we know little more of the community until it was refounded as a Benedictine monastery for men, probably in 970. Its first abbot, Byrhtnoth, brought the relics of St Withburga from Dereham, so that Ely was provided with four female saints from the same family.

below right: Winchester Cathedral, north transept

Nothing survives of the pre-Conquest buildings; the Normans rebuilt the entire complex. What is particularly characteristic of the present cathedral is due largely to two periods of intense creative activity – the Norman work of the early twelfth- and the Gothic of the early- to mid-fourteenth centuries. In addition to these, the east and west ends of the cathedral were altered in the thirteenth century.

The Norman abbey church was begun in the late eleventh century by Abbot Simeon from Winchester. The ends of the transepts show clear influence from the design of the Norman work at Winchester. The enormous size of the nave may well have been due to Abbot Richard, Abbot Simeon's successor, whose ambition it was to convert the abbey into a cathedral. He did not live to see the fulfilment of that ambition, but the abbey was given cathedral status in 1109 in the time of Abbot/Bishop Hervey. Since the nave is largely the place for the laity, such a huge structure seems hardly appropriate for the church of a monastery in a very small town. But the Normans introduced from the Continent the practice of requiring every parish in the diocese to send representatives in procession to the cathedral on the feast of Pentecost.[6] A great deal of space was needed for these gatherings, as it still is for special occasions such as ordinations

The Norman nave arcade

and Christmas services. Visitors to the cathedral on a quiet winter weekday find it hard to credit that sometimes this enormous building can be full to overflowing. Space in the nave was also needed for other processions. As we shall see (Ch. 2) the Palm Sunday procession was a complex and splendid part of the cathedral's ritual. Large numbers of visitors would also be expected for the feasts of local saints – in this place, most especially, St Etheldreda and her sisters.

The other great period of creative work at Ely was the fourteenth century. In response to the disastrous fall of the Norman central tower in 1322, the crossing and Choir of the cathedral were transformed. In other great churches where a Norman tower had collapsed, it was usually rebuilt on its Norman foundations, but in the latest style. Here the central space was opened out into a huge, luminous octagon. At the time of the disaster, foundations had already been laid for a large Lady Chapel, situated just to

The fourteenth-century Octagon interior

the north of the Choir. This also was brought to completion in an exquisitely elaborate form. This large and complex building programme was undertaken by a remarkable group of men: the bishop, John Hotham; the prior John Crauden; the sacrist Alan of Walsingham; a master mason by the name of John (probably John de Ramsey) and the master carpenter William Hurley.

The thirteenth century Early English gothic style can be seen at both ends of the building. The large 'Galilee' porch, abutting the west front, was added at that time. And at the east end the Norman church was rebuilt in extended form to provide a more spacious and fitting setting for the shrines of Etheldreda and her sisters. The latter, and perhaps also the former, are closely associated with the bishop at the time – Hugh de Northwold.

Succeeding centuries have both added to and subtracted from the work of these major periods. Two exquisite chapels were built at the east end of the cathedral in the later Middle Ages.

Most of the medieval imagery and some of the furnishings were destroyed in the sixteenth and seventeenth centuries; more of the medieval furnishings disappeared in the eighteenth-century re-ordering of the Choir and presbytery.[7] Many fine furnishings were added as part of a nineteenth-century restoration programme. More recently the passage leading from the Choir to the Lady Chapel has been rebuilt, and new imagery has been commissioned and placed in various parts of the building.

MEDIEVAL churches were consciously and deliberately imbued with meaning; with complex, inter-related layers of Christian meanings. This was evident to the educated and was explained to the uneducated. But over the intervening centuries these meanings were eschewed or simply forgotten. All that has been left is a sense of spiritual atmosphere, more evident to some people than to others.

The service in which a church was consecrated to use for the worship of God made explicit the significance of the building. It was acknowledged that God, who cannot be contained in any work of human hands, might nevertheless deign to be present here as in the Old Testament Temple in the earthly Jerusalem.[8] From the Book of Revelation was read St John's vision of the Holy City, in all its shining beauty, coming down from heaven.[9] A treatise which was much copied and highly influential in the later Middle Ages recommended meditating, pondering on, contemplating the Heavenly Jerusalem:

> Chosen city of God, built by the hand of the eternal builder: who could estimate, who could detail the beauty of the decorations of your wonderful construction?... The Lamb of God is your light... He, the King of Kings, is in your midst and his servants are around him. There are the hymn-singing choirs of holy spirits, the far-sighted company of prophets, the apostles passing judgment, the countless and victorious army of martyrs... Blessed is

Bishop Hugh de Northwold's thirteenth-century east end (l) and the fourteenth-century Lady Chapel (r)

The cathedral as a distant glimpse of the heavenly city

my soul, if it is given me to gaze on the abundance of your power and glory, the beautiful walls, the wonderful gates, the streets paved with decorative marble... and your king, our God, on the glorious throne of his majesty.[10]

This is based on biblical descriptions, especially that in the Book of Revelation. It is an incitement to think frequently about the heavenly Jerusalem in order to live a life that is fit for heaven. Modern spiritual writers have also recommended meditation on the heavenly Temple as an aid to prayer.[11] But the medieval description, as we shall see, also fits closely the details of this cathedral, and especially the interior of the Octagon.

The true, spiritual, heaven is difficult to contemplate. As material creatures, women and men need the aid of physical things – sight, sound and movement – to help in the task. All of these are provided by this building. Walking around and through it, one has an experience of following a pilgrimage route around and through the cross of Christ. Along the way are visual aids in the form of attention-catching imagery, together with the auditory aids of music and speech. This building is not, cannot be, heaven itself. But it represents heaven and is designed to help the attentive visitor across the threshold into an experience of spiritual contemplation.

What we call holy in the world – a person, a place, a set of words or pictures – is so because it is a transitional place, a borderland, where the completely foreign is brought together with the familiar. Here is somewhere that looks as if it belongs within the world we are at home in, but in fact it leads directly into strangeness.[12]

In a complex interweaving of significances, the church building is both heaven, and the soul of each person being built up into citizenship in heaven. Every Christian is, in the words of St Paul, a 'living stone'. The late medieval Church made much use of this metaphor in teaching people how to lead a good life so that, at the last, they might themselves be built into the very fabric of the heavenly city. *The Golden Legend*, an explication of the festivals of the Church's year and one of the most famous books of the Middle Ages, completes its description of the ceremony of dedication of a church by pointing out the spiritual meaning of that ceremony: 'Now at last we speak of the consecration or dedication of the spiritual temple, which is ourselves, namely the congregation of all the faithful, built up of living and polished stones.'[13] In St John's vision that city is adorned with gems and many-coloured marbles. These were emulated by the use of stained glass, polychrome painting and vari-coloured stones in walls and floors. Such implicit symbolism was complemented by explicit imagery – of Christ and his mother; of saints and angels; of stories from the Bible; of innumerable creatures great and small which are part of the natural world created by God.

The view into the Octagon from the nave

> 'The greatest accomplishment of medieval art is the comprehensiveness of its image systems. The Gothic cathedral, covered inside and out with a myriad of sculpted, painted and translucent images, conveyed a sense that there was a place for everything, that there was a complete world order... Human history from Creation to the Last Day, human labor from January to December, and cycles of nature from leaf to fruit and from mouse to monster, were all included.'[14]

Romanesque and gothic Ely has lost much of its medieval imagery and most of its colouring. But enough remains for us still to experience something of the intended impact. Moreover, since the cathedral continues in use for its original purpose, new imagery is being added. It, too, illustrates aspects of the Christian message.

Church iconography always points beyond itself to the spiritual world which cannot be directly imaged. So it is that the imagery is allusive, complex, and also deliberately attractive. Beauty of form and material was used in order to help the viewer transcend its materiality. 'Not everything has a name; some things lead us into a real beyond words. Art thaws even the frozen, darkened soul, opening it to lofty spiritual experiences. Through art we are sometimes sent indistinctly, briefly, revelations not to be achieved by rational thought.'[15]

It has taken much research by art historians and other scholars, to regain such insights into the significance of medieval churches and their decorations. Scholarly interpretation is based on evidence of various kinds. There are early Christian and medieval sermons, biblical commentaries and theological treatises, of which the most influential from the thirteenth century onwards was St Thomas Aquinas's *Summa Theologiae*. There are lyrics and poems, the greatest of which is Dante's *Divine Comedy*. Aquinas's summation of Christian theology included sections on the use and importance of church buildings and imagery. Dante presents in superb poetry the orthodox view of the Christian faith and is unequalled in his movingly imaginative portrayal of heaven. His work was known to, and read by, Chaucer. It was probably quite widely known among educated people in later medieval England.[16] By the fourteenth century there were many manuscript collections containing selections or popularised versions of the works of the great theologians. These became progressively more widely available throughout that and the succeeding century.[17]

Numerology, the symbolic use of numbers, is another of the means by which buildings gained significance. Recent scholarship has shown how medieval number theory worked and how highly regarded it was.[18] Its symbolism is known to underlie architectural proportions and shapes. Numerology was so embedded in the way of thinking that the writer of the *Liber Eliensis* found it natural to praise the local saints in a 'fantasy-impromptu'[19] on the number four. This likened them to, among other things, the four Evangelists (see Chapter 3, pp. 49–50), the four corners of the Earth, the four rivers of Paradise, the four Gospels and the four Cardinal Virtues.[20] So important was numerology that some composers of polyphonic music deliberately used the architectural proportions of churches for works which were to be performed in them. The deep consonance thus obtained between building, liturgy and music was not merely esoteric. It enabled all involved, whether explicitly aware of it or not, to experience more profoundly the ordered unity of all God's creation. This may or may not have been done at Ely, but local texts use such musical concepts as analogies. For instance, the *Liber Eliensis* refers to the *organum* (polyphony) of the prophets[21] to illustrate the way in which seemingly disparate themes in the prophetic writings of the Old Testament weave together into one message.

Studies of medieval memory training and meditative techniques make it clear that marginal images and grotesques were far from being mere doodles but added their own significance to books and buildings.[22] Such images could be, and were, used as part of the on-going project of explaining and then deepening the faith of the beholder.

But above all, the liturgy forms the basic evidence for how the building and its imagery were understood. The service of consecration of a church was considered above. Much more is to be found in the daily Mass and Offices. These, repeated in a continous yearly cycle, include most of the Bible. The Psalms were chanted in their entirety every week[23] – most clerics knew them by heart. In addition to this, the night Office of Matins included readings from the great early theologians, of the second through the sixth centuries. Prominent are those known as the 'Four Latin Doctors', so-called because they were the most profound and influential thinkers in the western, Latin-speaking, part of the Church: Sts Jerome, Ambrose, Augustine of Hippo, Gregory the Great. Many of the readings in the night office contain material which can illuminate our approach to the church building and its imagery. In this attempt at understanding, one needs to take the same approach as the early commentators did to the Bible text. St Augustine was in the habit of saying when about to preach on the Gospel passage which had just been read aloud: 'We have just heard the fact; now let us search for the mystery that lies hidden behind it.'

It is often said by Christians nowadays, in deprecation of any concern for historic church buildings, that the Church is people, not buildings. Like most clichés, this is misleading. Certainly the Church is people. It is the community of all the followers of Christ; indeed, it is his body in the world. But indi-vidual communities of Christians in particular places have, from the very early days of the faith, needed special buildings in which to join together as the body of Christ. As we have seen, the personal, spiritual, meaning of the church building was drawn out by commentators so that each individual might truly experience his or her own place as a spiritual stone, built into the Church, which is the body of Christ. These buildings have been decorated with imagery which reminds worshippers of the meaning of what they are doing, and also inspires them to follow more closely the God in whom they trust. 'Minimally, images instruct; maximally, they are capable

both: marginal grotesques in the Lady Chapel

The Nativity of Christ – nineteenth-century nave ceiling painting

of translating the worshipper to ecstatic states of contemplation, and the maximum was not beyond the reach of the humblest worshipper.'[24] Buildings have a permanence which itself witnesses to the faith across the ages. People die, but the church remains as a reminder to future generations that God has been worshipped in this place for centuries. 'They built in stone, …from a sense of the future: stone would last and when all the men had gone the stones would pray.'[25]

In my book on Lincoln cathedral[26] I concentrated mainly on the medieval work, and here also it is the medieval work that is most important and most rewards interpretation. But at Ely the medieval imagery in many parts of the building has been so defaced and the nineteenth century replacements are so much in evidence that I have paid considerable attention to the latter, especially in those aspects in which great care was taken to emulate medieval styles and imagery. Further imagery has been added more recently to enrich the building's message, and this also is considered in the light of the continuing use of the building for its original purpose – prayer and the worship of God.

'Look then upon this Cathedral Church... imagined by men's minds, built by the labour of men's hands, working with power upon the souls of men... the visible Temple of God.'[27]

View through the screen towards the High Altar

CHAPTER 1

Exterior

Walk about Sion... Consider well her bulwarks

'From whatever direction you go to Ely, you see the cathedral long before the journey's end. ... For long the horizon has been empty, the foreground unremarkable. And there, suddenly, the grey shape of the cathedral stands against the sky. Like a ship upon the crest of a wave, it rides at the head of a low hill... To the pilgrim of a thousand years ago, the solitary hillock in the desolate fens, crowned by a noble group of buildings, will have seemed a miracle made visible.'[1] This distant vision did indeed seem miraculous to at least one medieval pilgrim whose experience was

The cathedral from the south east

14

right: The cathedral from the south

below: the north flank of the nave, looking south west

The cathedral seen across the monastic buildings

recorded in the *Liber Eliensis*. Ralph the Schoolmaster was cured of a painful illness after praying to St Etheldreda, so he travelled to Ely to give thanks at her shrine. When he reached Kentford, before dawn on a July morning, he looked toward the cathedral and saw it miraculously illuminated, shining brightly in front of him.[2]

This building has frequently been seen as a ship and, as we shall see in Chapter 3, the Christian Church has been likened to a ship. A distant view of the cathedral's bulk in daylight seen floating, as it so often is, on the fenland mists, must have been a vision of security in a weary and troubled wilderness. The pilgrim will have arrived with a sense of wonder and achievement, glad to settle into the monastery's guest house before admiring the beauties of the architecture and visiting the shrines of the saints.

Throughout the medieval centuries frequent processions wound their way around the outside of the cathedral. Visitors and pilgrims then, as now, will also have walked around the exterior singly or in groups marvelling at its size and magnificence. It is unlikely that lay visitors were allowed to walk right around the cathedral. This is because, as we shall see in Chapter 9, the cathedral was also a monastery. Even today the area on the south side, where the monks' domestic accommodation was situated, is an enclosed garden and the former monastic buildings are private houses or part of the Choir School. When the monastery was functioning, that side of the precinct was largely closed to outsiders. But since the main accommodation for guests

The Octagon
crowning the cross-
shaped cathedral

was located just to the north and east of the cathedral it seems likely that its
west and east ends, the north flank and part at least of the south side of the
Choir would have been open to them (see the plan of the monastery on
p.156).

From here within the precinct, but even more from a distance, the exterior of the Octagon stands out as a crowning feature at the centre of the
building. It covers the place where the two arms of the cross-shaped
ground plan meet. The cross on which Christ died is the defining shape of
the entire building, implicit in every movement around it, both outside and
within. For Christians the cross is not just a reminder of that terrible death
but a sign of victory. For, in rising on the third day to new life, Christ overcame death itself to obtain eternal life for all humanity. In St Paul's Epistles
and in the Book of Revelation, that eternal life is represented as a crown for
which we strive in our attempts to live in accordance with God's good will
for us. The Octagon-crown hovers over a great, luminous space inside,
which, as we shall see, represents the vault of heaven with the risen and

The Octagon at the centre of the cross – view from the West Tower

The exterior of Steeple Gate, from the High Street

glorified Christ at its centre. This central crown might also be a reference to Ely's patron saint, Etheldreda. Queen and abbess, her shrine was the major attraction for pilgrims.

Most visitors to the cathedral, apart from those who came on business, would have entered through one of the gates from the High Street. Steeple

The Sacrist's Gate
from the High Street

Gate gave direct access to the lay cemetery and to the parish church of the Holy Trinity (no longer existing) which flanked the north wall of the nave. The two gates to the east of it led to the hostelry and to the north transept door. This latter gave access to the transept, the shrine and the Lady Chapel, the exteriors of which can still be seen in front of visitors entering, through this gate, from the High Street.

It may seem strange that with such a large cathedral church there should also have been a need for a, separate, parish church. But the devotional needs of local lay people were different, both from those of the monks and

from those of pilgrims who had come to visit cathedral and shrine. By the early thirteenth century many monasteries were providing the means of separating these functions. This was done by building parish churches and also, in this case, a Lady Chapel at a distance from the monastic quarters. One advantage for the laity of having their own parish church was that they were responsible for it and exercised more control over its decoration and use.[3]

The walls of the cathedral nave and of the north and south transepts are capped by battlements, a military feature which may seem incongruous on a church. Battlements, otherwise known as crenellations, were initially devised for a practical purpose in the defence of a castle under seige. But they later became a fashionable feature used on many kinds of buildings with no defensive purpose. On churches, though, they were not merely fashionable. The concept of a fortress or castle is deeply embedded in Christian religious symbolism. God himself is a fortress, as for instance in Psalm 144: 'Blessed be the Lord my strength... My hope and my fortress, my castle and deliverer, my defender in whom I trust...'

top: Nave, Octagon, North Transept and Lady Chapel

bottom: battlements on the transept

taunk de fu e de fufre. Vunt la mifericorde de deu nuf garde p fa pite. ki uit en regne en ferle de ferlef amen.

St John (bottom left) looks up into the Heavenly Jerusalem. The walls of the city are shown opened flat, with triple battlemented gates and Christ enthroned within.

Manuscripts of the Apocalypse, the biblical Book of Revelation, sometimes show the heavenly Jerusalem as battlemented. For instance the Trinity College Apocalypse and the Douce Apocalypse, both dating from the latter part of the thirteenth century, show St John's vision of the Heavenly Jerusalem in this way.[4]

A castle, or fortified city, can also represent the human soul, defended by the virtues from attacks of the devil. It is an image used by many theologians of the early and of the medieval Church, notably one of the most

The Lady Chapel,
West Front

influential, St Gregory the Great.[5] This is also the theme of a fifteenth-century play appropriately entitled 'The Castle of Perseverence'.[6] Such images of defence against 'the world, the flesh and the devil' will very likely have resonated in the minds of pilgrims looking attentively at the crenellated exterior of the nave. They certainly were recommended to the monks who worshipped daily in this building. Monks 'are closed in this holy monastery as knights in a castle, where we are beseiged with great multitudes of fiends... And therefore when we hear the bell ring to Matins we ought anon, as true God's knights, arise quickly and arm us with prayer... and haste us to the place of our defence, that is the church... and there we ought to lift up the long spear of fervent desire of our hearts to God... whereby our enemies shall be rebuked, and we kept in godly praisings, under the banner of his protection.'[7]

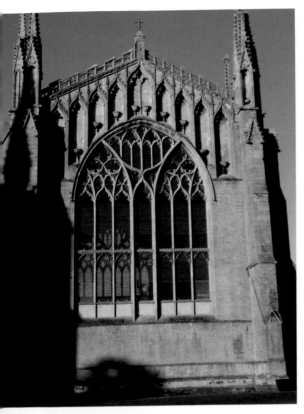

top: Lady Chapel east front

bottom: double niche at the centre top of the Lady Chapel east gable

Adjoining the North Transept is the large and elaborate Lady Chapel. During the thirteenth and fourteenth centuries many cathedrals built special chapels for devotions addressed to the Virgin Mary, mother of Jesus, most blessed of women, *the* Lady above all others. England was foremost in its devotion to Mary, so much so that she was taken as the patron saint of the country and England was said to be her dowry. St George was added as a subsidiary patron late in the Middle Ages and only ousted the Virgin as *the* patron of England after the mid-sixteenth-century Reformation. Lady Chapels were added to many of the great churches of England, from the late twelfth to the fifteenth century. They were placed in one of two possible positions; either at the east end of the church or in the 'shoulder' position, adjacent to the north side. This shoulder position was used in Ely, possibly in imitation of the Holy House at Walsingham, not far away in Norfolk.[8] Walsingham was the foremost pilgrimage shrine in Britain dedicated to the Virgin. The Walsingham Holy House was held to be a replica of the house in Nazareth, where the Annunciation took place and where the Holy Family lived after their return from exile in Egypt. Another similarity is that the Walsingham House was entered from inside the main church through a door half-way along its south side, as is this chapel. At Walsingham it was also possible to enter from outside, a possibility not provided here. Pilgrims to Walsingham from the south and south-west of England may well have included a stop here in Ely on their way, in order to offer their prayers to the local saints as well as to to the Virgin Mary in her splendid chapel.

The Ely Lady Chapel is one of the largest and most ornate of the chapels dedicated to Mary. On its exterior the buttresses and gables are adorned with niches which once held statues. No direct evidence survives to tell us which saints were portrayed there. But it is possible to make an informed guess at some of the imagery. The uppermost niches in the east and west gable ends differ from each other and are both unusual configurations. The gable end on the east has at its centre twin niches, for two slender figures side by side; the west has a wide central niche flanked by narrower ones and with a smaller niche above it. Since the chapel is dedicated to Mary the central imagery would most likely have referred to her.

Two of the most frequently portrayed scenes of the Virgin are the Annunciation and the Coronation of the Virgin; these represent the beginning and the end of the story of her part in the redemption of the world by Christ. The Annunciation is the name of the occasion when a young girl was visited by the angel Gabriel who told her that she had been chosen to become the mother of Jesus, the Son of God[9]. Her willing assent to this task enabled God's love to flow more fully into the world through the work of Jesus. The figures of Gabriel and Mary, turned towards each other in an Annunciation scene, probably filled the slender twin niches of the east gable.

The Coronation of Mary is not taken from the Bible. The Bible does, however, contain the idea of eternal life in heaven given as a crown after death to all faithful Christians. The crown is a sign of victory and of completion; we still talk of a difficult task being 'crowned with success'. The Virgin Mary, whose willing assent to God's plan made her the paradigm Christian, was thought to be appropriately crowned after death with heavenly life beside her son. Her coronation was variously portrayed, but in one of its forms it would make sense of the curious configuration on the west gable of the Lady Chapel. In this form the Virgin is crowned by the Trinity: Mary in the centre flanked on either side by Christ and God the Father. The Holy Spirit may be represented by a dove or, as on a cloister boss at Worcester, by a third human figure.[10] A fifteenth-century alabaster carving in the Fitzwilliam Museum shows the Coronation of the Virgin in a configuration very similar to that of these niches on the Lady Chapel gable.[11]

On the buttresses of the Lady Chapel and on the east gable wall of the cathedral are further empty niches which were probably intended to hold statues of saints. It is not known which saints were portrayed in these places. But the niches represent the many mansions in heaven[12] and the placing of the saints on the buttresses signifies their own 'buttressing' function. Their lives of holiness strengthened and supported the Christian community in their time and continue to support the Church as it remembers them. It may be that some of these niches were deliberately left empty, to show that there is room for many more in heaven and to encourage each

top: configuration of niches at the top of the Lady Chapel west gable

bottom: the Coronation of the Virgin by the Trinity: boss in the cloister of Worcester Cathedral

Buttress niches on the east front of the cathedral

visitor to live well. This church building thus reminds pilgrims of their own place in the spiritual building which is the Church: '...you are citizens with the saints... built upon the foundation of the apostles and prophets, with Christ Jesus himself as the cornerstone. In him the whole structure is joined together and grows into a holy temple in the Lord; in whom you are also built together spiritually into a dwelling place for God.'[13] As we shall see, inside the cathedral Christ is shown at the centre, joining the whole structure together.

The fruitfulness of this metaphor is shown in its constant use by theologians and devotional writers. Among the most influential of these were the Four Latin Doctors[14], the Venerable Bede in the eighth century, and Peter Damian in the eleventh century.[15] In the thirteenth century the writer of the *Metrical Life of St Hugh of Lincoln* used this metaphor in summing up the meaning of the cathedral built by the saint: 'Thus unconscious stones enclose the mysteries of animate ones, the fabric made with hands represents that of the spirit...'[16] In the late fourteenth century the poet William Langland recounted, as in a vision, the Christian Church as a building:

And Grace gave him the Cross, with the garland of thorns,
That Christ suffered on at Calvary for Mankind's sake.
And from his baptism and the blood that he shed on the Cross
He made a kind of mortar, and mercy was its name.
And with it Grace began to make a good foundation,
And wattled it and walled it with his pain and his passion;
And out of all Holy Writ he made a roof afterward;
And he called that house Unity, Holy Church in English.[17]

This metaphor of the spiritual stones was used in a set of instructions, dating from the fourteenth century, for people visiting the sick and dying. Visiting the sick was one of the good deeds recommended to all Christian people. The Church taught that there were seven of these, known as the Works of Mercy. They are:

to feed the hungry, give drink to the thirsty, clothe the naked, shelter the homeless, visit the sick, succour prisoners, bury the dead.

The list was taken from the instructions of Christ himself, as recounted in the Gospels.[18] There Jesus mentioned six of these; the burial of the dead

was added from another biblical source. The fourteenth-century treatise suggests that the dying be comforted with the prospect of taking their place as stones, built into the walls of the heavenly city: 'And therefore, before you go out of this world, you must polish your stone and make it ready... This stone is your soul, which you must make strong through right belief... You must cleanse it through hope of God's mercy; and perfect charity the while heals a multitude of sins.'[19]

About half way along the south side of the Choir two bays are quite different from the others. The majority of the upper windows of the thirteenth-century aisles were replaced with large fourteenth-century traceried windows.[20] But in two bays this was not done. Here, most clearly visible on the south side, the lower parapet and smaller lancet window openings of the earlier work survive. These openings are unglazed and there is no roof over the upper part of the aisle at this point. Walls on each side of these two bays close off what inside is the gallery or triforium and it is the inner arch which is glazed. It is a most unusual feature, expressly designed to mark out the most sacred part of the interior of the cathedral. Inside these bays the High Altar and the shrine of St Etheldreda were originally placed. The opening of the gallery, bringing the windows closer in to the central space, sheds a different quality of light upon shrine and altar. On sunny days the effect is to spotlight the area. Unfortunately the High Altar is now placed further east and the shrine no longer exists, so that much of the intended effect is lost. But the original position of the shrine, marked now by an inscribed slab in the floor, is still picked out in daytime by this special lighting.

top: pinnacle niches on the Lady Chapel

bottom: the two bays (centre) with inner windows lighting the shrine

High up on the buttresses of the north and south sides of the eastern part of the cathedral are various grotesque carvings of a kind generally known as gargoyles. This name is derived from the gargling noise made on rainy days by such figures functioning as down-spouts. Not all the carvings here

top: face-puller gargoyle

bottom: man in the grip of a ravening beast

have that function – most are simply decorative. But they all signify 'the works of the devil': blasphemy and vice, together with the results of such behaviour. Vicious people were likened to beasts: 'Pride turns man into a lion, for he wishes to be feared and respected by everyone, and... if anyone resists his presumption he is furious, and sets on him like a lion does on a lesser beast. ... Treacherous and covetous people who rob their neighbours of their worldly goods by threats and oppression become like ravening wolves.'[21] The most telling of these gargoyles is that which shows a human in the grip of a ferocious beast – is it a lion or a wolf? – whose open mouth is clearly ready to devour its hapless victim. Unlike the saints, these figures are not placed in niches. They squat or crouch on the buttresses, peering and leering excrescences rather than integral parts of the structure. They are a reminder that vicious behaviour works against peaceful co-existence in human societies.

Such meanings were widely understood. The mid-thirteenth-century French allegorical poem 'Le Roman de la Rose' describes a walled garden within which the rose of the title is to be sought. On the outside of the garden walls are pictures of vices. This poem was translated by Chaucer in the late fourteenth- or early fifteenth-century as 'The Romaunt of the Rose', and seems to have been quite widely known even before being translated into English. The descriptions of these vices are similar to many of the gargoyles found on church exteriors – as one might expect. Hate, for instance, is 'like a mad woman... grinning' with rage; 'full hideous was she for to see'.[22] Another of the vices, sloth, was described by the parson, in Chaucer's *Canterbury Tales*, thus: 'An idle man is like a place that has no walls; the devils may enter on every side or close at him all unprotected...'[23] Indeed, it is no surprise that the compiler of the cathedral's own chronicle referred to Picot the wicked sheriff – despoiler of the monastery's lands, the property of St Etheldreda – as a 'starving lion, a footloose wolf, a deceitful fox, a muddy swine, an impudent dog...'[24]

The gargoyles on the Choir buttresses date from the thirteenth and

fourteenth centuries. On the nave and westwork are carvings which probably carried a similar significance. Just below the projecting parapet at the top
of these walls there is a Romanesque corbel table. This consists of a series
of projecting stones, carved as heads, with small arches between them. 'No
two of them are alike, for they vary in shape, position and expression. Some
are very fine heads, male and female, others are heads deformed by fear or
hilarious laughter. Some heads look straight in front while others turn side-
ways, or even upside-down. Among the animal heads are some of cats, cows,
and lions, and here and there a few birds appear with sharply-pointed
beaks.'[25] Too few of the originals have survived for it to be possible to
discover in detail what they all represented. But it is known that similar carvings on corbel tables of about the same date signified vices and blasphemy.
One of the best preserved examples is the set on the church at Kilpeck in
Herefordshire, where such a significance has been demonstrated.[26]

The cathedral from
the south east, seen
across the meadow

In looking attentively at all these features of the exterior of the cathedral, the pilgrims will have been acting in accordance with instructions given long before, to Jewish pilgrims going to Jerusalem: 'Walk about Sion and go round about her; count all her towers: consider well her bulwarks; pass through her citadels...'.[27] The earthly Jerusalem was considered a representation of the celestial city. In walking attentively around its physical structures it was possible to reach in spirit beyond the material world and catch a glimpse of the spiritual reality of heaven. Medieval cathedrals were built for a similar purpose. They also represented the Heavenly Jerusalem. Their design, layout and decoration all aimed at helping the attentive pilgrim to an experience of transcendence.

CHAPTER 2

West Front

The Lord reigneth, he is clothed with majesty

The main entrance front of the cathedral is notable particularly for its Westwork: a broad western transept and corner turrets, with multiple layers of intricate arcading to cover them outside and in. The front was even wider before the northern section of the transept collapsed, seemingly some time in the fifteenth century. The arches of the arcading are mostly of the Romanesque, Norman, form, with semi-circular heads. Only in the upper-most stages are they slightly pointed, in the beginnings of the Gothic style. The top of the tower was added at a later date.[1]

The West Tower, transept and Galilee Porch

Romanesque architecture is so-called because in its forms it refers back to the buildings of ancient Rome, which were much admired throughout the early Middle Ages. Because of its military and diplomatic prowess, the Roman empire had spread widely around the Mediterranean and through northern Europe, to the Danube in the east and Hadrian's wall in the north. The peace and stability that was enjoyed within the empire encouraged a high level of civi-lized living, of literature, architecture, art and culture. It was in the Roman Empire that Christianity began and first spread, until eventually the Church understood itself as the legitimate suc-cessor and replacement of that empire. Splendid stone public buildings were

29

above left: The
Triumphal Arch of
Titus in Rome

above right: Arch of
Titus: the treasures of
the Jerusalem Temple
carried in procession
after the sack of the
city by the Romans

one of the ways in which Roman rule was asserted; they had a propaganda
function, showing who was in control. Victorious generals held processions to celebrate their victories and built triumphal arches to advertise
their contribution to the stability of the empire. The pagan emperors were
worshipped as gods after their death (and sometimes before) and stone
temples were built to honour them.[2]

Christianity took over such structures and reinterpreted them. St Paul
wrote of Christians as being part of the triumphal procession of Christ, a
reference to the fact that looted treasures were carried in such processions.[3]
Churches were built with triumphal arches to signify, not the warlike
exploits of military leaders, but the victory of Christ, the Prince of Peace.
Lincoln cathedral has, at the centre of its west front, triple arches with this
meaning. The three giant arches on the west front of Peterborough cathedral, although in the later, Gothic, style, were probably also intended to
convey this triumphal meaning. Here at Ely is a variant of the theme; rather
than three great arches, multiple smaller arches entirely cover the walls.
The windows, with their triple stepped-arch form, resonate with triumphal
arch associations. The other rows of arcading also have significance. At
about the same time as this was being built, churches and monuments in
Aquitaine were given similar treatment. It has been argued that this also
was a deliberate reference back to Roman imperial buildings: 'The arcaded,
multi-level structure, an emblem of deification and immortality in imperial times... served as a sign of the triumph over death through which all
Christians are guaranteed eternal life.'[4] There were close connections
between England and Aquitaine at the time, culminating in the marriage of
king Henry II to Eleanor of Aquitaine in 1152. Bishop Nigel of Ely was

sufficiently closely associated with Henry to have provided money to help him finance a military campaign in Aquitaine.[5]

Some scholars have misinterpreted Christianity's use of imperial imagery as a claim to secular power.[6] But, though doubtless the reality fell short of the ideal, its aim was quite the reverse. In its appeal to peace rather than war, to the reign of God rather than emperor, to victory over evil and death rather than over human enemies, the intention was to make use of imperial imagery for a different purpose. Jesus himself had done something similar when he rode into Jerusalem on an ass, accompanied by his disciples on foot.[7] His triumphal entry into the city was greeted by the populace with the enthusiasm due to an emperor. But an emperor would have been riding a tall horse and accompanied by armed soldiers. Jesus was deliberately appealing to, yet at the same time subverting, the meaning of an imperial triumph. The Gospel writers explain it as fulfilling an Old Testament prophecy about a new kind of king who would be sent by God to disarm all nations and establish in Zion (Jerusalem) a reign of peace: 'Rejoice greatly, O daughter of Zion!...Behold,

top left: The Triumphal Arch of Constantine in Rome

top right: the triple arch of the West Front of Lincoln Cathedral

bottom: multi-level arcading on the south-west transept

The triple arched windows of the south west transept, recalling Roman triumphal arches

thy King cometh unto thee... lowly and riding upon an ass... and he shall speak peace unto the heathen...'[8] In early Christian art Jesus was even shown on the ass riding side-saddle, a feminine mode which underlines the peaceful, anti-imperial nature of his coming.[9]

There were many occasions in the Church year when processions were held. There were also individual occasions that warranted a procession, such as the reception of a new bishop. Bishop Nigel was conducted in procession through the streets of the town, which were 'arrayed with hangings, tapestries and decorated seats' and thus conducted to his enthronement in the cathedral.[10] Most of the liturgical processions moved around the inside of the church and cloister. Those which celebrated special feast days went also around the outside of the church. Each year, as a remembrance of Christ's triumphal entry into Jerusalem, the Church held a great procession. This was on Palm Sunday, so-called because palm fronds[11] were held by the participants to emulate the crowd that greeted Jesus. For that procession this great west front of the cathedral represented the entrance to Jerusalem; its doors were the gates of the city. The source of this ritual procession is Jerusalem itself. We know that as early as the fourth century

Christ's entry was being re-enacted there each year as the people processed with their bishop from the Mount of Olives into the city.[12]

The Palm Sunday procession was unique in consisting of two processions. One, representing the people who went out to meet Jesus, moved around the outside of the building, perhaps even going out into the town. It is known, for instance, that the processions of Hereford and Canterbury cathedrals actually went outside the city walls, stopping to sing an appropriate verse at one of the city gates then moving back in and towards the west door of the cathedral.[13] It seems that each cathedral and city had its own particular way of arranging the route of this procession, depending on the unique geography of the place.[14] At nearby Peterborough, which was an abbey but not a cathedral during the Middle Ages, the procession seems to have remained within the grounds of the abbey.[15] Here in Ely, where the small town nestles just outside the cathedral precinct there are no city gates. But the outer gates of the precinct may have been used to represent the gates of Jerusalem, with the procession moving out and along the High Street for a short distance.

In Lincoln and other places the congregations of all the city churches took part in the procession. Ely has few parish churches, but people from nearby villages will have come to join the ceremony. This procession, as it moved back in toward the west door of the cathedral, was met by another, consisting of clergy and choir. They carried in their midst a shrine containing the consecrated bread of the Eucharist – the Host or Body of Christ. This was also carried in procession on another feast day – that of *Corpus Christi* which celebrated the presence of Christ in the Host. The people who went out to meet Jesus on Palm Sunday thus met with and greeted him under the form of the sacramental bread. As the joint procession neared the west front it was greeted with angelic singing from some of the choirboys.[16] At Wells cathedral there is special provision for this in the form of

The Entry into Jerusalem; Jesus, riding on an ass, is greeted by a crowd carrying palm fronds. This carving is part of the nineteenth-century High Altar reredos, inside the cathedral

The cathedral towers
signify the towers of
the heavenly city.

galleries inside the west front. Holes behind some of the carved angels are
set at the right height for young boys to sing through.[17] To those in the
approaching procession it must have seemed as if the angels themselves
were singing. What they sang was a hymn written for this very purpose in
the ninth century.[18] It has been translated into English and is still appropriately sung in Anglican churches on Palm Sunday. 'All glory, laud and
honour To thee redeemer king...'.[19]

It is possible that at Ely the so-called 'Galilee'[20] porch which shelters the
west door was used for this purpose. Peterborough also has a Galilee porch,
rather smaller than that at Ely, which was certainly so used.[21] No special
provision for the boys has been found, but some of the arches in the second tier on the west side of the south west transept appear to have been
open originally.[22] Before the construction of the Galilee the boys might
have sung from there. The original design of the Galilee porch included an
upper storey, as does that at Peterborough. The boys may have sung from

Fifteenth-century illustration of a Bishop carrying the Host in a container, processing with attendant clerics.

below: Quatrefoil with angel on the West Front of Wells Cathedral. Some of these have openings through which choirboys sang.

the windows of that. Alternatively, they may have used the interior of the porch. At Peterborough the porch is too small for this – the evidence suggests that a raised stage was set up for part of the ceremony, as was done at many parish churches. But at Ely the interior of the porch is very wide, and the two levels of stone benches which run along both sides are unusually deep to be merely decorative. As a comparison, the double arcading in St Hugh's Choir in Lincoln cathedral, from the design of which the Ely work is derived, is only about half as deep. Here at Ely the benches are deep enough for each to hold a row of singers, in stepped formation, safely above and out of the way of the incoming procession. This would be an appropriate formation in which the choir could greet the approaching Host, singing the words: 'As the Lord entered the Holy City...'.[23]

above: The Galilee
Porch from the west

above right: arcaded
benches inside the
Galilee Porch

The shrine then moved forward to the main door and was held aloft while the rest of those processing moved underneath it into the nave, thus symbolically passing through Christ, the Doorway to eternal life: '...everything was focussed down on the individuals passing beneath, and passing as they hoped to do in the future into the New Jerusalem.'[24]

The Palm Sunday procession was not merely a symbolic reminder of a historic event. As we have seen, the cathedral represents the heavenly, as well as the earthly, Jerusalem. To enter through its doors is to to be brought into contact with the eternal verities of the reign of God. 'For in entering the church in this sacred context the participants are not merely re-enacting the entry of Christ into Jerusalem, but at the same time prefiguring the entry of the blessed into the New Jerusalem, both in the real sense of the physical entry into the Holy City following the physical resurrection and also in the symbolic sense whereby ordinary perception is replaced by the perception of the real that stands behind the phenomenal world of mere appearances... The facade was to be understood as a threshold leading from the life in this world to the eternity that lies beyond it.'[25]

left: Double arcading
in St Hugh's Choir,
Lincoln Cathedral

below: The Galilee
Porch from the south
west

We have mentioned one possible use for the interior of the porch. We must now say more about this structure and its purpose. This Galilee porch was added to the west front of the cathedral in the early- to mid-thirteenth century – quite why is not known for certain. In the later Middle Ages wedding ceremonies were begun in church porches. Vows were exchanged and contracts signed here and then the participants moved into the church for the nuptial mass. It is unlikely that ordinary lay people would be married in a monastic cathedral; their own parish church would be a more appropriate setting. But an aristocratic wedding might well have required the more spacious, stately setting of the cathedral porch and nave.

A porch was also used during the rite of dedication of a church – a rite which was compared, by a major medieval commentator, to the marriage rite: 'The dedication of a church is the nuptial coupling of the Church and Christ'.[26] The dedication of a church might seem to be a very rare event but in fact dedications and re-dedications happened with some frequency. After any occurrence of

a sacriligious act the building would need re-dedication, as was required by
Canterbury cathedral after the murder of Thomas Becket. Likewise, exten-
sive rebuilding projects would, on completion, culminate in the ceremony
of dedication.[27] The Ely porch may well have been built by Bishop Hugh de
Northwold as an ancillary to his major extension of the east end of the
cathedral, to form a suitably impressive canopy for the initial part of the
dedication ceremony for his new work. The porch could thereafter function
as a ceremonial welcoming place and entrance for visiting dignitaries.

The breadth of the west front also requires explanation. In the century
after this was built, broad screen fronts became a typical feature of English

The interior of the
Galilee Porch,
nineteenth century
view

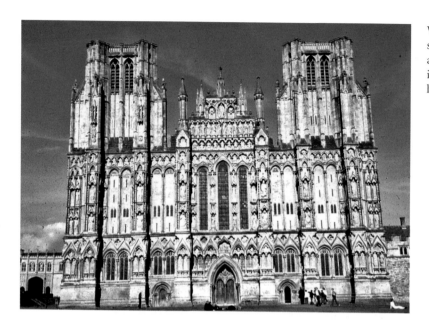

Wells Cathedral west screen front. The angel quatrefoils are in the spandrels of the lower windows.

cathedrals. They were used, as at Wells and Salisbury, for a display of statuary representing the inhabitants of the heavenly Jerusalem.[28] Here in Ely there are no statues but it is possible that the arches originally held painted figures.[29]

We have seen that the arcading itself carries the message of the triumph of Christ. As we saw in the previous chapter, blank niches may well also have carried a message, that these are some of the many mansions of heaven awaiting the faithful. There may be a yet further meaning to this western part of the cathedral. It has been pointed out that churches with a large western block – known as a Westwork – are characteristic of the Rhineland.[30]

Palm Sunday was the first day of Holy Week, the yearly remembrance of the Passion of Christ – his suffering, death and resurrection. We have seen that the exterior of this part of the cathedral played an important role in the ceremonial re-enactment of Christ's entry into Jerusalem. The interior of the western block in Rhineland churches was used for Holy week ceremonies and symbolised the Sepulchre of Christ in, or rather just outside, Jerusalem.[31] The place in which Jesus was executed and buried was, at that time, outside the walls of Jerusalem. But a few years later the city was extended. A further stretch of wall was built and in the process the hill of the crucifixion and of the sepulchre were incorporated into the city. The space just inside a cathedral could well seem appropriate to symbolise a place that is inside, but only just. It is a place of transition; the outskirts of the celestial city.

Eleventh-century
'Holy Sepulchre'
chapel, inside the west
end of the nave,
Aquileia Cathedral,
Italy

The solemn services of Good Friday, which commemorated the death and burial of Jesus, came to be marked by a dramatisation of his burial. Then two days later, early on the Sunday morning, the story was brought full circle with the announcement of his resurrection.

On Good Friday, after the reading of the Gospel story of Jesus' death on the cross, the Host, normally kept on or above the high altar, was taken in procession through the church and then deposited in the Sepulchre to symbolise his burial. A watch of prayer was kept until the midnight vigil of Holy Saturday. According to the Gospel account[32] three women followers of Jesus went out of the city, in the early dawn, to the garden tomb. They intended to anoint the body of their crucified teacher and friend, but they found the tomb empty and guarded by an angel. This is the scene which was dramatised at Easter. In many churches throughout Western Christendom, during the liturgy of the early hours of Easter Sunday young clerics representing the three Maries approached the tomb where another, dressed all in white, asked them: 'Whom do you seek?'. To their reply 'Jesus of Nazareth' he answered, using the words of the angel 'He is not here; he is risen'.

In the later Middle Ages in England the structure which represented the tomb of Christ – the Easter Sepulchre – was in most churches generally placed at the east end, on the north side of the main altar. But in the twelfth century, at the time when this west front was being built, some German cathedrals were placing the Sepulchre inside the Westwork.[33] Even where there was no westwork, for instance in Italy where such structures were not the fashion, replicas of the Holy Sepulchre were built in some churches at the west end of the nave. The circular chapel in the cathedral of Aquileia is a surviving example.

We do not know if some form of Easter Sepulchre was placed in the western part of this cathedral, but if, as in those great Rhineland churches, it was used for those ceremonies then a procession of the Maries along the whole length of the nave in the darkness would have been powerfully resonant. For those approaching from outside, this massive Westwork would stand as a potent reminder of the walled city of Jerusalem, of the empty tomb and of the resurrection of Christ. Those taking part in the Palm Sunday procession moving towards and in through the west door were, in any case, being drawn into a great, week-long drama re-enacting the climactic events on which their Christian faith was founded.

CHAPTER 3

Narthex
Stand at the crossroads and look

The Christian story of salvation is retold in two ways. One way is by providing images to illustrate God's work in history, as recounted in the Bible. This tells of the creation of the world, the Fall, the history of Israel, Christ's task of redemption, the end of the world, and our ultimate fate in the afterlife. All of this explains the nature of the universe, how we should behave, and the meaning of our existence.

The other way is to interpret each Christian life as a journey in hope toward God. This building which is an image of the Heavenly Jerusalem does both. It re-tells, especially in the great series of nineteenth-century ceiling paintings, some of the crucial episodes in the biblical story. It also aims at inspiring Christians to begin, and helps to fit them for, their own particular journeys. As one of the great leaders of the early Church put it: 'In order to give us a life that is simple and unencumbered by worry, [Christ] sets before us the life of a pilgrim, one that is easy to lead and easy to leave on our on-going journey to the attainment of eternal happiness. ...We will then become what we dare not hope for, what we dare not imagine.'[1]

Pilgrimage is a journey of the spirit which can be helped along by making journeys of the body. These could require travelling many miles from home: to Ely and its shrines of Etheldreda and her sisters; from Ely to the shrine of Our Lady of Walsingham; from

St James dressed as a late-medieval pilgrim to his own shrine, with scallop shell on his hat, staff in his hand; screen painting in Castle Acre church, Norfolk

London to the shrine of St Thomas Becket in Canterbury, like Chaucer's pilgrims; or further – to the shrine of St James at Compostela in Spain, to Rome or to the earthly Jerusalem itself. We know of one pilgrim, a knight from Arundel who prayed to St Etheldreda to be healed of a devastating illness. She obliged, and instructed him in a vision to go first to Ely and then to 'St James in Galicia' (i.e. Compostela).[2] Of course, not all pilgrims travelled for entirely spiritual reasons.[3] Chaucer's pilgrims are perhaps representative of his own times. They are a mixed lot: a few deeply religious; some conventionally so; some just going along as an excuse for a holiday; some quite cynically on the lookout for material gain.

On the other hand, not everyone who genuinely wished to make a spiritual pilgrimage could go on a long journey. Some were too poor to be able to afford it; others were prevented by ill-health or family commitments. Those who neverthless desired the spiritual benefits of pilgrimage could make a symbolic journey; '...devotional objects in various media allowed individuals to reap the rewards of pilgrimage without having to actually travel abroad'.[4] In this building which represents the celestial city the pilgrim is enabled in various ways to engage in such a journey. The long nave itself is a route along which to move attentively, beckoned forward by the heavenly light which floods down from the Octagon and by the shrines of the local saints beyond the Octagon. But first, just inside the west door, the imagery suggests a pause to reflect on the journey of life.

Immediately in front as one enters the narthex is the modern figure of Christ, made in 1981 by Hans Feibusch. Christ is shown welcoming the

The wounded Christ – sculpture by Hans Feibusch

The 'Way of Life'
sculpture on the
north wall of the
Narthex

visitor with outstretched hands – hands which show the imprint of the wounds which Jesus suffered out of love for humankind. This is the Saviour who said: 'Come unto me, all ye that labour and are heavy laden, and I will give you rest.'[5] In front of it is a candle stand at which many visitors light candles as physical tokens of their prayers to Christ, the Light of the World.

Running up the north wall is a modern sculpture, 'The Way of Life' by Jonathan Clarke. It was commissioned by the Friends of Ely Cathedral to mark the Millennium. This sculpture images the Christian's journey as a winding road, broad-based but gradually narrowing to a cross-road near the top. This is susceptible to a range of interpretations. It can be seen as suggesting an ascent to a place which, like so many cross-roads, requires a decision and a choice – which way to go? Take the straight path onwards and upwards or branch aside? Those who know the biblical psalms might be reminded that the very first psalm is a meditation on the two possible ways of life. The way of goodness is secure, aimed at and founded in God. But the way of the wicked, although it may seem successful, leads ultimately nowhere: 'whatever way they go on is trackless, directionless, doomed'.[6] The prophet Jeremiah envisaged the people of Israel standing at such a point of decision: 'Thus says the Lord: Stand at the crossroads and look, and ask for the ancient paths, where the good way lies; and walk in it, and find rest for your souls.'[7]

Even those who sincerely desire to walk in the right way find themselves deviating from it. Most Christians stray from the path and need to seek it

again and again. The seventeenth-century priest-poet George Herbert expressed this in a poem in which the thought constantly turns back on itself until at last focussed on God:

'A wreathed garland of deserved praise
Of praise deserved, unto thee I give,
I give to thee, who knowest all my ways.
My crooked winding ways, wherein I live,
Wherein I die, not live: for life is straight,
Straight as a line, and ever tends to thee...'[8]

On the floor just inside the west door is a very convoluted path. Marked out in black on the white marble is a labyrinth. Labyrinths are of two kinds. The kind that most people would recognize as a maze has numerous dead-ends and wrong turnings in which it is possible to get lost. One way of understanding life is to envisage it as a series of choices more puzzling than a simple cross-road. To discover oneself in a dead-end and find the right way again requires changing one's mind, admitting failure, turning around and making a fresh start. This is what Christians understand as 'repentance'; the Greek word which it translates is *metanoia* – which could also be translated as 'change of mind'.

Another sort of turning is required by the labyrinth here. It has only one

opposite: 'The Way of Life' and the labyrinth, seen from the south-west transept gallery

route but it twists and turns in all directions. All that is needed is to enter, begin and persevere in the journey; the end is assured. But the road takes many turns and frequently seems to be going in entirely the wrong direction before at last reaching its goal at the centre. What this requires is not so much a change of mind as persistence and faith. The aim is that of the Shaker hymn:

> 'To turn, turn, will be our delight
> Till by turning, turning, we come round right.' ....
>
> 'And when we find ourselves in the place just right
> 'Twill be in the valley of love and delight.'[9]

This labyrinth was laid out in the nineteenth century but is a copy of a medieval labyrinth such as can still be found in some French cathedrals.[10] There are labyrinths in the cathedrals of Amiens, Beauvais, Bayeux, Chartres. They functioned as one means of spiritual journeying for pilgrims who could not travel far from their homes. Some pilgrims would walk around; others would move around on their knees. Either way, the journey would be undertaken with prayer.

Those who knew their psalter by heart would pray in the words of the fifteen 'gradual' psalms, psalms 120–134. These psalms '...were part of the journey to grace, the route for the spiritually ambitious, the upward climb of the human soul towards God.'[11] They seem to have been composed for Jewish pilgrims travelling to Jerusalem for the yearly festivals[12] and as such were taken into Christian worship. In some monasteries, on feast days, they were chanted as the monks processed through their church, thereby reminding themselves of the purpose of their life and work. 'By degrees, by the steps of the Gradual Psalms, spiritual enrichment is gained. As a group, these fifteen psalms celebrate, petition, praise and instruct. Through metaphor and through rich imagery, this series of short psalms creates an atmosphere of dependence on God, in which to express joy and obtain comfort.'[13] The personal prayer books known as 'Books of Hours' contained the gradual psalms. Such books were produced mainly for the use of well-off women from the mid-thirteenth century and became gradually more widely available. Similar prayer books known as 'Primers' were produced in the later fourteenth and fifteenth centuries.[14] These also contained psalms as well as other prayers. It may be that the owners of such books would bring them in order to pray the gradual psalms while moving around the labyrinth and through the church.

Pilgrims who did not know the psalms and owned no books would repeat such prayers as they did know. Foremost among these was the Lord's Prayer, the 'Our Father', in Latin the *Pater Noster*. This was given to his disciples by Jesus himself as the very pattern of how to pray rightly. This prayer also

celebrates, petitions, praises and instructs, thus bringing the pilgrim to the centre of the labyrinth, to Christ in the valley of love and delight.

This recitation of prayers and psalms was, and still is, a major basis of Christian prayer. Initially the person praying may be distracted and inattentive, but the familiar words will gradually quieten the mind, opening it to the possibility of spiritual insight. 'The prayers that people use most frequently and find most helpful are probably the Our Father and the Psalms; ...[if the prayer is] uttered in a very low voice and with deep feeling.... [one's] soul is as it were in the presence of God'.[15] These meditations on life as a journey prepare the visitor for the road ahead, both physical and spiritual. The physical road ahead is marked by the long traverse of the nave, a straight path leading towards the light at the east end of the building, towards the sunrise and the High Altar which is also the spiritual goal and focus of the church. But before moving along that path there is more to experience here in the narthex.

Also in this western part of the cathedral is the font, set close to the entrance as a reminder that the baptism which takes place here is the entry to life in Christ. The present font dates from the mid-nineteenth century and is in the style of the mid-thirteenth century, with supporting pillars crowned by stiff-leaf foliage. These sprouting leaves, as we shall see later, represent growth and increase.[16] On the sides of the bowl are the symbols of the four Evangelists, the writers of the Gospels. These are represented by the four beasts, which Revelation describes as surrounding the throne of God: 'the first beast was like a lion, and the second beast like a calf, and the third beast had a face as a man, and the fourth beast was like a flying eagle'.[17]

The earliest recorded use of these beasts to symbolize the Evangelists is by St Irenaeus of Lyon in the late second century. Late in the following century, Victorinus of Pettau explained that the animal of each Evangelist is associated with the opening lines of their Gospels. Matthew is likened to a man because his Gospel begins with Christ's earthly ancestry and his human nature. Mark begins with a voice crying in the wilderness, as the lion roars in the desert. Luke is represented by the sacrificial ox, because his Gospel begins with the sacrifice offered by Zachariah. The eagle, which was thought to be able to gaze directly at the sun, is associated with John, whose Gospel opens with a direct statement of the divinity of Christ the 'Sun of Righteousness' and 'Light of the World'. The *Liber Eliensis* likens the four female saints of Ely to these four creatures: 'So that they may symbolize people entering from the four corners of the world, they are the followers, in number and merit, of those four-winged animals in Heaven'[18]. Here on the font these symbols aptly surround the water in which candidates for baptism are initiated into the new life of Christ by being washed and then signed with the cross.

Nowadays the font contains a small fountain of running water, another profound image. Water is one of the necessities of human life. We need it for drinking and for cleansing; we cannot long live without it. Water bubbling up out of the ground, fresh and clean, gives promise of new life and new hope. For Christians this new life and hope comes from God through Jesus who promised that those who tried to follow his way would be given 'a well of water springing up into everlasting life'[19]. Early churches in Britain, as elsewhere, were often built near or over a spring of water, which was used for baptism. Sometimes the spring would become a holy well, blessed by the presence and ministry of an early saint who had dwelt in that place. St Withburga's well can still be seen near her church in East Dereham.

The nineteenth-century font, carved with the symbols of the Evangelists

The angel – symbol
of St Matthew the
Evangelist

In baptism the candidate is signed with the cross. From early times, Christians would use this sign, tracing it with their hands as a gesture of blessing and of consecration to the service of God. In the fourth century, St Cyril of Jerusalem taught those who were preparing for baptism: 'Let us, then, not be ashamed to confess the Crucified. Be the cross our seal made with boldness by our fingers on our brow, and on everything; over the bread we eat and the cups we drink, in our comings in and goings out; before our sleep, when we lie down and when we awake, when we are on the road and when we are still.'[20] The sign of the cross is traced by the priest upon the forehead of the person to be baptised; it is also marked by individuals upon themselves, moving their right hand from forehead down to breast then from left to right[21], as they invoke the blessing of God, Father, Son and Holy Spirit.

The cross, the central Christian symbol, is found in many parts of this building. Indeed, it defines the entire layout since the ground-plan is in the shape of a cross. The intimate connection between the gesture of the sign of the cross and the layout of churches is shown in an anecdote from the life of an early English saint, St Oswald. He founded a church: 'and since he had protected it by the sign of the revered cross... so also therefore he began to construct the buildings of that place in the fashion of a cross.'[22]

The shape determines movement through the building and is constantly implicit in the way in which the interior space is experienced. Simply walking from the west door straight down the nave provides an awareness of how the transepts branch out from the middle, like the limbs of a tree or the widespread arms of a man. According to St John's Gospel Christ himself is the Way.[23] 'Christ is not only to be worshipped, but... he is also to be seen as a way along which we can travel. Every attempt to understand him implies a journey or a following. Only by following him and allowing ourselves to be transfigured into his likeness can we know him with whom we are dealing.'[24]

   The cross of Christ is also central to the great west window, which shows the Crucifixion. The glass dates from the sixteenth century and comes from the church of St John the Evangelist in Rouen. It was given by Bishop James Yorke in 1808. On the bottom level the third scene from the left shows Christ kneeling in the garden of Gethsemane; the panel to its right shows Jesus betrayed by Judas and arrested by the soldiers of the High Priest. On the upper level, reading again from left to right, there is Jesus being tried

Scenes of the Passion and Crucifixion of Christ, in the west window, upper level

'Christ the King' – modern stained glass in the south west transept chapel

before Pilate, his carrying the cross, his crucifixion, and the removal of his dead body from the cross (known as the descent, or deposition).

The emphasis in churches on this image of suffering and death is an aspect of Christianity that many people find puzzling or even repulsive. What Christians remember and celebrate in their constant turning to the crucifixion is a man whose trust in God was not extinguished by suffering and death, so that death itself was turned to new life. Since this man is also God we now know that, as St Paul wrote, 'neither death, nor life, nor angels, nor rulers, nor things present, nor things to come, nor powers, nor height, nor depth, nor anything else in all creation, will be able to separate us from the love of God in Christ Jesus our Lord.'[25]

It is often those who have suffered pain and evil who are able to see this religious meaning in their experience, rather than those whose faith has never been seriously tested. Faith is a matter of living through painful situations in as much joy, peace and love as we can receive from God, because this is what he wants and his presence enables us to do so. The Christian belief is that pain lived through in this way, for God and with God, leads to a new kind of existence in this world and the next, to a resurrection.[26]

In the small chapel in the southern part of this narthex the modern stained glass window shows Christ on the cross robed and crowned. Portraying him thus is a way of signifying the triumph and kingship of Christ. The cross was not just the instrument of his terrible death – the story did not end there. On the third day was his resurrection, followed by his ascension into heaven where he now reigns in glory. 'The earthly enthronement of Christ, the King of all creation, was upon the gibbet of the Cross. His royal power lies in the humility of his merciful love.'[27] St Paul connected the cross of Christ with the public processions of Roman generals, accompanied by captives and other spoils of their victories. Those victories, as we have seen, were commemorated by the erection of triumphal arches. St Paul speaks of the crucifixion of Jesus as the moment when the powers of this world were led like defeated captives behind a great victor.[28] In the seventeenth century the Anglican priest, Thomas Traherne wrote:

Defeated captives displayed in the triumphal procession; Arch of Titus, Rome

> The Cross is the Abyss of Wonders, the Centre of Desires, the Schoole of Virtues, the Hous of Wisdom, the Throne of Lov, the Theatre of Joys and the Place of Sorrows; It is the Root of Happiness, and the Gate of Heaven.[29]

The Chi-Rho, another sign of the triumph of Christ can be seen on the south-west transept ceiling, painted in 1878 by Thomas Gambier Parry. This sign is made up of the Greek letters which abbreviate the word 'Christ', superimposed on a cross. The Roman emperor Constantine, before a crucial battle, was awakened by an angel. "And Constantine saw in the heavens the image of a cross described in shining light; and above the image was written in letters of gold the legend: 'In this sign shalt thou conquer!'"[30] He had the sign attached to his army's standards; his army won the battle. It is often suggested that Constantine's vision marks the first use of the Chi-Rho symbol – that he invented it – but this is unlikely. It was already in use by Christians and was probably already known by Constantine, whose mother Helen was a Christian. This explains how he was immediately able to understand the meaning of the symbol seen in his vision.[31]

In the light of all these meanings it is not surprising that Christians revere and cherish the cross of Christ. In one of the greatest of medieval English poems the fourteenth-century poet awakes on Easter morning and calls to his wife and daughter:

The south west transept ceiling, nineteenth-century painting by Thomas Gambier Parry

Arise and go reverence God's resurrection,
And creep to the Cross on knees, and kiss it as a jewel,
For God's blessed body it bore for our good…[32]

And in the seventeenth century John Donne remembered the cross inscribed on him by the priest at his baptism, experiencing it still guiding his spiritual life:

Who can blot out the Cross, which the instrument
Of God, 'dued on me in the Sacrament?...
Be covetous of Crosses, let none fall.
Cross no man else, but cross thyself in all.
Then doth the Cross of Christ work fruitfully
Within our hearts, when we love harmlessly…[33]

As we saw in the previous chapter, this western part of the cathedral may have been used in the twelfth century for the dramatisation of the Maries' visit to the Sepulchre of Christ. That ceremony ceased with the Reformation in the sixteenth-century and may, indeed, have been shifted to the eastern part of the church before that time. But the proclamation of the Easter message is still celebrated in another ceremony, one which dates from early Christian times. Clergy, choir and people gather here by the font in darkness late in the evening of the Saturday in Holy Week for the Easter

The Chi-Rho symbol on the south west transept ceiling

Vigil. It is probably this service that is referred to in the *Liber Eliensis* as the 'Twelve Readings'.[34]

The darkness is the darkness of the tomb in which Jesus was buried. In this darkness the Church keeps vigil as it awaits the resurrection. A fire is lit, symbolising the new light which came into the world with Christ's return to life. A large candle on a tall candlestick stands near the font, symbolising the close connection between baptism and Christ's resurrection.[35] The candle is lit from the new fire which then is passed from person to person, each holding his or her own small candle. The light spreads as they pass it on to each other, just as faith in Christ has spread down the ages and across the continents.

The large candle is lit to mark the victory of light over darkness, of life over death, of good over evil. So the specially large candlestick which holds it retains this symbolism even when the candle is not lit. One such candlestick, in a church in Rome, is inscribed: 'I announce the feast day, the good news that Christ is resurrected. I am the witness of such a great gift.'[36] During the Easter Vigil service the lighted candle is hailed as 'the light of Christ' and the deacon sings the *Exultet*, an ancient hymn of praise:

> Rejoice, heavenly powers! Sing, choirs of angels!
> Exult, all creation around God's throne!
> Jesus Christ, our King, is risen!
> Sound the trumpet of salvation!
> Rejoice, O earth, in shining splendour,
> radiant in the brightness of your King!
> Christ has conquered! Glory fills you!
> Darkness vanishes for ever!

right: angel bearing
shield with the cross

below: font and
Paschal Candle

The *Exultet* ends with the prayer: '...grant that this Easter candle may make our darkness light; for Christ the Morning Star has risen, never again to set...'

Readings from the Old Testament then recount the history of God's dealings with the people of Israel. Central to this story and to the meaning of this night is the Exodus, a memory of liberation from oppression. The Israelites had been enslaved in Egypt but, with the power of God, Moses led them across the Red Sea to liberty in a land of their own. Ever since, for some three thousand years, Jewish families have celebrated this liberating experience annually at the Passover. It was during the Passover, and in fulfilment of its deep meaning, that Jesus died and rose again. He passed over from death to life, and in so doing liberated all his people, all those who follow him.

The Easter candle represents the column of fire that led the way for the Israelites as they journeyed through the desert after escaping from slavery in Egypt. God was with them all through their journey, as a cloud by day and a pillar of fire by night:

'Marvellous things did he in the sight of our forefathers, in the land of Egypt...

He divided the sea and let them go through... In the day-time also he led them with a cloud: and all the night through with a light of fire.'[37]

This is a night of jubilation, a joyous celebration which is marked by the repeated singing of the Alleluias. Alleluia (or Hallelujah) is a Hebrew word meaning 'Praise God'. It is much in evidence in the psalms; indeed, the whole collection of psalms is called in Hebrew by a word which means 'praises' and many of the psalms sing the praise of God. But the jubilant Alleluia has not been heard throughout the forty days of the season of Lent, the time leading up to Easter, during which Christians examine their lives and seek to turn away from those things which hinder their spiritual life. Now the word returns in force, to express the joy of life restored and renewed.

'Alleluia, that is a word of joy, and praising, and especially it betokens that unspeakable joy that is in heaven endlessly...'[38] 'And therefore it is most sung in Easter time for joy of our Lord's resurrection, by whom we shall all arise in the end of the world, and come to everlasting joy in soul and body.'[39]

Looking up from the font containing the water of new life, one can see the west tower ceiling which is painted with images of God as Creator, the One whose Spirit brooded over the face of the primeval waters at the very beginning of time.[40] This ceiling was painted in the mid-nineteenth century by Henry Styleman le Strange. The design was described in detail soon after its completion:[41]

top: the twelfth-century Paschal Candlestick in S. Paolo fuori le mura, Rome

bottom: inscription on the candlestick: *'surrexit Christus'* – 'Christ is risen'; monstrous figures below it represent the powers of evil overcome by Christ

> The subject... is the Creation of the Universe. Stems and branches of foliage embrace and sustain five circles placed crosswise. In the upper circle toward the east, is depicted the *Dextra Domini*, the "Right Hand of the Lord," as the emblem of the Almighty Father. The central circle contains our Saviour in an aureole [a halo], in the act of exercising creative power. In his left hand He holds the globe of the world; and He is surrounded by the sun, moon, and stars. About Him is written the text, "I am before all things, and by me all things exist." In the circle beneath is the Holy Dove, brooding over the

Tower ceiling painted by Henry Styleman le Strange: The Creation of the Universe

waters of the newly created earth. Rays of light proceed from the *Dextra Domini* in a threefold manner, and embrace within their influence the other two persons of the Godhead. In the other circles are figures of cherubim and seraphim holding scrolls, on which are the words, "Holy, Holy, Holy, Lord God of Sabaoth." Round the whole is the text: "Thou art worthy, O Lord, to receive glory and honour and power: for Thou hast created all things, and for Thy pleasure they are and were created."[42]

With this great image of God in Trinity reigning over the lovingly created universe, the pilgrim is ready to continue on a journey into deeper under-standing of the divine nature and of the Christian story.

CHAPTER 4

Nave and Transepts
Our feet shall stand within thy gates, O Jerusalem

The nave is so called from the Latin word *navis*, a ship. It is the part of the church in which ordinary, lay people generally worship as they are carried forward on the sea of life. In Chapter 1 we saw that the exterior view of the cathedral also has this connotation – hence the cathedral's popular designation as 'the ship of the fens'. This meaning is explicit in one of the

The nave interior, looking east

prayers of the baptism service in the *Book of Common Prayer*: 'Almighty and everlasting God, who of thy great mercy didst save Noah and his family in the ark from perishing by water... mercifully look upon these thy servants... that they... may be received into the ark of Christ's Church; and being steadfast in faith, joyful through hope, and rooted in charity, may so pass the waves of this troublesome world, that finally they may come to the land of everlasting life...' The Church, like Noah's Ark, carries a rich range of creatures safely to shore.

'The first and abiding impression as one looks along the nave is one of repose: the repose of the trees of great forests in their prime with numberless years behind and before them.'[1] The small-scale columns and arches of the exterior walls are repeated here as large forms. They accompany the pilgrim, marking the stages of the journey with their regular rhythm. It is a rhythm in which large rounded columns alternate with clusters of more slender columns, with tall mast-like colonnettes thrusting up the full height

between them. 'It is these lance-like shafts which create the unity that is so apparent as one looks down the cathedral from the west door. The three arched storeys of the nave are framed and enclosed, and their members united.'[2] Through every arch at the lowest level an opening gives a glimpse into the further spaces of the aisles on either side. Above each is another arch, the gallery, subdivided into two smaller arches, and above those a third level with a central window flanked by smaller blank arches. The beauty of the design was praised in a versified Life of St Etheldreda, written about the same time as the nave was being completed: 'The columns are worth looking at; they are slender and beautiful; and they match other columns in shape and position. Although these columns are full of light, our eyes[3] cannot get their fill of them. This work of art, this ornament and adornment among churches, shines bright with what the artisan bestowed upon it, just like the temple of Solomon. The hall is adorned outside, but inside too it is full of adornment. The artisan's skill will never have its like.'[4]

above: the three-storeyed elevation of the nave

opposite: the rhythmic repetition of alternating bay designs is unified by the strong vertical emphasis of the intermediate shafts

The admiring author of this description draws especial attention to the light shining within the building. This comes from the side windows but most of all from above into the centre of the nave. The upper level of windows is known as the clerestorey, through whose openings the clear light can penetrate. Light is an image of God. We talk about being enlightened when the truth becomes clear to us. Christ himself is the Truth and the Light. Christians at their baptism become children of light.

One very obvious feature of the nave is its great length, which would have been even longer before the construction of the fourteenth-century Octagon truncated it by one bay. This feature seems to have been significant: ...'the great length of the more important Anglo-Norman churches is an attempt to emulate the size of the largest Early Christian basilicas in Rome.'[5] Here again, these great cathedral and abbey churches look back to ancient Rome, centre of the Roman Empire; in this case back to a Rome just beginning to become a Christian state. The full length would not have been evident from the west end of the nave because, as we shall consider later, there were screens closing

The interior of the cathedral of St John Lateran, Rome; still essentially the church built by Constantine but with Baroque alterations.

off the east end to form an enclosure for the monks' Choir. So this great size is not only symbolic – it also had a practical function. Most of the great churches possessed the relics of saints, which could draw large crowds on occasions such as the saints' feast days. Moreover, a cathedral is the mother church of a wide-spread diocese, a building which needs, on occasion, to house large crowds of people. It was the custom for parish clergy to bring their parishioners to the cathedral at Whitsun.[6] Many would have come, as they still do, at Christmas and Easter. They also came, as we have seen, on Palm Sunday to join in that day's special procession. Those who lived at great distances could hardly do this – or at least, not often. But still, throngs of people would have arrived for the great festivals. The feast-day of St Etheldreda was especially popular.

The three storeys of this nave are particularly well proportioned. The one, two, three ascending sequence of arches, resonates with the Church's belief that God is both one and three, a trinity of persons in a unity of being: God the Father, God the Son, and God the Holy Spirit. The number three, as expressing the very nature of God, permeates Christian thought, especially in the Middle Ages. In the early fourteenth century Dante expressed it thus: 'That One and Two and Three who always lives, and reigns in Three and in Two and in One, not circumscribed, and circumscribing all, was sung three times by each of those spirits...'[7] The threefold song heard by Dante in heaven was the Sanctus, the angelic acclamation heard also by the prophet Isaiah in his vision of heaven: 'Holy, holy, holy is the Lord of hosts; the whole earth is full of his glory'.[8] Christian interpreters of the Old Testament understood this as one of many implicit references to the nature of God as Trinity.

The nave has a wooden roof, its contour rather reminiscent of the hull of a ship. Indeed, some of its beams may have come from a ship. According to the *Liber Eliensis*, St Etheldreda saved a shipful of sailors and merchants caught and buffeted by a storm. When they at last arrived safely ashore they hastened to Ely to tell of the miracle. Giving thanks to the saint, they donated the timbers of their ship to St Etheldreda.[9] It is not known where these timbers were in fact placed. They may have been used for repairs here or in the monastery buildings. But the connection between seafarers and the church is nicely displayed in this story. The sailors who were helped safely to land by St Etheldreda must have felt rather like the, otherwise unknown, people whose simple graffito survives on a wall near the rock of Golgotha in Jerusalem. That inscription was probably made in the early third century by pilgrims who had completed the arduous journey to the place of Christ's death and resurrection. It shows a boat at last come to harbour, its sails furled, and below it the poignant phrase: *Domine ivimus* – 'Lord, we have arrived'.[10]

above: the painted nave ceiling

left: sketch of a boat, left by an early Christian pilgrim to the place of Christ's resurrection

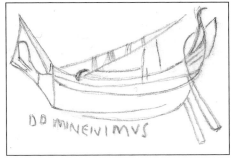

The nave roof may originally have been painted, as was done at Peterborough, where the glorious thirteenth-century painted ceiling still survives.[11] But the present painting at Ely dates from the mid-nineteenth century when a range of imagery was provided for all who look up, while traversing the nave. Here are portrayed scenes from the Bible. They were painted by two amateurs, who asked no payment for their hard work. As we saw in the previous chapter, the first, Henry Styleman le Strange, had already painted the ceiling under the west tower. He was careful to choose a design and a type of painting which would complement the medieval architecture, both in style and content. The style was based on his study of twelfth-century manuscript illuminations, of stained glass designs and of surviving Romanesque ceilings in German churches. In the nave he originally intended to portray a Tree of Jesse – showing the ancestors of Christ. This was a medieval way of depicting the genealogy of Christ – his 'family tree'. It is based on the Gospels, two of which contain accounts of Jesus's ancestry.[12] This was important because the Saviour, prophesied in the Old Testament and longed for by the Jewish people, was to be 'of the House of David' – descended from King David. Thus Jesus was, by his ancestry as well as by the facts of his life, death and resurrection, recognised as the one who had been promised by God.

'But as the painting advanced, the introduction of large sacred subjects seemed far more desirable on so enormous a surface', and so what was decided upon was 'the principal incidents of reference to our Lord, from the creation of man by "the Word of God" to His final coming in glory.'[13] Starting at the east end Le Strange painted six scenes before his death in

The eagle symbol of St John the Evangelist

1862. The series was completed by his friend Thomas Gambier Parry. Prophets flank some of the central scenes. In roundels along each side of the design are the ancestors of Christ, joined together by entwining vines – thus incorporating the essentials of a Tree of Jesse, in fulfilment of le Strange's original intention.

As we have seen, the four Evangelists, whose writings convey to humankind the good news about Christ, surround the font in which people are baptized into the Church of Christ. The Evangelists' symbols are also painted on the nave ceiling 'in order to exhibit the unison of the old dispensation with that which was to follow' – the unity of message between the Old and New Testaments.[14] The Bible tells the story of a gradual deepening of the knowledge of God, through the Old Testament and into the New; but both parts communicate the message of God's goodness and loving kindness.

The large central scenes on the ceiling illustrate some highlights of this story, moving through the Old Testament and the New, from west to east.

As we have seen, the ceiling of the west tower shows God as creator of the universe; as it were, the beginning of the great story. The first scene on the nave ceiling shows the beginning of the human story: the creation of humankind, in the very image and likeness of God.[15] God placed the first two people – Adam and Eve – in a beautiful garden, the garden of Paradise, to live there forever in love, peace and joy. But all did not continue to go well.

The two westernmost scenes on the nave ceiling: the creation of Adam (bottom), and Adam and Eve eat the forbidden fruit (top).

The second scene portrays what is known as the Fall: the moment at which the first human sin was committed, causing pain and death to enter human experience. Adam and Eve are shown standing on either side of a tree, around which is curled a serpent. Tempted by the devil-serpent, they disobeyed God's command and ate the fruit of the tree of the knowledge of good and evil. In this way evil came into human life and Paradise was lost.[16] This, of course, is a myth. It was never meant as what the modern world considers a scientific or historical account. Nevertheless, in a simple story it captures a profound truth about human life. The world around us, and human nature itself, are essentially good. Evil and pain exist, indeed sometimes they seem predominant; yet they are alien and go against the way things ought to be. The story of the creation and the Fall tells us that God saw that all that he created was very good. Evil entered the world as a result of human choice; but once it had entered, human choice was unable to defeat it. That first sin warped our very nature in a way that has passed down to all the descendents of those first ancestors. Unaided, human beings cannot stop the evils that have been let loose in the world; only a new creation by God could achieve that.

The story in the Bible goes on to show how things went from bad to worse. One of Adam's sons, Cain, murdered his brother Abel. The human race grew, but grew also in wickedness, until at last God decided that a new beginning had to be made. He sent a great flood to cleanse the world of all the evildoers, saving the one good man, Noah, and his family. From them, after the Flood had receded, humankind was reconstituted. In thanks for being brought safely through the flood, Noah made a sacrifice to God – shown in the next scene. God promised Noah that never again would there be such devastation. A new means would be found to do away with evil.[17]

The following scene shows a further stage in the story. Abraham and his wife Sarah were promised a son in their old age. That son was Isaac. When Isaac was grown, Abraham believed that God was commanding him to sacrifice his son. So Abraham took Isaac to a distant hill and made an altar for the sacrifice. But an angel preventing him from killing his son, gave him instead a ram for the purpose. The scene on the ceiling shows Abraham on the way to the place of sacrifice, with Isaac behind him carrying the wood for the sacrificial fire.[18] The story of the father who was willing to give his own son, and of the son carrying the wood for his own death, is seen as a prefiguring of the sacrifice of Jesus the son of God who carried his cross to the hill of Golgotha.

Next can be seen a reclining figure with, above him at an angle, a ladder on which angels are climbing up and down. This illustrates the Old Testament story[19] of how the patriarch Jacob, another of the ancestors of Christ, dreamt that in the very place where he lay a ladder stretched from earth to heaven. Angels were climbing up and down the ladder; it was a place of connection between earth and heaven, between the bodily and the spiritual worlds, as is this cathedral.[20] The service for the dedication of a church incorporated Jacob's words when he awôke: 'How dreadful is this place! this is none other but the house of God, and this is the gate of heaven'.[21]

The marriage of Ruth and Boaz is shown in the following scene. Ruth was a gentile woman married to a Jewish man.[22] The expected Saviour would be descended from both Jew and gentile; he would come to save people of all races and nations.

The next scene portrays another reclining figure, Jesse, the grandson of Ruth and Boaz. A later prophet spoke of how a rod or shoot would grow

from Jesse, who would be the promised Saviour. Thus Jesse is shown with a tree growing out of him, the genealogical tree which the painter originally intended to be the main feature of this set of paintings.

Jesse's youngest son was David, shown in the succeeding scene playing a harp. He was the great king and the great musician of the Bible. He was also a great saint and a great sinner. None of these aspects of his character are denied or forgotten. We shall consider him as a musician in Chapters 6

top: Jacob's dream at Bethel – a ladder stretching from heaven to earth

bottom: Jesse and the rod or tree which is the genealogy of Christ

King David playing
his harp

and 8. Of David, saint and sinner, St Gregory the Great had this to say: 'Sometimes Holy Scripture shows us, not only how the saints fought bravely, but also how they fell, that we may see by the example of the mighty, not only what weapons we must take, if we would conquer, but also what snares we must keep clear of, if we would avoid falling.'[23]

The later scenes are from the New Testament, showing the conception, birth and final glory of Christ, the descendant of David; the saviour promised by God. First is the Annunciation, in which the Archangel Gabriel brings to the Virgin Mary the news that she has been chosen by God to bear his Son. Mary's acceptance of this task is the beginning of the life of Jesus, God become Man.[24] After this the next scene shows the birth of Jesus – the Nativity.[25]

The Adoration of the child Jesus is shown next. Shepherds come from one side and Kings from the other, bringing gifts to the child.[26] These signify the Jewish people and the gentiles alike paying tribute to the Saviour sent by God.

The story which began at the west end with the creation of the first human beings, ends with the consummation of that creation at the end of the world. Here is portrayed the great vision from the Book of Revelation: Christ in Glory surrounded by angels and saints representing the whole of redeemed humanity enjoying eternal life, joying in the goodness of God.[27]

Looking down at the floor one sees a pattern of different coloured stones, laid during the Victorian restoration – a delicate visual expression of variety in unity. The poet George Herbert considered the different coloured stones of a church floor as an image of the human heart in relation to God – yet another use of part of a church building to represent spiritual insights:

'Mark you the floor? That square and speckled stone,
   Which looks so firm and strong,
      Is *Patience*...
But the sweet cement, which in one sure band
   Ties the whole frame, is *Love*
      And *Charity*...
Blessed be the *Architect*, whose art
Could build so strong in a weak heart.'[28]

top: Gabriel greets
Mary at the
Annunciation

bottom: kings (on the
left) and shepherds
(on the right) adore
the Christ child

It is not unlikely that a patterned floor existed in the Middle Ages, if not here in the nave then elsewhere. The south transept contains the remains of a fine medieval tile floor, thought perhaps to have come from the original passage from the Choir aisle to the Lady Chapel. Westminster Abbey has a complex mosaic floor around the shrine of St Edward the Confessor; Canterbury also had such flooring, as did many major churches on the Continent. The Westminster floor contains an inscription which makes it clear that the pattern incorporates cosmic symbolism.[29]

The east end of the nave originally was screened off by a stone wall or pulpitum which stretched across the central space, one bay west of the crossing, and returned toward the east on each side to enclose the Choir.[30] Another screen, the rood screen, was placed to the west of the pulpitum. This was probably an open wooden screen, similar to those which survive in many parish churches. It has been plausibly suggested that the screen that now encloses the chapel of St Edmund in the north transept is what remains of the nave rood screen.[31] Above the latter was placed the figure of Christ on the cross – the Rood – flanked by the Virgin Mary and St John. This carved group formed the first focus and goal for all who walked from the west door along the nave.[32]

These screens would have considerably shortened the perceived length of the nave at ground level, although the full length remained open to view at the upper levels. Passage was allowed along the aisles to the Choir, transepts and shrine, although such passage along the south aisle would have been restricted because of the nearness of the monastic cloister and because there was a screened-off chapel at its east end. The cathedral functioned as the church in which the monks offered their prayers throughout the day and during the night as well. Some modicum of privacy was required for the monks in their daily lives, and also for the Choir area of the church where their regular services were held.[33] The eastern parts of the original side screens must have been destroyed when the Norman crossing tower fell. They were replaced by fourteenth-century screens and Choirstalls. The pulpitum across the nave survived until the late eighteenth century, but was then removed in a major restoration of the church. A visit to Norwich cathedral can give some sense of how the view along the nave to the east would have

opposite top: Christ in Majesty adored by saints and angels – the final scene on the nave ceiling

opposite bottom: the patterned stone floor of the nave

St Alban's Abbey – the screen across the nave

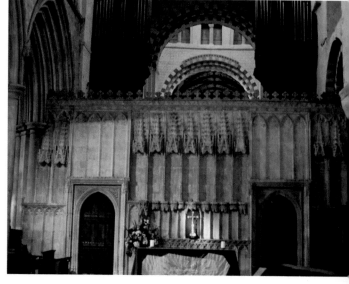

Norwich Cathedral – nave interior showing the placement of the screen towards the east end

looked when it was in place. To the west of the Rood screen, below the Crucifix from which it had its dedication, was the altar of the Holy Cross.

Because of these screens and because of the way the route wound along the aisle, across the north transept and then into the north choir aisle, pilgrims who moved along the nave towards the shrine experienced a series of transformations.[34] This would have been true also for the many pilgrims who entered, not through the west door or the Prior's door[35] but directly into the north transept. Different parts of the building are visible at different times and from different perspectives. 'The cathedral has created a new kind of reality which obviates for the moment the dictates of a uniform and consistent physical world.'[36] Even here in this internal space the pilgrim has a sense of discovering new places – as would have been the case on a longer, more hazardous journey to foreign lands. But all the time there is a strong emphasis on the easterly direction.

Most ancient and medieval churches were oriented – that is, they faced east. The altar was placed at the east end of the building so that the worshippers would look towards the sunrise during their morning prayers. The rising sun is a symbol and reminder of the resurrection of Christ. Various passages in the scriptures make use of the imagery of light to refer to Christ. One of these, the *Benedictus*,[37] was and still is used at Morning Prayer. It greets Christ as the dawn, or day-spring, from on high. As we have seen, the *Exultet* which is sung early on the morning of Easter Sunday greets Christ as the Morning Star. There are good reasons to suppose that from the time of the Apostles Christians prayed facing east. This signifies two things. First, that all Christian prayer is uttered in the name of the 'dayspring from on high' and, second, that all Christian prayer looks forward in hope to the time when, like the sun, the day of Christ's return will dawn.[38]

As one reaches the east end of the nave, the light and space of the Octagon are already commanding attention; but before considering the wonders of that space let us branch aside into the transepts. The north transept was the entrance for many medieval pilgrims. As we have seen, the central space under the Octagon was screened off at ground level, so the transept area

top: the martyrdom of St Edmund – wall painting in St Edmund's chapel

bottom: Christ the High Priest – altar retable in St Edmund's chapel – given in 1898

would have caught their attention before the Octagon itself. On the east side of both transepts are chapels. The southern chapel of the north transept is dedicated to St Edmund, the king of East Anglia after whom the nearby town of Bury St Edmunds is named. There on the upper part of the north wall are the remains of a painting of his martyrdom. He was killed after losing a battle against marauding Danes in 870. Taken prisoner, he was shot through with arrows and beheaded. A wolf is said to have guarded his head until the Danes left and his surviving followers returned to remove his body for burial. The picture shows him bound and shot through with arrows as more archers aim at him from either side. This scene is, as we shall see, repeated at the foot of Bishop Hugh de Northwold's monument, in the north Choir aisle. St Edmund's chapel also contains a beautiful modern retable above the altar, carved with the figure of Christ the High Priest. He is shown robed in a chasuble, the specifically priestly vestment, arms wide open in a gesture which represents both welcome and prayer, but also carries echoes of the cross. This wide-armed gesture is the ancient *orans*

Early Christian
funerary inscription,
now in the porch of
S Maria in Trastevere,
Rome

pose. The earliest images of Christians at prayer show them standing in this attitude. Along the base of the retable is a Greek inscription, taken from that part of the Letter to the Hebrews which speaks of the eternal priesthood of Christ: 'He is able to save completely those who come to God through him'.[39]

Both transepts have fine wooden hammer-beam roofs with two rows of carved angels. Those on the ends of the hammer-beams are full size; the lower ones are shown just from the waist upwards. All have outspread wings. The roof and angels are polychrome, in a largely modern re-paint but a potent reminder that most of the cathedral and all of its decorations were originally picked out with colour. The angels are in various poses. Some hold shields with heraldic devices; some hold objects connected with the liturgy, such as the chalice and host or a book; some play musical instruments and others are in an attitude of prayer. They represent the heavenly hosts, gathered in the presence of God to sing their praises together with all those who are gathered below. Those in heaven and on earth are joined together in one fellowship.

In the later Middle Ages the lower part of the south transept would not have been open to view from the north transept. But now there is a fine vista across the central space to the opposite wall. In the south transept is a modern sculpture by David Wynne. It shows Christ and Mary Magdalene at

Musician angels on
the transept hammer-
beam roof

left: the south transept interior

below: Christ and Mary Magdalene – sculpture by David Wynne

the sudden point of amazed recognition in the garden on the morning of the Resurrection.[40] The grieving Mary had gone to the tomb in which Jesus was hastily buried after his crucifixion, only to find it empty, the body gone. As she searched, anxiously trying to discover what had happened, Jesus appeared to her, alive. She did not immediately recognize him, until he called her by her name. Here is how Lancelot Andrewes, Bishop of Ely from 1609 to 1619, described the scene:

> And now, lo Christ is found; found alive. Who was sought dead. A cloud may be so thick we shall not see the sun through it. The sun must scatter that cloud, and then we may. Here is an example of it. It is a strange thick cloud had so covered her, as see him she could not through it; this one word, these two syllables, Mary, from his mouth, scatters it all. No sooner had his voice sounded in her ears but it drives away all the mist, dries up her tears, lightens her eyes that she knew him straight, and answers him with her wonted salutation, *Rabboni.*[41]

Christ in another guise can be seen over the pulpit. The pulpit itself is a grand nineteenth-century construction, with statues of Sts Peter and Paul on its flanks. Peter carries the keys which are his distinctive attribute, for

right: the nineteenth-century pulpit

below: carvings on the pulpit – *right:* St Paul, *left:* St Peter – both are shown treading dragons underfoot

Jesus had said 'I will give you the keys of the kingdom of heaven'.[42] Paul is shown holding the sword with which he was martyred. Both are shown trampling underfoot the dragon which is Satan. They take their place on the pulpit as the foremost preachers of the good news of Christ; Peter the leader of the Apostles and Paul the one who first carried the good news to the Gentiles. Those who preach today from this pulpit are passing on the same message to their own generation. Above the preacher is the figure of Christ, by Peter Eugene Ball. Christ is shown with his right hand in the gesture of blessing and his left pointing down toward the preacher – a reminder that Christ himself will speak through the preacher to the attentive listener. The pilgrim who has travelled to this point in the cathedral has already experienced a series of transformations; but there is yet more in store for those who travel further.

The Christ figure above the pulpit
– sculpture by Peter Eugene Ball

CHAPTER 5

Octagon
The Glory of the Lord is its Light

The vault of the
Octagon and the nave
ceiling

The crowning glory of the cathedral is the great Octagon, suspended over the crossing to allow light to flood down into the centre of the building. Its very shape is symbolic and in its original form the entire space from floor to vault displayed a carefully designed programme of imagery. It was created in the fourteenth century, after the Norman central tower had collapsed, destroying in its fall also the three Norman bays of the Choir.

> The genius of its builders preserved the exhilarating sense of light and space which the disaster had revealed to them, and also gave it a form which intensely conveyed the idea of the unity of earth with Heaven, of man with God, and of God with this small part of his whole creation which, though infinitely small indeed, was a microcosm of the medieval world and was therefore also a space infinitely large in a little room.[1]

By its eight sides, the octagon represents eternity. In this world of time we experience a succession of seven-day weeks, in a pattern which of itself can seem simply meaningless repetition. 'I saw all the deeds that are done under the sun; and see, all is vanity and a chasing after wind'.[2] But at the last, when time is no more, eternity will be our everlasting eighth day, the day of the new creation when 'death will be no more; mourning and crying and pain will be no more'.[3] In the light of this 'mystique of the eighth day',[4] which

A view of the Octagon interior, soon after the nineteenth-century restoration

already featured in early second-century Christianity and may have been present even before that, the succession of weeks has an eternal significance. Within time, Sunday is the first day of each new week. But Sunday also partakes of the nature of the eighth day, the day out of time, as the Christian community gathers, together with the whole company of heaven, to worship the eternal God.

The octagon, a transitional shape between square and circle, symbolises

The octagonal baptistry of the Lateran in Rome – early fifth century

the connection between seeming opposites: earth and heaven, human and divine, represented respectively by square and circle.[5] This meaning of the square is still in use: we still describe something as being 'foursquare' if it is physical, solid and 'down to earth'. Early Christian Baptisteries and Martyr's shrines were built in octagonal form to engage with this symbolism. In baptism the Christian passes through the waters of death to a new, heavenly, life in Christ. The octagonal Lateran baptistery in Rome, attached to the Pope's own cathedral, was probably the earliest and was certainly very widely known. Free-standing baptisteries in this shape continued to be built, especially in Italy, well into the Middle Ages.[6]

Martyrs also passed through death to new life, with Christ, in heaven. The places where their bodies were buried also took an octagonal form to signify that earth and heaven were especially connected by the presence of the relics of these great heroes of the faith. Jean Bony suggests that the Ely Octagon is a deliberate reference to the churches of early Christian martyrs 'to pay special honour to the remains of St Etheldreda and to all the Saxon saints whose bodies had been venerated for centuries in that old fenland sanctuary.'[7] Two of those buried here, Byrthnoth and Eadnoth, had been killed by the pagan Danes. St Edmund was also killed by the Danes. His body was not buried here but, venerated as a local East Anglian martyr-saint, he was commemorated in the nearest chapel in the north transept. Although Etheldreda and her sisters had not been killed for their faith, Etheldreda had preserved her virginity at some cost. As a king's daughter she had been twice married off in order to ensure political alliances, despite her early and constant belief that she was called by God to a life of dedicated celibacy. She convinced her first husband to respect that conviction; the second she seems to have had to run away from. The medieval Church considered freely chosen life-long virginity to be a form of martyrdom,[8] hence the appropriateness of architectural reference to the early martyrs of the faith in what was, first and foremost, Etheldreda's church.

The octagonal shape also recalls the shape of the Church of the Holy Sepulchre in Jerusalem, burial place of Christ, the supreme martyr, and a major site of Christian pilgrimage. The sepulchre in which Jesus was buried was primarily revered as the place of his resurrection, and so references to the sepulchre were not simply to his death but also to his risen life. Appropriately, it is the resurrected Christ who is portrayed above, on the central boss of the vault here in Ely.

For those who knew their psalms, a number of passages would come to mind in this part of the building. Those who had come to the shrines in hope of healing for mind or body would gain hope as they gazed on that central image of Christ, remembering Psalm 102: 'For he hath looked down from his sanctuary: out of the heaven did the Lord behold the earth; that he might hear the mournings of such as are in captivity: and deliver the children appointed unto death...'[9] Standing beneath the Octagon, where the height and breadth of the building are most evident, they might remember Psalm 103's evocation of the extent of God's loving kindness: 'For look how high the heaven is in comparison of the earth: so great is his mercy also toward them that fear him. Look how wide also the east is from the west: so far hath he set our sins from us.'[10]

Those who did not know the psalms could have the building interpreted

The widened space under the Octagon

for them. Cathedral guides are not only a modern phenomenon. The original guides would have been monks, well versed in the meanings of their church. 'The parallels could be brought out in sermons and in the liturgy, which together provided a constant commentary on ecclesiastical buildings and the rituals which took place within them.'[11] Medieval clergy, when describing church buildings, concentrated on the imagery. They were used to writing sermons, using the biblical passages which the pictures illustrate. 'They can tell their readers what the image shows and what it is about; they probably did so quite often. ...describing the content of an image...to carry a moral message.'[12] Medieval descriptions of images are generally explanations of their meaning. And still today the significance of the building is explained by guides, on displays and, from time to time, in sermons.

We have seen that the nave can be understood as Noah's Ark, carrying its passengers safely through the waters of destruction. Alcuin, one of the great educators of the eighth century[13] interpreted Noah's salvation with reference to the significance of the number eight. There were eight souls aboard the Ark, and with these began the re-birth of the human race after the flood. There were also said to have been eight survivors from the Danish sack of this monastery who later returned, patched up the buildings and continued, as best they could, the monastic life.[14] All of these resonances of the Octagon suggest re-birth and new life.[15]

Moreover, according to numerology, eight is the number of perfection. Ancient and biblical writers understood the number eight in this way. The longest psalm in the Bible (Ps. 119) is a meditation on goodness and on the sort of life that is worth living. The text is traditionally divided into groups of eight verses, signifying the blessedness and perfection of heavenly life. It is an acrostic: the first eight verses all begin with the first letter of the Hebrew alphabet, the second eight all begin with the second, and so on. Thus the psalm moves through the entire alphabet meditating, as it were, 'from A to Z', on God's goodness and faithfulness.[16] 'This psalm is the Teacher of the faithful, a paradise of all fruits, the storehouse of the Holy Ghost...'[17] Jesus summed up the essence of Christian holiness in eight beatitudes[18] and he himself is 'Alpha and Omega, the beginning and the end, the first and the last.'[19] This psalm is known as a 'wisdom' psalm; the wise person is one who knows how to lead the perfect life. For Christians such a life is life in Christ, for Christ is himself Wisdom. 'We preach Christ crucified... Christ the power of God, and the wisdom of God...'[20] It is this connection with wisdom that explains the prevalence in England of octagonal Chapter Houses. These were buildings where discussion about the practical affairs of monastery or cathedral took place, and where it was important to make wise decisions.

Originally the choirstalls were placed under the octagon; their backs formed an enclosing screen (see the plan on p. 156). People entering the cathedral through the door in the north transept, from the town, would encounter the screen and the Octagon rising above it. It must have been a stunning experience and a fitting preparation for their subsequent visit to the shrines and the Lady Chapel. The pictures on the screen together with the sculpture, stained glass and paintings on the surrounding walls and vaults represented the heavenly hierarchy.[21]

Buried at the base of the stalls on the north side were the seven Saxon benefactors of the monastery; Wulfstan archbishop of York, Osmund, Aelfwine, Aelfgar, Eadnoth, Aethelstan and Byrthnoth.[22] Pictures of them were painted above, on the back wall of the stalls. A similar effect can be found in Carlisle cathedral, where there are late-medieval paintings on the Choir screen. On the Ely screen most of the images were

The late-medieval painted Choirscreen in Carlise Cathedral

of local East Anglian people, not all of them formally recognized as saints by the Church but revered as having led good Christian lives. Entombed here, they are the 'living stones' from which the New Jerusalem is constructed. One was the hero Byrthnoth, whose courageous last stand, in 991, against the pagan Danish invaders was immortalised in a great epic poem 'The Battle of Maldon'. As he and his men, facing certain defeat, formed themselves into a shield-wall to fight to the death:

> 'He looks to Heaven: 'Lord I thank Thee
> For all the pleasures I have plucked from this place,
> O mild, though Mighty, I have most need
> To ask that my soul may sojourn safely with thee.'[23]

His headless body was brought to Ely for burial in the abbey, to which he had given a generous bequest of land.

On the arches, through which the diagonal walls open to the aisles, is carved a series of heads. There is a queen, a king, a bishop, two other clerics and a secular figure. They have been variously interpreted as historical personages but there is no certainty about any of these interpretations.[24] They represented the Estates of Society, the various classes of people and the concord that should exist, under God, between religious and secular authority. More generally they will have been understood as representing the whole range of people who, like the benefactors below, may hope to take their place at last among the saints in heaven. The hierarchy of sanctity is thus grounded, localized and shown to be continuous with the daily life alike of monks and lay people.

This is emphasized by the seemingly anomalous figures on the southwest arch, a devil and a lion. They are a reminder that those who are still pilgrims on earth, hoping at last to be with the saints in heaven, must beware of the wiles of the Devil. A Bible reading frequently used in the monastic services made this clear: 'Keep alert. Like a roaring lion your adversary the devil prowls around, looking for someone to devour. Resist him, steadfast in your faith.'[25] The monks moved past these devilish figures to and from their work and their rest, in and around the cloister. The carved devil is shown armed for battle, holding a weapon and a round shield. During the final service of each day – Compline – the monks chanted Psalm 91, in which they were assured that God would defend them and enable them to overcome the devil: 'My God, in whom I trust... ' 'His faithfulness is a shield and buckler.' 'The young lion and the serpent you will trample under foot.'[26] This south west angle of the Octagon led directly

Carvings on the
Octagon arches –
1: head of a bishop,
2: head of a king,
3: roaring lion,
4: armed devil

to the monks' dormitory, to which they processed immediately after Compline.

Such demonic figures scattered around the enclave were meant to instill a salutory circumspection. The monks were to be on their guard against, rather than terrified by, the power of evil. Indeed, as we saw in Chapter 3, it was their task to engage in battle with the demons. But at night, Compline prepared them to sleep in peace under God's protecting hand. 'And in what soul ever these two things are, that is, unity and peace with all others, and love and joy in God, there liketh our Lord to rest and to abide. And therefore, if ye say well your Compline... then bless you, and go to bed, and sleep restfully and safely, for our Lord Himself resteth in you, and He will keep you while ye sleep.'[27] Many modern Christians end their day by praying the service of Compline, so that they likewise may sleep secure in the hand of God.

Nearby is a further sculpted reference to Psalm 91. On the south side of the easternmost south nave pier is a corbel that once held a statue. It, together with the painted decoration which still survives on the vault in this bay of the aisle,[28] may have been part of the decoration of a chapel which seems to have been located here. This chapel may have marked the place of Etheldreda's original burial,[29] a spot which continued to be revered by the community after her translation to the shrine behind the high altar. The chapel would have been frequently visited by monks entering the church through the south-east door from the cloister.

Lion on corbel in the south aisle of the nave

Much damaged though the corbel is, one can still make out a lion and a dragon/serpent. The statue above would have been, in effect, trampling them underfoot. It is not known which saint the statue represented. But its position here where there may have been a chapel dedicated to her suggests Etheldreda as a possibility.

Above and to either side of the diagonal arches, Etheldreda's story was portrayed in a series of small relief carvings. These would originally have been painted in a way that made their details easier to see. The pilgrims standing in the north transept had come to visit Etheldreda's shrine, just a few yards to the east, beyond the High Altar. Here, on corbels supporting the Octagon vaulting ribs, her story is placed in the context of the whole company of the saints. In sequence clockwise

starting from the north west pier, the reliefs show scenes from the story of her life, death and subsequent miracles.[30] The story begins with the westernmost corbel on the north west pier of the Octagon. Here is a relief in two scenes. On the left is the saint's marriage to her first husband, Tondbert;[31] on the right his death.[32] The placement of this relief is significant, standing as it does above the place where the seven benefactors were buried, since Tondbert was believed to have given Etheldreda the Isle of Ely as a wedding present.[33] The next corbel shows the saint's second marriage, to Egfrid.[34] Etheldreda is shown being pushed and pulled into the marriage ceremony, to indicate her unwillingness to enter this marriage. The third corbel shows the saint being veiled as a nun, having at last gained Egfrid's consent to this.

The fourth corbel contains the Miracle of the Sprouting Staff: as Etheldreda slept on her journey to Ely, watched over by two of her companions, her staff, which she had placed upright in the ground, put forth leaves. The saint is shown lying asleep in the centre, with the staff sprouting behind her and one attendant raising a hand to point at it in amazement. The next corbel portrays the Miracle of St Abb's Head. Egfrid, who had unwillingly consented to his wife's decision to enter a convent, changed his mind and intended to remove her by force. She, being forewarned, set out towards Ely only to be overtaken by Egfrid and his followers at St Abb's Head. A miraculously high tide prevented the king from reaching Etheldreda and her companions until Egfrid gave up and returned to York. The carving shows the saint and her

Life of Etheldreda corbels: *(top to bottom):*
marriage with Tondbert/death of Tondbert;
marriage with Egfrid;
Etheldra being veiled as a nun;
Etheldreda's flowering staff

maidens in the centre, surrounded by waves, with the king and his men baffled on either side.[35]

The sixth corbel shows Etheldreda's installation as Abbess of Ely. She is enthroned at the centre of the composition with the Archbishop, St Wilfrid, and his monks on one side, Etheldreda's nuns on the other. The following corbel is divided into two scenes. The death of the saint is shown on the left; on the right is the translation of her body, sixteen years later, into the antique sarcophagus brought from Cambridge.[36] When the original coffin was opened, Etheldreda's body was found to be incorrupt, a miracle which further confirmed her sanctity.

The series is completed with the eighth carving. This deals with one of Etheldreda's posthumous miracles: the release of Bricstan from prison. Bricstan, having been unjustly convicted and imprisoned, prayed fervently to Saints Etheldreda and Benedict who at last appeared to him and broke his chains. Bricstan is shown in the prison with hands held in prayer towards the figures of the two saints. Benedict is kneeling to break the chains. This miracle had particular relevance because Bricstan entered Ely as a monk and his chains were displayed beside the shrine of Etheldreda (see Chapter 7, p.120).

These two latter corbels are placed close to the lion and devil, mentioned above. This placement may well have been meant to represent the way in which the saints, both in their own lives of heroism and as channels of God's miraculous intervention, are able to overcome all the assaults of evil.

Life of Etheldreda *(top to bottom)*:
The Miracle of St Abb's Head
Etheldreda's enthronement;
Etheldreda's death and translation;
Bricstan released from prison

It is perhaps difficult for a modern reader to believe that Etheldreda could have preserved her virginity through two marriages, and harder still to understand why she would want to do so. Nowadays virginity is considered a merely negative thing – a regrettable lack of sexual experience. But for the very new Christians of seventh-century England virginity was a powerful ideal. It was a means of following the courageous example of the early Christian virgin martyrs, those who had been faithful to Christ through persecution and terrible tortures. Moreover, for a high-born woman of the time it must have offered the only possibility of independence. Such women had little or no choice about whom to marry, or whether to marry, since they were politically useful in forming alliances between potentially warring factions.[37] Virginity was an ideal for men as well as women, which goes some way towards explaining why Etheldreda's husbands complied, even if reluctantly, with her wishes. They would all have known the story of Saint Cecilia who, having been married against her will, convinced her newly-wed husband to embrace virginity – and martyrdom for the faith – with her.[38] Etheldreda would also have known the story of St Radegund who, a century earlier in what is now France, had founded a monastery after fleeing from a forced marriage.

Above the local saints are placed further layers of saintly figures. In the windows are images of saints of the wider Church. The present glass dates from the nineteenth century but the original windows seem to have portrayed a similar range of individual saints. The carved figures in groups of three on the diagonal walls represent the twelve Apostles, founder members of the Church. These fine seated figures were carved by J. R. Redfern and installed as part of the nineteenth-century restoration. Although the

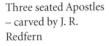

Three seated Apostles – carved by J. R. Redfern

original statues did not survive the Reformation, there was sufficient evidence to show that the niches contained carved figures and that they were seated. Their position in the scheme of imagery and the fact that they are twelve makes it a reasonable assumption that they were always meant to be Apostles. Between these niches is a series of small head-corbels. These heads wear a special kind of hat, which is identical to hats worn by Old Testament Prophets in contemporary manu-scripts and on contemporary carvings else-where in Europe. This suggests that they repre-sent the four major and twelve minor prophets – those who prophesied the coming of the Messiah, the Christ who was proclaimed by the Apostles.

Above that level, on the tops of the arched openings into nave, Choir and transepts, are the four Evangelists. The Evangelists, whose Gospels contain the recollections of the life and teachings of Jesus which form the basis of the Christian faith, and the Apostles[39] who were the first to preach that faith are suitably part of the structure of the building. They are spiritu-al supports of the Church in general, as their images are physical supports of this particular church. Above this great company of saints are angels; nineteenth-century in the lantern of the

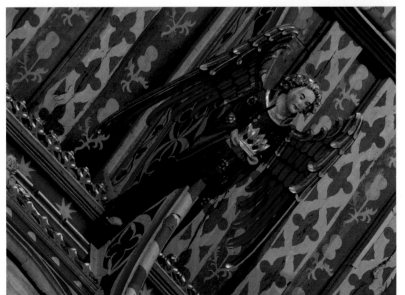

top: medieval carved heads of the prophets, flanking the seated Apostles

above: musician angel on transept roof; the lower angel points to the Book of Life

left: angel holding the Crown of Life

both: nineteenth-century painted angels on the panels of the lantern

octagon itself and medieval on the hammer beams of the flanking transept roofs.

The heavenly hierarchy could thus be seen to stretch in unbroken continuity from this very place and from each one of the varied pilgrims who visit it, some of them, perhaps, also saints. It moves up through the local saints, then to the heroes of the wider Church, then on to the founder members of the Church, and so to the heights of heaven. All are connected together in a bond of love and all are centred on God. It was recommended that the dying should be comforted with the assurance that they, too, were going to take their place in this heavenly hierarchy: '...it seems that you are moving quickly from this life towards God. There you shall see all the patriarchs, apostles, martyrs, confessors, virgins, and all men and women that have been saved. And for gladness of such fellowship, be then of good comfort in God...'[40]

The summit and culmination of this ascending imagery is Christ himself, carved in the centre of the upper vault, 'at the still point of the turning world'.[41] The upper vault is designed to give the illusion that it is floating weightlessly and, like the heavenly firmament,

The wounded, risen
Christ at the centre

turning. The effect is due to the fact that, although made of wood, it
masquerades as a stone vault. But a stone vault of such span with an open
lantern in the centre was impossible at the time this was built.[42] Also, the
upper vault has been given a half turn in relation to the octagonal space
below, so that its windows are above the piers and its supports are above the
lower windows and diagonal walls. On a windy day of alternating sun and
cloud it can indeed seem as though the vault is slowly turning: '...turned by
love, The love that moves the sun and the other stars'.[43] That love is shown
in the wounds displayed by Christ, the wounds of his willing self-sacrifice on
behalf of humankind. It is also the love to which the pilgrim's journey
should be tending; for the desire and will of each can be transformed, to
move in union with the love that moves the universe.[44]

Light floods down from the windows around the lantern, as if in illustration of Jesus's own prediction of the Last Day: 'You will see the heavens
opened and the Son of Man coming on the clouds of the sky, with power
and great glory.'[45] This symbolism of light in church buildings was well
understood from early times and frequently referred to. 'The message is
this: in the temporal realm, the closest we can come to seeing God is

through the light that emanates from heaven.'[46] The light scintillating from mosaics in the churches of Rome, one of the major pilgrimage destinations, was explained by a sixth-century inscription in one of them: 'God's residence radiates brilliantly in shining materials; the precious light of the faith in it glows even more. The secure hope of salvation comes to the people from the [saints] and from the sanctity this place derives honour.'[47] A similar interpretation was applied in the twelfth century to the glistening golden doors of St Denis, the great royal abbey on the outskirts of Paris, by Abbot Suger:

> '...being nobly bright, the work
> Should brighten the minds, so that they may travel, through the true lights,
> To the True Light where Christ is the true door.'[48]

Christ himself is the Light of the World whose glory shines on all creation and illuminates the members of his Church. 'For God, who said, "Let light shine out of darkness," made his light shine in our hearts to give us the light of the knowledge of the glory of God in the face of Christ.'[49] And this light of Christ transforms his followers. 'As light strikes the eyes of those who come out of darkness into the sunshine and enables them to see clearly things they could not discern before, so light floods the souls of those counted worthy of receiving the Holy Spirit and enables them to see things beyond the range of human vision, things hitherto undreamed of.'[50]

So much has been lost of the original imagery of the Octagon that we cannot be sure of the exact details of every part. But the general scheme is clear. It corresponds to the classic pattern of decoration in eastern, Byzantine, churches. In this the key figure is the Pantocrator – Christ as ruler of the world – in the summit of the dome: '...the image in the summit of the dome is crucial. It is the touchstone of the reality of the Incarnation.'[51] There is one difference between the Byzantine image and that in Ely. Here, as we have seen, Christ is shown, not so much as Ruler but as Saviour of the World – the compassionate one whose wounds show the extent of his love for humankind. Below him is a descending hierarchy of single figures, grouped to form different ranks and categories: angels, prophets, apostles and evangelists, martyrs and bishops. Entailed in this grouping is a time sequence, an unfolding through the ages of God's preordained plan for the redemption of the human race from Original Sin. The prophets foretold the Incarnation – God becoming man; the disciples and martyrs bore witness to it; and the bishops represent the living Church which continues Christ's redemptive work here and now.[52] All were shown here in Ely, ranged in tiers around the octagon of eternity, completed by the living people of each age, all looking to Christ, just as Dante saw the blessed in heaven:

'This realm secure and full of gladsomeness,
Crowded with ancient people and with modern,
Unto one mark had all its look and love.'[53]

Light floods down
from the Octagon
lantern

It is to this Christ that the monks looked and sang:

O Lord, shining King of heaven's citadel,
save your people in your loving kindness.
The choirs of Cherubim unceasingly proclaim your glory;
the noble Seraphim respond with hymns of praise.
The nine angelic orders worship you in your beauty;
the Church throughout the world unites to sing to you;
the sun, moon, and stars, the earth and sea all serve you,
O Christ the King enthroned on high.[54]

To this day the choir sings similarly in the *Te Deum* at Morning Prayer on
Sundays:

We praise thee, O God: we acknowledge thee to be the Lord...
Thou art the King of Glory: O Christ...

We have seen how the explicit imagery unfolds vertically, uniting earth and
heaven. There is also implicit, horizontal, meaning. This place is the centre
of the cross which forms the ground-plan of the cathedral. It is the place
from which all paths branch out; or, looked at the opposite way, it is the

The Octagon at the
centre of the cross

uniting point for those coming from the four directions of the compass. A
treatise on the cross had this to say:

> 'All things come together in this cross because on it suffered Christ, the
> creator of all things. For the Passion of Christ holds up the heavens, rules
> the world, and harrows hell. The angels are confirmed in their righteousness
> by it, the people are redeemed, the hostile are confounded. It secures the
> structure of the world, breathes life into the living, keeps feeling in the
> sentient, illumines the intelligent.'[55]

Here, beneath and among the Hosts of Heaven, the monks sang their services, day after day and night after night worshipping God with psalms,
prayers and scriptural readings. Their prayers rose up to heaven; prayers
for themselves, for their benefactors, for all of creation whom they represented before God. 'At the house of the Lord musicians play before him...
but because this little place by symbol leads over the threshold of his heavenly palace, there the Lord is praised as in his most holy abode, the Lord
enthroned over the sky vault which blazes with his glory; and there... is
gathered up the praise of every breathing thing.'[56]

Although the Choirstalls, which were originally meant to be here, have been moved to the east of the screen, it is appropriate that the modern choir, sanctuary and altar are placed in the Octagon which symbolises eternity. Here as was originally intended, the choir sings the music of heaven. Here the worshipping community joins 'with angels and archangels and the whole company of heaven', lifting up hearts and voices to Christ their Lord and God. 'At the words of the priest, the heavens be opened… and earthly joined to heavenly, and… one thing is made of visible and invisible'[57] here during the Eucharist, the Holy Communion, celebrated on Sunday, the first day of the week.

'The First Day is also the Eighth, because to partake of the life of God is to participate in that which is beyond time. So the Eighth day becomes the figure of life everlasting, the symbol of eternity in which we now live because of Christ. Therefore it is the day without evening, the last day, because no other day can follow eternity. Hence the Eucharist always makes the Church what she is, the Body of Christ and the Temple of the Holy Spirit.'[58]

CHAPTER 6

Choir
Sing unto the Lord a New Song

The elevation of
Bishop Hotham's
Choir bays

The Octagon opens out to show the length and breadth, height and depth of the spiritual universe; God can there be understood and praised as the creator of all that exists. To the east of the Octagon the Choir and sanctuary offer a different experience. Here one is in an enclosure sheltered from the nave and the surrounding aisles. This area is like a church within a church, turned inward in an act of concentration, to encounter the God who is to be found within each human heart. It is here that the daily sung services are held; Evensong most days sung by the cathedral's own choir or by a visiting choir. This is an intimate, reflective service. 'There is much rest in it, much time to ponder, and pray, and to relax in God... spreading our souls out in the sunshine of heaven, strengthening our inner life by the fellowship of the Common Prayer, and lifting up tranquil hearts...'[1]

These services continue the regular offering of worship in the tradition of the nuns and monks who formerly prayed in this place. In fact the stream of daily praise and thanksgiving has rarely been interrupted. After the devastating Danish attack in 870, when most of the community were killed or taken prisoner, the site was unoccupied for an unknown period of time before eight of the survivors returned. Thereafter services ceased for one day (October 27th, 1071) in the turmoil resulting from the conquest of the Isle by William the Conqueror, and then again when all the cathedrals were forcibly closed down for some years in the mid-seventeenth-century, during the Commonwealth period. Even in the latter period the tradition was not forgotten. It was reborn as soon as the building became available with the restoration of Monarchy and Established Church in 1660. Apart from those enforced breaks, daily worship has been offered in this place since the time of St Etheldreda.

The daily offices still contain the same ingredients as those used by the medieval monks. At the centre of each service are Bible readings, psalms, hymns and prayers. Since the very beginning of Christianity the psalms have been the Church's main prayer book.[2]

> 'For as Saint Augustine says: All that the old law; all that the prophets and all that the Gospel and the new law bid and ordain is contained in these holy psalms, and therefore... the singing of them pleases God much... Each man and woman and child, young and old, may find in these psalms that which shall teach them and that which shall delight them. ...For our lord God has made a drink by his servant David which is sweet to taste and effectual to heal the wounds of sinners by its virtue. This drink is these psalms, that are sweetly heard when they are sung, and they go through the heart when they delight.'[3]

The psalms are sung antiphonally, that is, one verse by one side of the choir and the next by the other side, turn and turn about. It is a manner of

Choir interior with medieval stalls

singing said to have started in the eastern Church after St Ignatius, late-first-century bishop of Antioch, experienced in a vision angels singing in this manner. The angels ranged on either side of the transept roofs, like the choir in their stalls, are no doubt singing and playing antiphonally.

In the daily services the psalms are followed by readings, first from the Old Testament and then from the New. These are interspersed with psalm-like 'canticles' taken from the New Testament. The first canticle for Evensong is the Magnificat, the song sung by the Virgin Mary when she was greeted as 'the mother of the Lord' by her cousin Elizabeth.[4] This canticle has for many centuries been popular in part because it is set in the first person singular – '*My* soul doth magnify the Lord…' – which allows the faithful a very personal way to experience the joy of God's promises soon to be fulfilled.[5]

Angels on either side of the the transept roof

In a fifteenth century play which dramatises the life of Mary, the significance of this song is spelled out. Mary recites it in Latin and Elizabeth comments on it in English, verse by verse.

MARY: 'For this holy psalm I begin here this day:
             Magnificat: anima mea dominum
             et exultavit spiritus meus: in deo salutari meo
ELIZABETH: By the Holy Ghost with joy God's son is in thee come,
             That thy spirit so enjoyed the health of thy God…

At the end of the Magnificat Mary explains:

This psalm of prophecy said between us two,
In heaven it is written with angel's hand;
Ever to be sung and also to be said,
Every day among us at our Evensong.'[6]

And thus it has indeed continued 'at our Evensong' as those at prayer follow the advice of St Ambrose, late-fourth-century bishop of Milan: 'May Mary's soul reside in each one of us to glorify the Lord; May Mary's spirit reside in each one of us to rejoice in God. According to the flesh there is only one Mother of Christ, but by faith Christ becomes the fruit of each one.[7]

The choir at Evensong sings from the wooden seats which were made in the 1340s for the choir of monks. These are, although much restored, the Choirstalls which originally stood under the Octagon. They have been twice moved and a third of the original seats are missing. In particular on each side the medieval stalls for bishop and prior have been lost. But the majority of the medieval stalls still remain in use. The stalls and their canopies are intricately carved. They were originally painted; the present uniform brown appearance dates from the mid-nineteenth century restoration.[8]

As part of that restoration, replacement stalls were provided at the west end for the bishop and the dean and an extra, lower, line of stalls added.[9] Carved scenes were also placed in the upper canopies of the stalls. It is thought that the architect in charge of the restoration, Sir George Gilbert Scott, found evidence that carvings or paintings were originally placed there. The nineteenth-century carvings represent subjects from the Old Testament on the south and scenes of the life of Christ from the New Testament on the north.

The choir stalls. The back row and canopies are medieval; many of those below are nineteenth-century replacements, as are the carved scenes in the upper canopies.

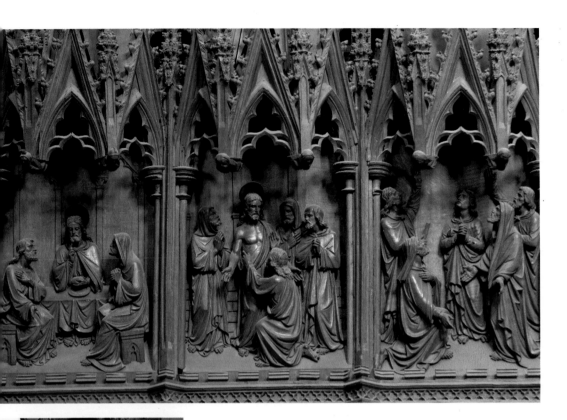

On the carved ends of the upper desks are nineteenth-century angels; some play musical instruments, others hold scrolls which represent music which they are singing. At the ends of the stalls is a series of small figures representing the builders of the various portions of the cathedral, from St. Etheldreda, who holds a model of a Saxon church, to Bishop Alcock, who exhibits his chapel.[10] On the lower range stall ends are carved the lion, eagle, ox and angel which, as we have seen in Chapter 3, are the symbols of the four Evangelists.

Also among these nineteenth-century additions is a copy of one of the most frequently represented of medieval images – the pelican, placed on the end of one of the bottom desks on the south side. A pelican is shown pecking her breast to draw blood with which to feed her young – a symbol of Christ who feeds his people

Nineteenth-century carvings on the Choirstalls:
above: New Testament scenes: the Supper at Emmaus; Doubting Thomas; the Ascension of Christ; *left:* St Etheldreda holding a model of her church

far left: the ox of St Luke

left: the Pelican feeding its chicks

with his own body and blood in the Eucharist. Various Fathers of the Church, including St Augustine of Hippo, interpreted Psalm 102 verse 6 as referring to Christ. They understood his suffering and death alone on the cross as foreshadowed by the psalmist's cry: 'I am like a pelican in the wilderness'. Ancient bird lore, perhaps through misunderstanding the way that pelicans regurgitate food for their young, thought that the pelican feeds her chicks with her own blood. So Christ, who in the Eucharist feeds his people with his own blood, shed on the cross, is doubly likened to the pelican.[11]

The pelican, seated above its nest and pecking its breast to feed the chicks below, became a favorite symbol both in church decoration and in heraldry. It was the sign used by the many guilds dedicated in the later Middle Ages to *Corpus Christi*, the (Eucharistic) Body of Christ. It will generally have brought to mind the love and sacrifice of Christ, present in the church at every Eucharist and in the reserved Sacrament; Christ whom the poet Dante could affectionately call: *nostro pellicano*.[12]

The monks stood for many hours, day and night, chanting the psalms. For the elderly or infirm such long standing was difficult, so special seats were provided. The seats when tipped up have a small shelf on which to rest while still remaining upright – they are 'mercy' seats, which is the meaning of the Latin word *misericordia* from which the term 'misericord' is derived.

Misericords have been much studied, but usually in isolation from their

Some of the carved spandrels above the stalls seem to portray spiritual warfare

context. Choir stalls generally have, as here, elaborate backs to keep off draughts, canopies above and armrests between the seats. From an iconographical perspective, only the misericords have been studied in any detail. And concerning these, the scholarly consensus seems to be that, apart from a few overtly religious subjects, the imagery consists mostly of humorous, everyday or genre scenes.[13]

Yet what has been written of contemporary manuscripts with similar imagery is surely true of this carved imagery; that it exhibits a range of different meanings which need to be studied both as a complete, individual set and also in comparison with such imagery found in other contexts.[14] So far none of the surviving sets of cathedral stalls has been studied in its entirety.[15]

With some of the original stalls missing it is probably now impossible to discover what, if any, overall meaning there may have been here at Ely. Still, it is worth scrutinising the work that survives, especially that on the upper, back, row of stalls which are largely medieval. Like most such Choirstalls, the ones here have carvings on the stall elbows and shoulders as well as on the misericords.[16] The significance of the carvings on the elbows and shoulders has not so far been studied. The elbows have heads

carved on the ends, some of which are human, some bestial. Above, the end of each of the shoulders has three figures: a central head flanked on each side by the head of a recumbent figure whose body stretches back along the seat. Many of the latter are human from the waist upwards but bestial below. Such semi-human figures represent the conflict, to which all people are subject, between reason and the baser passions. 'Their form begins in the likeness af a man but terminates in the extremity of a beast. ...And like a man ending in a beast, sin – while beginning in the likeness of reason – passes on to an end devoid of reason.'[17] On the two eastern-most sets of the north side the recumbent figures are gnawing at the arms of the central figure. On another, two lions are gnawing at the legs of a king. This latter is a particularly dramatic way of portraying the attack of irrational impulses, for reason should wear the crown of authority. The tenth from the east on the same side shows recumbent figures gripping and pulling at their hair. One of the crouching figures on a misericord is similarly pulling his or her hair in what was a conven-tional image of Wrath. The other recumbent figures are beasts or monsters. 'Such monsters may evoke generally the threatening forces named in the psalms: the unjust, the iniquitous, the enemies that harry, oppress and ter-rify ...'[18]; they signify the assaults of the devil on those

top: shoulders and elbows of stalls

above: head on a stall elbow

left: shoulder carving: crouching king with a lion gnawing his foot

who here prayed in the words of the psalms.

This context suggests a new appraisal of the misericords. Certainly a few of these have obvious religious or moral significance. Indeed, it has been suggested that, of all the surviving sets of stalls, Ely has the largest number of saints portrayed on the misericords.[19] Each of the misericords consists of a main, central section flanked on either side by a smaller carving. The latter are known as 'supporters'. The supporters may show further scenes in the same story as the main section, or they may form part of one extended scene together with the centre; they may comment upon the central scene or they may simply provide a decorative frame for it.

Let us first consider the overtly religious subjects. The story of the Fall[20] is shown on two of the seats. One is carved with the beginning of the story, showing Adam and Eve in Paradise eating the forbidden fruit. The supporters show the

top: human-headed beast on stall shoulder

bottom: the Fall: Adam and Eve, tempted by the Devil, eat the forbidden fruit.

animals, with whom the first humans lived at peace, sitting under trees laden with the fruits provided by God for their sustenance.

The other seat continues the story in three scenes. In the middle, the angel with a fiery sword is thrusting naked Adam and Eve out of Paradise. Before eating the forbidden fruit they were unaware of, and unembarrassed by, their nakedness;[21] afterwards they attempted to cover themselves. The supporters show later scenes in the story, in which both are clothed. On the one side Adam delves and on the other Eve spins. These are the tasks that they had to undertake in order to get their livelihood after forfeiting the rest and ease of the Garden of Eden. They are accompanied by their two children, Cain and Abel. That they all are clothed is a sign of their fallen nature.

Another seat shows Noah's Ark[22] with three octagonal, battlemented turrets. Thus the connection between the Ark and the Church, that we considered in a previous chapter, is not only made but also related to the octagonal features of this very building.[23] The threefold turrets refer to the three persons of the Trinity; it is God who is carrying the human race to safety. This story also is shown in three scenes. On the left a carrion bird pecks at a drowned animal; in the centre Noah looks out of the Ark, and on the right the dove is shown plucking a branch from a tree growing on dry ground. The dove's return with the branch is the sign to Noah that at last the flood is over and he, his family and their cargo of animals can disembark safely. The return of the dove to Noah is understood to signify the descent of the Holy Spirit at baptism, after the candidate has been carried through a symbolic death in the baptismal water, to new life in Christ.[24]

Another biblical scene is that of Samson wrestling with the lion, tearing its jaws apart with his hands.[25] This was understood as an Old Testament 'type' or prefiguring of Christ, who in his death and resurrection grappled with the forces of evil and definitively overcame them.

Another symbol of Christ is the Lady and Unicorn image. Of the unicorn it was said:

> '...it is a little beast.. and extraordinarily swift. It has a horn in the middle of its brow, and no hunter can catch it. But it can be caught in the following fashion: a girl who is a virgin is led to the place where it dwells, and is left

Samson overcoming the lion

there alone in the forest. As soon as the unicorn sees her, it leaps into her lap and embraces her, and goes to sleep there. Then the hunters capture it... Our Lord Jesus Christ is the spiritual unicorn... He is called very swift, for neither principalities nor powers, nor thrones nor lordships could capture him; the underworld could not hold him, and not even the most cunning devil could understand him. But by the will of the Father alone He descended into the Virgin's womb to save us.'[26]

The misericord which portrays the martyrdom of St John the Baptist shows, on the left, Salome dancing in front of the table at which her mother is feasting with King Herod. Salome is shown bending over backwards, as if about to turn a backward somersault. This was the standard medieval way of portraying her dance. In the centre is St John's beheading; the right supporter shows Salome presenting his head, on a platter, to her mother.

Other saints are portrayed – the hermit St Giles shelters an exhausted and wounded deer as the huntsmen, bows at ready, approach from the supporters on either side. The saint is shown sitting in a leafy bower, with a rosary in his left hand. He comforts and protects the deer with his right hand, through which can be seen the arrow which has wounded the deer.

below: the Martyrdom of St John the Baptist

bottom: St Giles shelters a deer from hunters

The saints epitomise the good life. Also shown on the misericords are warnings about vice and temptation. One misericord shows a devil perched between two women. This is Tutivillus, whose special work is listening in on the conversations of those who gossip rather than paying attention to their prayers. He also keeps a check on the clergy and choir, writing down any mistakes that they make due to laziness or inattention[27] and noting any monks who took an inordinate pride in their singing.

Tutivillus is an example of the comic devil, designed to make a serious point. At the Last Judgment he will turn up with a sack full of transcripts of mistakes and gossip to be weighed against each person's good deeds. In this way he was portrayed in the medieval mystery plays. On the misericord's supporters are subsidiary devils. One is holding the end of a scroll in his

mouth while pulling the other end with his hands. He is trying to stretch it, because there is so much to write down. The other is busily writing. A relative of Tutivillus is carved in stone on the west side of the north Octagon arch label. There a man's head leans out; his right ear, angled towards the space where the monastic choir was originally placed, is very large. It is as if he is listening intently for mistakes in the monks' chanting. According to a manuscript in Oxford the monstrous race of the Panotii use their giant ears to hear evil.[28] So these carvings are reminders that the devil has, as it were, hidden microphones all around, listening out for misdeeds.

Some of the misericords portray vices, or the assaults of the devil in various guises. Gambling and drunkenness go together on the misericord which portrays two men playing at dice. On one of its supporters is a man beside a barrel; on the other is a man holding a cup and flagon.[29] Domestic strife is illustrated in the scene of a man and a woman fighting.[30]

Another man grips his knees in agony while an ape-like demon-dentist wrenches at

top left: Tutivilus the devil tempts two women to gossip instead of praying

top right: devil stretching a piece of parchment

centre: devil writing down the gossip

bottom: big-eared devil listening for misdeeds

top: demon dentist

bottom: stag eating a
snake

a tooth. Like the gargoyle on the south exterior, this is a graphic illustration of the violence and pain that can be wreaked by evil in human life. It also can hardly have failed to remind the monks of one of St Etheldreda's miracles, in which she healed a man suffering agonies of toothache.[31]

A story concerning Etheldreda's sister Withburga seems to be portrayed on another misericord. She is shown on the right supporter, praying inside a chapel. The central scene is of a huntsman falling headlong from his foundered horse, and on the left supporter the hunted deer move safely away from him, followed by his hounds. St Withburga is said to have been provided with milk by tame deer until they were killed by an evil huntsman. As punishment he was killed by falling from his horse, but the saint prayed forgiveness for his soul.[32]

The monks may well have understood the deer who have been saved from the hunter as a reference to themselves, protected by God from the assaults of Satan. Psalm 42 compares the human soul to a deer: 'Like as the hart desireth the water brooks: so longeth my soul after thee, O God.' And Psalm 91 assures the believing soul that there is no need to fear the hunter. The stag on one of the supporters is shown eating a snake, which the Bestiary interprets thus: 'if the devil (-snake) enters their body after they have committed a sin, they hasten to Christ... and are renewed, laying aside their old guilt.'[33]

The image of a falling rider is frequently portrayed as a dramatic illustration of the saying that 'Pride goes before a fall', a message eminently appropriate to this story. Pride is the worst of the seven deadly sins and the root of all the others.[34] Other sins may be implicitly referred to on other misericords: a man and a woman seated side by side may seem innocent enough. But his legs are crossed, with one leg at an acute upward angle pointing towards his companion. It has been argued that such images have sexual connotations,[35] in which case this carving would represent the sin of lust.

This may also be the meaning of another misercord on which a single, bearded male figure crouches holding a sword pointing upward into the seat above. There is surely deliberate humour, as well as a serious moral point being made, in placing all these carvings here beneath the backsides of the praying monks.[36] John Maddison has pointed out that another misericord may also portray lust[37], but in this case lust being overcome. A bear is shown, shaking apes out of a tree; on the supporters are hares. Apes and hares were emblems of lust but the bear could symbolise Christian conversion and hence the fight against vice.

Many of the carvings show Atlas-type figures.[38] These are crouched beneath the seat, carrying its weight on their shoulders or on upraised arms. Such figures are often to be found supporting vaults. They represent sinners oppressed with a heavy load of vice from which they cannot free themselves.[39] Some of these figures have on the supporters images which underscore this meaning: lions and dragons with devilish import or, as on one seat, male and female centaurs playing musical instruments, like the ne'er-do-well strolling minstrels that they resemble.[40] Centaurs, being half-human, half-beast, represent those who are driven by their baser instincts. The Atlas-figures include people of all kinds; young and old, men and women, sometimes in couples, sometimes alone; even a king and queen. Their position is undignified and many of them look extremely bored by the tedium of their task.[41] Others seem to be asleep. One on the north side crouches between two curled-up lions; all three are asleep.

Drowsiness must have been a frequent problem for the monks, especially during the long Night Office. But physical sleep was also a metaphor for spiritual inattentiveness, as in the scriptural calls to stay awake, alert for the coming of Christ. Caesarius of Heisterbach, in a

top: crouching man with upright sword

centre: centaur playing a fiddle

bottom: king and queen 'bored by the tedium of their task'

top: serpent monster on stall shoulder

bottom: the fox, disguised as a bishop, preaches to a group of birds

thirteenth century text which was well-known in later monastic circles, told of a monk who saw a serpent, image of devilish influence, crawling over the back of one of his drowsier brothers.[42] It is very likely that the serpent-tailed creatures, carved on the shoulders of the stalls, would have reminded the monks of this cautionary story.

The fox was frequently used in sermons and moral tales as a devilish figure. Crafty and cunning, he pretends to virtue in order to seduce the foolish, as on the supporter of one misericord. This shows the fox dressed as a bishop, preaching to some silly birds, upon whom he will pounce when they least expect it. He holds a scroll, upon which was probably written: '*Pax vobiscum*' (Peace be with you) – the opening words of his sermon.[43] The central carving here shows a fox running off with a cockerel in its mouth, chased by a woman brandishing her distaff. A man working at the grain harvest looks on from the other supporter, clutching his scythe, as if unsure whether he should attempt to intercept the fox. Chaucer, in 'The Nun's Priest's Tale', gives a similar story of the cunning fox which runs off with the cock Chanticleer, chased by a woman with her distaff and by a group of men. The poet's tongue-in-cheek narration leaves it unclear whether a moral is to be drawn from that particular re-telling of the tale.

Images of the crafty fox masquerading as a preacher were much used in the later Middle Ages. They were carved, as here, on Choirstalls and also on nave benches in parish churches.[44] Most recent interpreters have seen in these images a political satire on the corruption of the clergy. That may be so, but here such a general application seems unlikely. These misericords were placed in the innermost part of the monastic church and may have been seen by few people apart from the monks themselves. It may be a monkish reference to the difficulties of having an abbot who was also diocesan bishop,[45] but this carving would also have served as a reminder of the Bestiary stricture that the fox 'is a clever, cheating animal' and that it is 'a symbol of the devil'.[46] The predatory owl, a denizen of night and darkness, was another devilish figure, prone to pounce on the unwary. One misericord shows an owl clutching a mouse, while smaller birds hide in foliage on the supporters.

The Bestiary stories were well-known and much enjoyed. The young novices in monasteries were taught by means of them; and the monks whose task it was to preach and to guide pilgrims would make use of these same racy and humorous stories as examples.[47] It is all too easy to be patronising about the medieval liking for moralised animal tales. Yet the fact is that Aesop's fables are still popular and we still, successfully, use animal stories and comparisons as a light-hearted way of making a serious moral point.[48]

There are also religious or moral messages implicit or explicit in those misericords which show scenes which a medieval viewer would have recognised as part of everyday life. The carving that is generally taken to show a hare hunt may be simply such a scene.[49] But is the animal portrayed really a hare? It could as well be a rabbit, and if so there is a meaning implicit here. A medieval observer would have known of the rabbit's bad reputation: 'for no other wild beast in England is called 'riot' save only the rabbit'.[50] Even well-trained and otherwise well-behaved hunting hounds would lose all discipline when chasing a zig-zagging rabbit. That may be why the two hounds with their master in the central carving are being held on the leash, to keep them under control as they strain forward after the rabbit dashing into the wood ahead of them. Since the rabbit was another symbol of lust, this scene is a reminder to the celibate monks of the need for self-discipline.

The labourer shown beside a field of ripe corn and the man harvesting grapes are also scenes of everyday life. They represent two of the Labours of the Months, a series of twelve scenes frequently shown on or in churches throughout medieval Europe as a reminder that God creates and provides all the gifts of man's cultivation. But the grapes are reminiscent of the wine of the Eucharist and the wheat of its bread. The harvest scene also resonates with the great call of Jesus for the harvest of souls and his demand that his disciples pray the Lord of the harvest to send reapers.[51]

Moreover, the monks themselves

Man with scythe harvesting a field of grain

were likened to the labourers in the vineyard, their chanting of the psalms works of mercy.[52] Indeed, this metaphor was embedded in the very charter in which King Henry I set up the diocese of Ely. The reason for carving a new diocese out of the enormous diocese of Lincoln was given as: 'The harvest of the church in my reign is plenteous and, moreover, the tillers of the soil are few, and for that reason struggling with the harvest...'[53] (That is, there were not enough priests within the Lincoln diocese to care properly for all of its widely-spread parishioners.)

Above all, it is important to remember the context of all these carvings, since they cannot be fully understood when studied in isolation from their original purpose. These stalls were produced to furnish the Octagon, with its tremendous programme of imagery portraying the heavenly hierarchy. They contain the seats upon which the monks leaned as they chanted the psalms of the daily offices. The psalms compare God's work in the world to everyday activities of human beings. God is shepherd; God is vine-grower, 'God's activity is closely connected with real life. ...What God has done, does and will do for his people is as real, as normal and as natural as what the shepherd does for his flock or the vine-grower with his vineyard. The impression conveyed by these comparisons is this: when the psalms speak of God, they are speaking of reality.'[54] The vividness of the carved scenes on the misericords likewise speak both of everyday reality and of the reality of God's care for his creatures.

In these stalls the monks chanted their Offices day and night.[55] Most of the words that they used were taken from the Bible, the Word of God. 'Plainsong was therefore an intense form of prayer, returning to God (as prayer was supposed to do in its purest form) the words that He Himself had spoken... The ideal of monastic devotion was a meditative quiet in which eyes, ears, body and mind were thoroughly occupied, then becalmed and eventually stilled, so that a monk could hear the voice of his Creator... the "whole machine of the body" labouring to praise and comprehend God.'[56]

This sense that music can bring the whole person, body, mind and soul into harmony with God explains the continuing importance of music for Christian prayer. The seventeenth-century poet George Herbert, musician and priest, envisaged himself as a stringed instrument whose music would only be truly harmonious once it was centred on God:

> 'My music shall find thee, and ev'ry string
> Shall have his attribute to sing;
> That all together may accord in thee,
> And prove one God, one harmony.'[57]

And the enclosed Choir area of a cathedral was a metaphor of heaven itself to Herbert's contemporary, John Donne:

The enclosed room of the Choir – view from the east gallery level

> Since I am coming to that Holy roome,
>   Where, with the Quire of Saints for evermore,
> I shall be made thy Musique; As I come
>   I tune the Instrument here at the dore,
> And what I must doe then, thinke here before.[58]

In these stalls the choir, clergy and congregation have continued to sing the regular services, using the same biblical words and sometimes even the same plainchant melodies that were sung by the monks. From the stalls to the vault, this is a place for heavenly music, a place where humans have the privilege of joining with the heavenly host in praising the perfection of goodness and love which is God.

'Therefore sometime ye sing, sometime ye read, sometime ye hear, now one alone, now twain together, now all. Sometime ye sit, sometime ye stand, sometime ye incline, sometime ye kneel... [singing] Hymns with Psalms... and Lessons with Responses, and Responses with Verses... And all to the praising of our Lord Jesus Christ ...and so to exercise the body to quickening of the soul; that therewith all such bodily observances should not be found without cause of ghostly understanding... Now join to all this the fruit of that thing that is sung and read; and thereto the fellowship of Angels amongst you in time of God's service, and most of all the miraculous and unspeakable Presence of God Himself... and see whether it is not nigh another heaven to serve and praise God in the choir.'[59]

The meaning and continued importance of church music after the Reformation is aptly summed up in another piece of verse. Not great poetry, like that of Herbert and Donne, but a simple epitaph to a choir man in Durham cathedral, inscribed on a stone in the floor of the Galilee chapel:

Iohn Brimleis body here doth ly
Who praysed God with hand and voice
By musickes heavenlie harmonie
Dull myndes he maid in God reioice
His soul into the heavenes is lyft
To prayse him still that gave the gyft.
    1576

CHAPTER 7

Shrine and Retrochoir

Let the Congregation of Saints
Praise Him

The major goal for most Ely pilgrims was the shrine of St Etheldreda. She was the foundress of the original monastery on this site and was buried here. The shrines of her sister St Sexburga and her niece St Eormenhilda were here also; the body of her sister St Withburga was brought to join them in 974[1]. Here their physical remains reposed in splendid shrines; their souls rejoice with all the other saints in heaven. The shrines with the bodies of the saints formed a tangible connection between earth and heaven, a reminder that we are surrounded by 'a great cloud of witnesses'.[2] The shrines of the saints in English churches were destroyed during the Reformation but some have been reconstructed from recovered fragments. These can give an idea of how Etheldreda's shrine would have looked.

The word 'saint' means 'holy', set apart for God. In this sense all Christians are saints, set apart by their baptism and called to lead lives which demonstrate the love of God in the world. But not all Christians live up to their calling. Those people who are especially designated as saints are the heroes of the faith, recognised by ordinary people as having lived as fully as possible a life of responsiveness to the divine will.

> Who were the saints? Women and men of God, belonging to the good world of God, who in their earthly lives did what they could to alleviate… great need and who in their heavenly existence continue the task in God's name, but now more powerfully and more surely, led by the finger of God. The invocation of the saints has been encouraged both by lament over suffering, pain, loneliness, and injustice,

The reconstructed shrine of St Alban in St Alban's Abbey

and by certainty that the heavenly patrons were able and prepared to lighten this yoke.[3]

Heaven was not a vague and distant future but an immediate and daily way of life, filled with friends. What we have seen of the imagery of the Octagon is simply a formalisation, a reminder, of this sense of being surrounded by helpers and well-wishers. Each day could begin with a sense of the companionship of the saints and angels, as is seen in this prayer for morning:

> 'May we walk in prosperity this day of light:
> in the power of the most high God, greatest of gods,
> In a manner pleasing to Christ,
> In the light of the Holy Spirit,
> In the faith of the patriarchs,
> In the merits of the prophets,
> In the peace of the apostles,
> In the splendour of the saints...
> In abundance of peace,
> In praise of the Trinity,
> With our senses alert,
> With constant good works,
> With spiritual powers,
> With holy life,
> In these things is the journey of all labouring for Christ
> who leads his saints after death into eternal joy.
> That I may hear the voice of the angels,
> praising God and saying Holy, Holy, Holy.'[4]

The architecture and decoration of the entire building were carefully designed to lead up to and focus upon the shrine area. The east end of the Norman cathedral was rebuilt and extended in the mid-thirteenth century by Bishop Hugh de Northwold.[5] Ely is just one of a number of such extensions made to churches in that century, the aim of which was to provide extra room around major altars and shrines. More space was needed for pilgrims visiting the shrine, to provide more altars and probably also to allow room for processions to move comfortably around the eastern part of the church. It was in the thirteenth century that the diocese of Ely adopted the customs of the cathedral of Salisbury – known as the Sarum Rite.[6] This rite laid considerable emphasis on processions, both inside and outside the church building. Many extensions, of parish churches as well as cathedrals, seem to have been wholly or partly motivated by the need to provide space for such processions.

The decoration of the cathedral becomes more elaborate as one moves eastwards, with a decorative culmination around the original position of the shrine and high altar. The design of the presbytery was influenced by that of the Lincoln nave, but is more elaborate.[7] This richness at Ely may be explicable simply as the personal choice of patron or designer. But at Lincoln there is a progression of increasing elaboration from west to east, even though most of the building work actually progressed from east to west.[8] A similar effect of greater richness at the east end was achieved at Westminster Abbey, where the spandrels in the Choir and transepts are enriched with diaper patterning. The architect of the nave, which was built about a century later than the eastern part of the church, omitted this patterning. This effect at Westminster has been interpreted as a deliberate crescendo, intended to lead up to and focus attention on the sanctuary and shrine area. Likewise, at Salisbury there is evidence 'to establish that the architectural vocabulary was consciously selected and deployed to express the division of the building into identifiably discreet [sic] parts'.[9] So it seems likely that at Ely also, elaborate carved decoration was considered an appropriate way of signalling the importance of the presbytery as compared with the austere Norman nave.

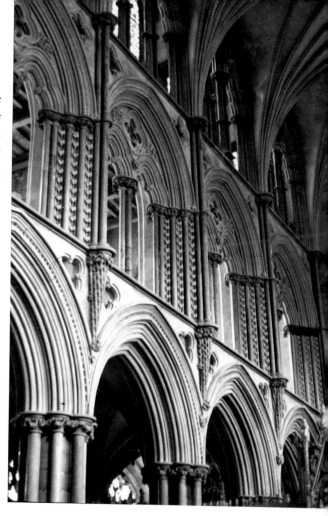

The thirteenth-century retro-choir of Bishop Hugh de Northwold

It has been plausibly suggested that the foliated brackets between the arches of the main arcade are a reference to the miracle of Etheldreda's sprouting staff (see Chapter 5, p.86). These '...can be seen to change their form as they approach and surround the site of the shrine. At the east end

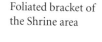

Foliated bracket of the Shrine area

The patterned rib vaults of Bishop Hotham's Choir (top) and Bishop Northwold's presbytery (bottom)

they are tightly furled... But around the shrine, in the two western bays – where Etheldreda slept as she had done on that grassy bank in Lincolnshire six hundred years before – they miraculously burst forth.'[10]

The fact that only the bays to the east of the Crossing have stone vaults may also be part of this symbolic marking out of the sanctuary and shrine area. In many medieval churches the apse or chancel are the only vaulted areas. This functions as a mark of the significance of the altar and of Christ, whom the altar signifies. The use of stone vaults in this position is yet another way in which medieval architects looked back to Early Christian usage. The great fourth-century churches of Rome were wooden-roofed except for the apse which contained the altar. That was vaulted. 'The rib-vault ... provided... a dome of heaven, over the high altar'.[11] And if this ceiling represents the vault of heaven it is entirely appropriate that, as we shall see, it is inhabited by carved images of saints.

Just as the cathedral as a whole is connected, by its form, its symbolism and its consecration, with heaven, so too the earthly shrine of the saint was connected with her heavenly presence. It was believed that, having spent much of her life in this place, she retains in heaven a fondness for it. To those who visited and prayed at her shrine she would extend her own prayers for them before God; sometimes she persuaded God to work miracles. On the tomb of one of the great saints of the early Church, St Martin of Tours, is an inscription which explains this connection between the saints and their relics: 'Here lies Martin the bishop, of holy memory, whose soul is in the hand of God; but he is fully here, present and made plain in miracles of every kind.'[12] So they came, to Etheldreda as to Martin; the devout to obtain her blessing, the guilty to seek her intercession, the sick in hope of a healing miracle.

A further analogy with St Martin is provided by his tomb, which was given a splendid, probably antique, marble cover at some time about the year 500.[13] Etheldreda was enshrined in a similar antique coffin, as was reported by Bede not long after.[14]

> [Etheldreda] was succeeded in the office of abbess by her sister Sexberga, who had been wife to Erconbert, king of Kent; who, when her sister had been buried sixteen years, thought fit to take up her bones, and, putting them into a new coffin, to translate them into the church. Accordingly she ordered some of the brothers to provide a stone to make a coffin; they accordingly went on board ship, because the country of Ely is on every side encompassed with the sea or marshes, and has no large stones, and came to a small abandoned city, not far from thence, which, in the language of the English, is called Grantchester [modern Cambridge], and, presently, near the city walls, they found a white marble coffin, most beautifully wrought, and neatly covered with a lid of the same sort of stone. Concluding therefore that God had prospered their journey, they returned thanks to Him, and carried it to the monastery.[15]

In the early 970s the casket containing her body was raised up into a shrine near the high altar of the church which preceded the present cathedral. Her sister Sexburga, who became abbess after Etheldreda's death, was enshrined nearby. So also were Sexburga's daughter Eormenhilda, and – after she had been translated (or stolen) from Dereham[16] – Etheldreda's other sister, Withburga.

In the late eleventh century Bishop Wulfstan of Worcester, who was himself soon to be canonised as a saint, had in his portable prayer book this prayer for the feast of St Etheldreda: 'Almighty and eternal God, the author

The reconstructed Shrine of St Thomas Cantilupe in Hereford Cathedral

St Etheldreda
enthroned as Abbess;
carved boss on the
vault above the site of
her shrine

of virtue and lover of virginity, you deigned to lead blessed Etheldreda on this day to the joys of heaven. We humbly implore your mercy, that as we celebrate her sacred feast here on earth, we may rejoice in her benevolence among the stars. We ask this through Jesus Christ our Lord. Amen.'[17]

As we saw in Chapter 5, virginity was a high ideal at which many aimed. But not all were able to withstand the political and social pressures to which high-born women, and to a lesser extent men, were subjected in their time. Yet all of these relatives of Etheldreda were referred to as virgins, even though at least two of them had married and borne children. This usage also applied to the early saints who went away into the Egyptian desert. 'Their understanding of chastity was that, for any Christian, the only virginity possible is that of the indwelling life of Christ. They therefore remained celibate after they were in the desert and were, in fact, referred to as virgins whatever their previous experience.'[18] The island in the desolate fens that was seventh-century Ely served as an English approximation of the rigours of desert life.

Hanging near the shrine were Bricstan's[19] chains, a reminder of one of Etheldreda's miracles, portrayed on the eighth Octagon corbel (see Chapter 5, p. 87). Bricstan, a local man from Chatteris, had for some years led a dissolute life. But after recovering from a serious illness he repented and decided to enter the monastery of Ely. Before he could do so he was falsely prosecuted, condemned, and thrown into prison in chains. He was there for some months, praying to St Etheldreda and St Benedict for release. At last they appeared to him and struck off his chains. This miracle ensured his acquittal and release; so he entered Ely as a monk, bringing with him his chains as proof of the miracle.[20] The chains hung near the shrine, to the north of the altar, as a reminder of the saint's power to help her petitioners. They may also have carried, for medieval pilgrims, a further, implicit, reminder. The most famous chains in Christian devotion were those of St Peter, revered in an early church in Rome. In the near vicinity of Ely is the church at Coveney, dedicated as St Peter *ad vincula* and very likely possessing some relic of St Peter's chains. In the vault above the site of Bricstan's chains is a carved boss portraying St Peter.

THEFT and vandalism have always been a hazard in places where valuables, whether material or spiritual, are kept. Throughout the Middle Ages relics of the saints had both a spiritual and a material value. In addition, their shrines were covered with jewels and precious metals, gifts of the visiting devout and rich. We know that this was so with the shrines in this place. Somewhere near this shrine there will have been a watching loft.

Such structures have survived in St Alban's Abbey and Oxford Cathedral, in each case close to the shrine of the abbey's patron saint. These structures have two storeys, the upper one providing a small compartment in which a monk-custodian could keep discreet watch over the pilgrims at the shrine. The present, modern, wrought-iron screens and gates at the west end of the chancel aisles are shut each evening, after a careful scrutiny of the area to the east of them. Similar gates and screens protected this part of the building in the Middle Ages and custodian monks had the task of overseeing its security. 'The security of the shrine and of the church was dependent on the controlled opening and locking of a sequence of doors and gates and on the continuous presence of a custodian. This often involved the locking of these doors and entrances from the inside, necessitating various members of the community spending the night within the church and within the shrine area.'[21]

Originally the High Altar was placed just to the west of the spot now marked on a floor slab as the site of Etheldreda's shrine. So this area was doubly sacred. Its sanctity was marked in further ways. Two bays of the intermediate, gallery, level are provided with

top: the Shrine of St Alban with two-storey watching loft in the background

left: the present High Altar with the site of St Etheldreda's shrine in the foreground

right: modern inscribed slab marking the shrine site

opposite: inner windows to light the shrine area; to their left the colonnette of the Norman Triumphal Arch runs up from floor to vault

windows set not, as with the other bays, on the outside wall but on the inner wall above the arcade. In Chapter 1 we considered these from the outside. Here we can see how their placement alters the lighting of these two bays, allowing more light to fall directly upon altar and shrine. This, in effect, spot-lights them. On a sunny day it is particularly effective. Light, as we have seen, is both physical and symbolic. It allows us to see more clearly both material and spiritual things. The correspondences were brought out explicitly by one of the great teachers of the early Church, discussing the nature of sanctity:

> As when a ray of light touches a polished and shining surface, and the object becomes even more brilliant, so too souls that are enlightened by the Spirit become spiritual themselves and reflect their grace to others... The grace of the Holy Spirit enables them to focus their minds on their heavenly citizenship, and to dance with the angels.[22]

The thick, plain colonnettes which run on each side up the entire elevation just at the end of the choir stalls are another way of marking out the sacredness of this area. They are all that remains of the great arch which framed the apse of the Norman cathedral. Such arches have been interpreted as triumphal arches signifying, as we have seen, the victory of Christ. What the triumphal arch celebrates here is the presence of Christ in the Eucharist at the altar. When the Norman apse was demolished and the east end was extended in the thirteenth century and again when the choir bays had to be rebuilt in the fourteenth century after the collapse of the Norman tower, these colonnettes were left in place. It has been argued that this was a deliberate retention of their triumphal significance. The High Altar

both: grimacing heads at the base of the vault brackets

remained in the same position throughout, its importance signalled by these vestiges of the triumphal arch.

Tucked into the angles of the arcade are human heads grimacing grotesquely. Why should there be such grotesque images lurking in the holiest part of the building? The cathedral signifies the Heavenly Jerusalem, but it is not yet heaven itself. Here on earth we can experience the dawning of the light of eternity but the darkness of evil has not yet been completely overcome.

> Although dawn intimates that the night is over, it does not yet proclaim the arrival of the full light of day. While it dispels the darkness and welcomes the light, it holds both of them in tension, the one mixed with the other, as it were. Are not all of us who follow the truth in this life daybreak and dawn? While we do some things which already belong to the light, we are not yet free from the remnants of darkness.[23]

John Bunyan made a similar point in *The Pilgrim's Progress*, in which the characters Ignorance and Vain-Hope get very close to heaven before being thrust down: 'Then I saw that there was a way to hell, even from the gates of heaven...'[24] As we have seen, the cathedral is oriented so that those worshipping here during the main, morning, services are facing the dawn which signifies the light of Christ. This is rising upon the world but does not yet have full possession of the hearts and minds even of those who profess and call themselves Christians.

St Etheldreda's shrine was in the place of honour, immediately east of the High Altar, with the shrines of her sisters and niece nearby. The Body of Christ, present during the Mass at the High Altar, and the shrines of the local saints were thus held together in close proximity. The significance of each was enhanced by that of the other. Etheldreda looks down in blessing from a carved boss in the middle of the vault bay above the shrine area. Her physical relics below, her soul in heaven: both were able to convey blessings on those seeking her aid. The eternal triumph of all the saints in heaven is signified by a boss over the next bay which portrays the Coronation of the Virgin.

All other altars in the church were subsidiary to the High Altar. The main Mass of the day was sung here with great ceremony and the complex of shrine and High Altar was the most sacred part of the building. This is why most of the medieval monuments are collected around this area. The bishops and lords, who had wielded great power and carried great responsibilities, felt a need to be buried close to Christ and the saints in the hope of clemency for their failures in this life. The local saints, to whom they had been devoted, would surely remember to intercede for them when they came to be judged.

The present High Altar is backed by a sumptuous nineteenth-century screen and reredos, designed by Scott and carved by James Rattee, founder

The nineteenth-century High Altar reredos, carved by James Rattee

of the firm of Rattee and Kett. Rattee had previously worked on the oak screen at the west end of the Choir and on the replacement choirstalls.[25] The complex imagery of the reredos was explained in admiring detail soon after it was put in place:

> Immediately over the altar are five compartments filled with sculpture; above which rises a mass of rich tabernacle-work. The sculptures, which are in alabaster, represent – Christ's Entry into Jerusalem; Washing the Disciples' feet; the Last Supper; the Agony in the Garden; Bearing the Cross.

High Altar and reredos, showing the design of the original embroidered altar frontal

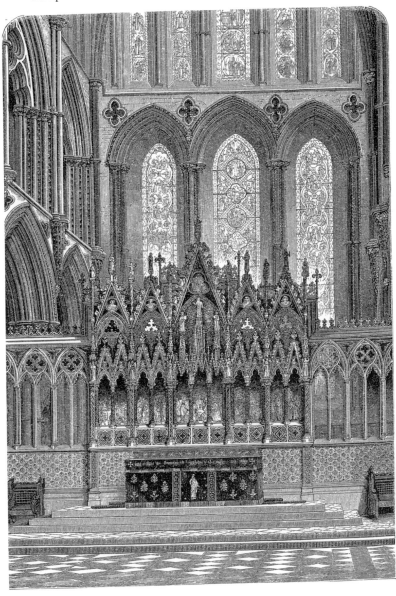

High Altar carved scenes:
top: the Last Supper
below: The Transfiguration (Christ flanked by Moses and Elijah)

Shafts of alabaster, round which a spiral belt is twisted, inlaid with agates and crystals on a gold ground, divide these compartments, and support the arches above. The tabernacle-work is crowded with figures of angels bearing the instruments of the Passion,[26] and with medallion heads in relief: those on the north represent Isaiah, Jeremiah, Ezekiel, and Daniel; those south, the four Doctors of the Latin Church – Jerome, Ambrose, Augustine, and Gregory. Each compartment terminates in a gable, of which that in the centre is highest. In this gable is the Saviour, with Moses and Elias [Elijah] on either side; above is a medallion of the Annunciation; and on the highest point a figure of our Lord in Majesty. On the side gables are figures of the four Evangelists, with their emblems on the crockets. In trefoils, set in the

High Altar carved
scenes:
above: the
Annunciation
above right: Christ in
Majesty, supported by
symbols of the
Evangelists, with
pelicans below

gables, are projecting busts; those north representing Mary Magdalene and
Mary the mother of James; those south St. John the Baptist and St. John the
Divine[27]. On spiral pillars between the gables are figures of Faith, Hope, and
Charity, north; and of Justice, Prudence, and Fortitude, south. All the
details of this very important work of modern art – in which the spirit
rather than the letter of ancient examples has been followed – deserve the
most careful observation.'[28]

It does indeed deserve careful observation; for its superb craftsmanship;
for its design which aims to fit sympathetically within this great medieval
building; and also for its imagery which displays for meditation such a
range of the major features of Christian belief.

In the area behind the High Altar are two chapels – Bishop Alcock's on
the north and Bishop West's on the south; these are discussed below in
Chapter 11. Between these is a chapel dedicated to St Etheldreda, containing a modern statue. This was carved by Philip Turner in 1960 and shows
her holding the crozier which signifies her status as abbess.

Until the present Lady Chapel was built there existed a Lady Chapel in
the south Choir aisle. This was probably provided by screening off part of

the aisle, in the way that aisles of parish churches came to be partitioned with parclose screens to form chapels. It must have been highly inconvenient for the monks to have the chapel in that position. Their processional route around the eastern part of the cathedral would be impeded to some extent. Worse, since chapels dedicated to the Virgin Mary were popular with women, it would have brought them uncomfortably close to the monks' domestic quarters. It was not necessarily misogyny that motivated the transfer of chapel and female visitors to the other side of the building. For a group of men vowed to a life of celibacy the frequent presence of women must have been a serious and troublesome temptation. Because of this, from the early thirteenth century, there were papal pronouncements requiring greater segregation for those devoted to the monastic life.[29] Bishop Walpole's visitation injunctions of 1300 suggest that a solution must be found for this problem.[30] It is understandable, then, that the chapel should have been moved away.[31] Yet it seems that even after the new chapel was built, some sort of Lady chapel continued to exist in this place for the monks' use.[32] The move also allowed for a larger and more sumptuous space to be dedicated entirely to the Mother of God. By the early fourteenth century the monks were committed to singing an extra series of services: the Little Hours of the Virgin and a Saturday votive mass of the Virgin. Some of these services were musically elaborate. The earliest polyphonic music seems to have been composed in honour of Mary. It was fitting that a splendid new chapel should house such services and also provide room for the lay people who wished to attend. Its fine acoustics mean that it is nowadays frequently used for recordings of church music. The chapel is entered through the broad doorway in the north Choir-aisle, opposite the spiral stairs to the organ loft.

St Etheldreda: statue by Philip Turner

North Choir aisle with doorway to Lady Chapel passage

CHAPTER 8

Lady Chapel
A Garden Enclosed

The Lady Chapel, although almost entirely free-standing, is entered not directly from outside but from the interior of the cathedral. The chapel was thus in close physical and symbolic proximity to the shrines of Etheldreda and her sisters, as indeed the previous chapel in the south Choir aisle had been. For this new chapel a magnificent doorway was pierced

Doorway to Lady Chapel passage

through the Choir aisle north wall. It was originally flanked by statues in the niches and with the seated Virgin and Child above it. Of the latter the lower part – the lap of the Virgin – remains in place. Below and to either side, in the spandrels of the arch, are censing angels.

Incense was burnt during festal services. Its fragrance was redolent of heaven and the meaning of the rising smoke was found in both the Old and the New Testaments: 'let my prayer be counted as incense before you, and the lifting up of my hands as an evening sacrifice'[1] 'And the smoke of the incense, with the prayers of the saints rose before God from the hand of the angel'[2]. St Paul likens the knowledge of Christ to the fragrance of incense as it spreads through the world.[3] The singing of psalms was also likened to incense: 'For even as incense that is cast into the fire maketh a sweet smell by its smoke rising in the air; so a Psalm sweetly and softly sung... giveth forth a fragrant smell before the face of our Lord Jesus, and before all the Court of Heaven.'[4] The pleasant fragrance was said by St Thomas Aquinas 'to show the effect of grace, wherewith

Top: top of doorway to Lady Chapel, with remains of a statue of the seated Virgin and Child

below: West doorway with censing angels, Salle church, Norfolk

Christ was filled... From Christ it spreads to the faithful through his minis-ters...'[5] This connection between the physical object and the spiritual state which it symbolises is similar to that between the two meanings of the word 'church': 'For in censing, God is honoured just as he is honoured in the grandeur and beauty of a material church. For the grandeur of a material church signifies the image of the spiritual church which is the Kingdom of Heaven, or the soul of the just...'[6] Here on the doorway the censing angels are honouring the Incarnate God, the child Jesus, with his mother Mary who represents the Church in which Christ is made manifest.

The major niches, at eye level on either side of the doorway, probably showed the Annunciation, with Mary being greeted across the opening by Gabriel. In a similar position, although set higher up, are the figures of Gabriel and Mary on either side of the entrance to the chapter house of Westminster Abbey. Smaller relief carvings of the Annunciation frequently flanked doorways or porches of parish churches, especially those dedicated to the Virgin. In this way those entering would be dramatically drawn into the story of redemption. The empty doorway 'is, so to speak, the space where God holds his breath, attendant upon the consent of the Virgin'.[7] As we shall see, Gabriel's greeting to Mary would be echoed in the prayers said within the chapel. Dante envisages this prayer echoing eternally in heaven, as Gabriel greets Mary in an everlasting Annunciation.[8] Those who pray in this way to the Virgin here on earth are thus drawn into the life of heaven.

Gabriel and Mary in the Annunciation scene of the west doorway of Amiens Cathedral, France

The chapel was originally approached through a passage which was destroyed some time after the Reformation. Its modern replacement, designed by the architect Jane Kennedy, stands partly on the original foundations. Carved bosses in the roof (by Peter Eugene Ball) represent the Annunciation, the swaddled Christ Child, the Virgin and Child and the head of the adult Christ. The windows have patterns of grisaille (grey coloured) glass based on medieval designs. Small roundels portray St Etheldreda and the MR for *Maria Regina*, which signifies the Virgin Mary.

Between the two parts of the inner doorway of the Lady Chapel is a corbel which once held another statue of Mary. On it is carved the small figure of a kneeling monk, signifying that the monks were dedicated to prayer. It served also as a reminder of what was expected from pilgrims entering the chapel: prayer to God in honour of Mary, and a serious attempt to live in obedience to the will of God.

The chapel interior today is drastically different from its original state. Its carvings destroyed or severely damaged, its paint whitewashed over, its windows mostly filled

The modern passage to the Lady Chapel, designed by Jane Kennedy

far left: Virgin and Child by Peter Eugene Ball

left: MR – *Maria Regina* – Mary, Queen of Heaven

with clear glass, it has suffered from deliberate iconoclasm, A great effort of the imagination is required to recover its original effect; but it is worth the effort. It contained 147 statues, none of which remains intact; the large upper ones have entirely disappeared. In the spandrels of the lower canopies the long series of scenes from the life and miracles of the Virgin have been battered. Not a single head remains on any of the figures; some of the scenes have been cut away so completely as to be unreadable. Traces of paint survive on the eastern walls and in some of the upper niches on the side

top: Lady Chapel interior looking east

left: north wall and arcading

walls, showing that those sections, and probably all, of the arcading were coloured. This is
suggested by an account published in 1807
which tells of traces of colouring and gilding
found when later whitewash was 'scaled off'.[9]
Of the original stained glass, just the tracery
glass in one window exists, and this has been
pieced together from remnants which had survived in a number of windows. But it provides
evidence of the predominantly green and gold
tones which were fashionable in the first half of
the fourteenth century, when the chapel was
built.

With its wall arcading flowing around the
lower level, its statue niches, stained glass windows and vaulted ceiling, it has been likened to
the small shrine structures which housed the
relics of saints. And it is indeed a shrine of
sorts, although it contains no relics. Yet there is
an even more compelling comparison. In the

midst of these dipping and waving wall-canopies, edged in carved leaves,
with a green-gold light all around, this chapel will surely have called to
mind a garden. Small enclosed gardens were well known.[10] They gave a
modicum of privacy in an age when most of life was lived in public. Walls
or fences were usually covered with bushes and creepers, or the perimeter
consisted of a living hedge. Such gardens were a medieval fashion; they

top: niches showing
painted outlines of
the original statues

left: fourteenth-
century stained glass
in Lady Chapel
window – all that
survives of the
original glazing
scheme

The elaborate foliated arcading flows around the walls

were also a biblical image. The lover in the Song of Solomon sings of his virginal bride as 'a garden enclosed'.[11] This lyric found a place in the Bible because Jewish interpreters understood it as referring to God's love for the people of Israel. Christian theologians, for whom the Church is the new Israel, interpreted it as a love song of Christ and his bride, the Church. The image of the bride who is an enclosed garden was deemed appropriate to the virginity of Mary.[12] As a Middle English verse addressed her: 'Forsooth, Mary, thou art a garden of all sweetness.'[13]

The enclosed garden also contained overtones of Paradise, Eden, that delightful garden given by God to Adam and Eve but forfeited by their disobedience.[14] Mary's obedience to God's choice of her as mother of the Saviour was understood as reversing the loss of Paradise. She was thus an indispensable part of the redemption won by her Son. The call from God came to her through the angel Gabriel, who greeted her: 'Hail, full of grace' – in Latin *Ave gratia plena*. On one of the carved stone bosses up in the vault the scene is shown, with Gabriel holding a scroll on which this Latin text is written.[15] Throughout the Middle Ages clerics loved to pun upon the greeting as they explained that this 'Ave' reversed the name 'Eva' as Mary reversed the consequences of the sin of Eve: '...for just as Eve's talking with the fiend was the beginning of our perdition, so our Lady's talking with the angel, when he greeted her with this Ave, was the entry of our redemption.'[16] The contrast between Eve and Mary is made in hymns, some at least of which would have been sung here and would have been familiar to devout lay people.[17] The pun on the names is made explicitly in at least two of the special Masses for feasts of the Virgin.[18]

Gabriel's greeting became the first part of the standard prayer to Mary, still used by millions of Christians throughout the world: 'Hail Mary, full of grace, the Lord is with thee. Blessed art thou among women and blessed is the fruit of thy womb.' The second part of the prayer is Elizabeth's greeting to Mary.[19] This prayer, composed of scriptural verses with the name 'Mary' added, emerged in the twelfth century. In the late thirteenth century the name 'Jesus' was added at the end, to clarify the aim of the prayer.[20] Faithful

Vault boss of the Annunciation showing modern re-painting

lay people were encouraged to use this prayer frequently, preferably at those times when the church bells rang to announce the services that were conducted every few hours in the course of each day. Also, since the ordinary people had no access to books, they were advised to repeat many times the few prayers that they knew by heart as a substitute for the psalms which formed the basis of the prayers of the literate. The 'Hail Mary' and the Lord's Prayer (the *Pater Noster*) formed the basis of their devotions. One hundred and fifty repetitions would mimic the number of the psalms.[21] An early thirteenth century treatise written for anchoresses – women hermits[22] – bids them repeat these and other prayers while meditating on the Five Joys of Mary. The Joys are: the Annunciation, the Nativity, Jesus' Resurrection, his Ascension, and her Assumption.[23] The first four of these are biblical, but the Assumption is taken from apocryphal writings. It was said that, after the Ascension of Christ, Mary had lived with John 'the beloved disciple'. At length she died and was buried; her soul was immediately taken to heaven by Christ himself. But on the third day after her death she was resurrected and her body taken by angels straight to heaven. She is thus the first of the faithful redeemed by her son. As his mother she was not required to await the end of this world, when all the rest of humanity will share in the resurrection of the body.

Late in the thirteenth century clergy began to suggest that lay people should pray similarly, repeating these simple prayers while meditating on scenes from the life of Christ and of the Virgin. Those who prayed in this way would be deepening their understanding of the story of redemption. At first the suggested scenes were too many for memorizing. Users were advised to pray in front of pictures – just such pictures as are carved around the walls of this chapel. For here we have, in the spandrels of the canopies, a series of scenes from the life of the Virgin. Many of these are also scenes

Scenes from the life
of the Virgin Mary
sculpted in the
spandrels of the
arcading

from the life of Christ but some – those on the north wall in particular –
depict stories of the miracles worked by Mary.

Five or ten repetitions of a prayer were recommended for each scene.
Strings of beads were held in the hand and used to count the prayers. This
was the beginning of the development of that form of prayer known as the
Rosary, the rose garden.[24]

By the late-fifteenth-century the rosary devotion had taken the form
which, with minor variations, it has retained. The number of scenes was
cut down to allow for easy memorisation. Fifteen 'mysteries' (as they came
to be called) were chosen, from the life of Christ together with the apocryphal stories of Mary's Assumption and Coronation. These were divided
into three sets of five. The strings of beads also acquired a standard form.
Fifty beads are divided into five groups of ten, with a single, larger bead
between the groups. So the person praying would choose one of the three
sets of mysteries and pray ten Aves while meditating on each of them. On
the large single beads a *Gloria*[25] would mark the end of one mystery (thus
using the standard ending of the psalms when they are prayed) and a *Pater
noster* would be said as the start of the next. The entire rosary, working
through all fifteen mysteries, would require moving three times around the
beads and would bring the total number of Aves to one hundred and fifty
– the number of the complete book of psalms. Because of the amount of

time and concentration needed for the entire rosary it was, and is, normal to pray just one circuit at a time.

In some parish churches, by the early sixteenth-century, sets of beads were provided for use by anyone who wished to pray but had forgotten to bring their own. In Acle church, Norfolk, the beads were accompanied by a written placard containing this verse recommending their use:

> 'Man, in the church not idle thou stand,
> But take thy beads in thy hand.
> And if thou have here none of thine,
> I pray thee, take these for the time, …
> And when thou wilt no longer stand,
> Leave the beads where thou them found.'[26]

It is very likely that prayer beads would also have been provided here at Ely. Churches in parts of Germany still possess paintings and sculptures which portray the mysteries of the rosary. As we have seen, people were advised, if possible, to pray in front of pictures. The total sensory experience, involving sight and touch together with mental effort, was thought to aid the inner transformation which is the aim of all prayer. Nevertheless, for this way of praying, pictures are not necessary. Even beads are not needed, since at a pinch the ten fingers will serve for counting the prayers. The great advantage of this means of prayer is that, once the basic prayers and the mysteries have been learnt, it can be used anywhere at any time.

This building, which is itself a garden, seems to have been conceived as a stage for meditating on the sculpted scenes while praying the Mary prayer. It is devotional architecture at its most focussed; a rose garden because Mary herself was both the garden and the rose. In the fourth century St Ambrose referred to Mary as 'the rose of modesty' and in the early fourteenth century the poet Dante hailed her as 'the rose in which the Word of God became flesh'. One of the prayers which will have been said in the chapel greets her thus: 'O Mary, flower of virgins, as the rose or the lily, make prayers to thy son, for the help of all Christian men.'[27] She was especially the 'rosa sine spina' – the rose without a thorn. By the early fifteenth century, and perhaps earlier, English lyrics took up the rose theme:

Man praying with rosary beads, encouraged by angels; capital on the arcade in West Keale church, Lincolnshire

> There is no rose of such virtue
> As is the rose that bore Jesu...
> For in this rose contained was
> Heaven and earth in little space...

> Then leave we all this worldly mirth
> And follow we this joyful birth;
>   *Transeamus.*[28]

Transeamus – 'let us cross over'. This building, like Mary herself, represents 'heaven and earth in little space' in which anyone willing to make the effort of meditation on the story of redemption can be enabled to 'cross over' in spirit into heaven. It is the paradise garden restored to those who 'follow [Christ's] joyful birth'.

Because Mary was considered to be the first Christian, she was taken as a model for each individual believer. So the enclosed garden also represented the heart, the place of the soul's communion with Christ, a garden of delight available for the devout soul.[29] St Jerome suggested that Christians should emulate Mary, the garden of the virtues. It is as the pattern of a virtuous person that Mary is shown in the most readily recognizable of the carved scenes.[30] About half way along the south wall of the chapel one of the scenes shows a small figure mounting a flight of fifteen steps. Two larger figures stand behind her and another is in front at the top of the steps, facing her. The small figure is Mary, who was said to have been presented in the Temple as a young child. Like the infant Samuel in the Old Testament, Mary had been born of elderly, barren parents and had been promised to the service of the Temple. The early stages of the story are portrayed in the sculpted scenes to the east of this one. At the age of three, Mary was taken to be dedicated and was able to ascend unaided the steps up to the altar.[31] The number of steps is highly significant. They are the fifteen steps of the Temple in Jerusalem and Mary, even at an early age, was said to have known and been able to recite the appropriate gradual psalm on each step as she ascended. We became acquainted with these fifteen psalms in Chapter 3.

The 'gradual' psalms[32], from the Latin word '*gradus*', a step, are also known as the psalms of 'ascent' or of 'degrees'. They were sung by Jewish pilgrims on their way to Jerusalem and seem also to have been sung within the Temple. Tradition had it that one of these psalms was sung on each

The child Mary climbs the fifteen steps in the Temple, accompanied by her parents Anna and Joachim

of the steps within the Temple precinct.[33] These fifteen were known as 'the little psalter' because they encapsulate the teaching of the 150 psalms which comprise the complete Book of Psalms. 'Whatever their first occasion and their subsequent employment may have been, at any rate there is no doubt of the religious fitness of the old Jewish comment on this Jacob's ladder of prayer and praise, that each psalm of the series is a "Song on the steps by which God leads the righteous up to a happy hereafter"'.[34]

About a century after the chapel was built, this scene was dramatised in a play containing episodes from the early life of Mary – that same play from which was quoted the later episode of the Magnificat in Chapter 6. This, for the audience, would have been not unlike an animated version of some of the chapel carvings. In the scene of Mary's presentation in the Temple she uses the psalms, in turn, as she climbs the steps toward the bishop. He is waiting at the top, by the altar, to receive her. She gives a short explanation of each psalm, followed by its opening verse, first in English and then in Latin. Before she begins her ascent the bishop encourages her, and encourages the play's audience to emulate her, with a comment on the spiritual meaning of the psalms:

> BISHOP: 'From Babylon to heavenly Jerusalem this is the way.
>   Every man that thinks his life to amend,
>   The fifteen psalms in memory of this Maid say.'
> MARY (as she ascends the first step; psalm 120):
>   'The first degree spiritually applied
>   It is holy desire with God to be:
>   'In trouble to God I have cried,
>   And with speed the Lord hath heard me.'
>   *Ad dominum cum tribularer clamavi;*
>   *et exaudivit me.'*[35]

The average lay person could not be expected to know these psalms by heart; repetitions of 'Ave Maria' and 'Pater noster' were counted an appropriate substitute. But many would have recognized the first lines, known as *incipits*, of some of the psalms, for these were frequently repeated and explained in much the same way as Mary explains them in the play.[36] As the pilgrims moved around the chapel, praying the life of Christ and the Virgin, they were themselves on the road from Babylon to heavenly Jerusalem.

According to the apocryphal story on which this episode is based, Mary then stayed in the Temple dedicated to a life of prayer, until the time of her betrothal to Joseph. Her life of reclusion must have seemed particularly appropriate and inspiring to the monks, whose own lives were similarly dedicated.[37]

For lay visitors, women and men, who came to honour the Mother of Christ there was much here to teach and inspire. If they looked up from the scenes between the canopies to the upper walls, windows and vault, they would be put in mind of the heaven at which they were aiming. The large niches originally contained statues of the inhabitants of heaven. There were angels, including the Cherubim who surround the very throne of the Most High.[38] There were also saints, placed as if they were functioning physically as the 'pillars of the Church' which they are symbolically.[39] The pilgrims were surrounded by the images of saints and angels, in sculpture, painting and glass; heaven was all around. If their visit coincided with one of the regular services held here in honour of Mary, they would also have heard, from beyond the screen which originally marked out the sanctuary and altar, the angelic singing of choir boys. Had they looked attentively at the small statues in the niches under the canopies, just above eye-level, around them they may have recognized the greatest musician in the Bible: King David.

The series of seated figures represented the Old Testament kings who were the ancestors of Christ. One on the south side showed a king with a harp. It is so damaged that now only the lower part of the king and the bottom of the harp can be seen. But the harp's folded leather bag can still be recognized on the figure's right leg. This bag, made of a very soft leather, would have been drawn up to protect the delicate instrument when it was not being played. One of the angels in the retro-choir of Lincoln cathedral

King David playing his harp

is shown playing just such a bagged harp. Here in Ely the figure is David: king, singer and instrumentalist, he was thought to have composed the psalms. '[B]oth men and women filled with the spirit of God made songs and psalms to the praising of God, and specially the king and prophet David, whom God chose from childhood to the great gift, that he should be prince of singers of God's marvels and maker of psalms to our Lord's praising.'[40]

The only other king that can be identified is the one, to the east of the entrance, holding an unsheathed sword. This is David's son Solomon, celebrated as a wise judge; the sword represents the power to administer justice.[41] It will also have resonated with the biblical story in which Solomon discovered which of two women was the real mother of a baby claimed by both. He ordered the child to be divided in half; one of the women gave up her claim in order to save its life. Thus she was revealed as the true mother and her, unharmed, son was given back to her.[42]

God had promised to David that his lineage would never fail and his throne be established for ever.[43] This was taken to mean, not simply that his family would continue, but that from his line would come the Saviour, the one whose reign would last for all eternity. Thus Gabriel, at the Annunciation, told Mary that her son would be called the Son of God and he would be given the throne of his father David.[44]

The Annunciation was shown in the spandrel carving just above David, but the scene has been cut flat to the wall and only the outline of the two figures can be seen. The biblical story in the spandrels follows from this around to the right – clockwise. Next to the Annunciation is the Visitation; Mary greeted by her cousin Elizabeth. These two scenes are also shown on carved bosses in the vault. The fourth scene along shows Mary riding an ass, preceded by Joseph and an angel, representing the journey to Bethlehem. The next few scenes show the birth of Jesus, the visits of the shepherds and of the Wise Men. The flight

above right: King Solomon holding the sword of justice

right: the Visitation

above: the Adoration of the Magi

above right: the Assumption of the Virgin; she is shown in a mandorla – now partly broken away

into Egypt continues on the west wall. Further along, in the sixth bay, the public career of Christ begins with his baptism. This seems to have been followed immediately by the crucifixion. There is no crucifix in the scene but it is thought that perhaps that was shown on the, now mutilated, finial of the canopy.[45]

The series continues with further scenes from the life of the Virgin, culminating on the north wall with her death, burial and assumption into heaven. The latter can be seen in the left spandrel of the fourth arch from the west. She is shown, as so often in the late Middle Ages, surrounded by a mandorla (an almond-shaped halo – part of it broken off) and carried up by angels. The mandorla is shown as a hard-edged shape, similar to what we shall see surrounding the figure of Christ on the Prior's Door (see Chapter 10). This is also the form it takes in early fourteenth-century manuscript illuminations, as for instance one dating from about 1315–25 in the Bodleian Library in Oxford.[46] By the fifteenth century, the mandorla would be portrayed as sunrays surrounding her. The sunrays show her as the Woman Clothed with the Sun of the Book of Revelation[47], a woman who also represents the Church.

It is strange that the Assumption is portrayed in such a tiny format, taking up only half of one spandrel, since this was a very important scene: '...intercession was a theme central to the Assumption... In the medieval imagination, it was the Assumption, above all, that established the Virgin's efficacy in the salvation of man. As prophesied in the Song of Songs, the Assumption was long regarded as a metaphor for the salvation of the human soul.'[48] And not the soul only, but also the body – for the belief was that Mary was taken bodily into heaven, the first of the faithful to share in Christ's resurrection. In her assumption 'the human body is glorified to eternity. The Assumption is God's highest benediction upon the human carnal kind made in his own image.'[49] However, it is very likely that the Assumption was portrayed in larger format in the stained glass, perhaps even as the major image in the west window.

The Assumption of the Virgin, fifteenth-century stained glass in East Harling church, Norfolk

Following this, along the north wall, is a series of scenes showing the posthumous miracles of the Virgin. These portray her clemency toward repentant sinners and her power as intercessor for those who pray to her. They are part of 'a substantial tradition' of such miracle scenes 'already well established by the late thirteenth century'.[50]

It is very likely that this imagery was explained to visitors, in order to increase its usefulness as a devotional aid. There may even have been, available in the chapel, a book with the stories of the Virgin's life and miracles. One such book is the so-called 'Vernon Manuscript'. This is a large, very heavy volume meant to be kept on a lectern 'for a community or a household... where individuals could look and read for themselves or to others, few or many, according to the circumstances'.[51] Most of its text is in English, so a book of this kind could be consulted by the monks for their private devotions or to help in the guidance of pilgrims. It could also be used by any lay person, man or woman, who was able to read. We know that books of prayers and readings were frequently made available in churches and chapels, very likely chained on a lectern to prevent theft; one is recorded in the Lady Chapel of a parish church in Salisbury.[52]

It is possible that even the floor of the chapel was intended to have imagery which complemented the overall message. Elsewhere in Ely is a tiled floor dating from the early fourteenth century. It contains mosaic patterns, figures of lions and the scene of Adam and Eve eating the fruit of the tree of the knowledge of good and evil. This floor was laid in the small chapel built as part of the prior's house and known as Prior Crauden's chapel. The imagery seems too large for its setting and it has been suggested that perhaps these tiles were made as part of a far larger scheme for the floor of the Lady Chapel. When in 1322 the central tower of the cathedral fell down, this elaborate scheme was abandoned as too expensive. The tiles that had already

The Fall: Adam and Eve eat the forbidden fruit; tiled floor of Prior Crauden's chapel

been made were then adapted to pave
the much smaller chapel.[53] As we have
seen, Mary's free acceptance of God's
will allowed for the reversal of the sin
of Adam and Eve, so this scene would
have been highly appropriate for the
Lady chapel. When the vault was
designed and erected one of the
bosses was carved with a portrayal of
the Fall, perhaps as a substitute for the
imagery originally intended for the
floor.

In 1834 the vault bosses were said
to 'represent the Nativity, the
Crucifixion and parts of the history of
the Virgin Mary; the figures... painted
of many colours, and gilded; scrolls
are annexed to some of them, on
which are inscribed fragments of the
hymn Magnificat, and the prayer *Ave
Maria*'.[54]

above: The Fall: vault
boss

left: Annunciation
and Visitation: vault
bosses

One of the bosses is of the head of
John the Baptist. Mary visited his
mother Elizabeth when the latter was
six months pregnant and remained
'about three months'. It was believed
that she had stayed for, and assisted
at, the birth of John thus becoming, in
effect, his Godmother. John is celebrated by the Church as the one
whose preaching and baptizing paved
the way for Christ's own mission.

In 1852 the vault was said to have
been 'painted azure blue and studded
with silver stars'[55] It is quite possible
that this represented the original decoration. Similar effects are found
elsewhere, most notably in the exquisite small late-fourteenth-century
chapel dedicated to the Virgin Mary,
known as Our Lady Undercroft, in
the centre of the crypt of Canterbury

Chapel of Our Lady
Undercroft;
Canterbury
Cathedral crypt

cathedral. These canopy-vaults represent the firmament, which marks the boundary between the earth, which can be perceived by the senses, and the invisible spiritual realm.

WHY, then, were all these carvings so thoroughly smashed by the reformers? This seems to have been done in the mid-sixteenth century under Bishop Goodrich, rather than a century later during the Puritan ascendancy.[56] It might be considered that some of the scenes carved here in the chapel provide reason enough for the iconoclasm. Much of the north wall has images taken from the stories of miracles worked by the Virgin on behalf of penitent sinners who were undeserving, except in their devotion to Mary. It is hardly surprising that those should have aroused anger. The tales of the early life of Mary, carved on the east spandrels of the south wall, are not scriptural; the reformers repudiated the use of apocryphal material, so these scenes were considered to be without proper authority. But it is a great pity that the reformers were so extreme in their attack as to spare none of the scenes, not even those that are biblical and central to Christian belief.

By the sixteenth century it seems that the devotion had changed. The emphasis on Mary, already outweighing that on Christ in these scenes, had become so extravagant that she seemed to some to have taken Christ's place as mediator and advocate with God. The repetition of prayers in the Rosary had for at least some of its users ceased to be a devout meditation on Christ's redemption of humankind and become what one writer has termed 'a vehicle for stockpiling... spiritual insurance for oneself and one's friends.'[57] Emphasis was on how many repetitions could be clocked up to gain indulgences, rather than on the devotion with which the prayers were offered or on the holiness of life which should have flowed from them.

Worse, Mary had come to be addressed in terms more suited to God than to a human being. Some of the major prayers of the liturgy were altered and directed towards the Virgin. For instance the *Te Deum* was so treated. The original dates from the early centuries of Christianity and is still in use at Morning Prayer on feast days. It is a hymn of praise to God the Father and to Christ: 'We praise thee O God; we acknowledge thee to be the Lord. All the earth doth worship thee, the Father everlasting...' From the late thirteenth-century onwards, variations of this became available as hymns in praise of Mary: 'We praise thee O Mother of God, we acknowledge thee to be the Virgin Mary. All the earth doth worship thee, bride of the everlasting Father...'

Even the Lord's Prayer, the *pater noster*, was adapted by a German theologian as a prayer to Mary: 'Our Mother, who art in heaven, give us this day our "supersubstantial" or daily bread.'[58]

These alterations narrowly avoided endowing Mary with attributes only appropriate to God; but the distinctions were very fine and the possibility of misunderstanding was great. It is not suprising that a nineteenth-century scholar described these alterations as 'extremely hazardous'.[59] To the sixteenth-century reformers they must have been further evidence that devotion to Mary had got dangerously out of hand. 'We tend to forget how fervent the devotion to Mary was in those ages. For it was Mary, Mother of Mercy, rather than Christ, the Judge, in whom the people had put their hope – *in te dulcis Maria speramus; ut nos defendas in aeternum.*'[60] The final phrase of the Te Deum, changed from 'in thee O Lord have we trusted...' to 'in thee sweet Mary have we trusted...'. This text, like contemporary images of Mary sheltering the faithful from the arrows flung by an irate Christ or God the Father, subverts the most basic Christian belief, that Jesus alone is the one who can be trusted to bring us to eternal life.

The reformers abolished the devotions to Mary and destroyed the imagery. But the Church of England, unlike the more Protestant denominations, retained some of Mary's feast days, as celebrations of Christ together with his mother, so that her true importance continued to be celebrated.

But, properly understood, the Rosary has a continuing use in the life of the Church. It is, indeed, only one way of praying; but for some people in some circumstances it is a fruitful method. Although it tends to be considered specific to Roman Catholics, there are today many Anglicans, Methodists and members of other Christian denominations, who use it. It was, in fact, used by John Wesley, Anglican priest and founder of Methodism, and his rosary beads still survive. Those who pray in this way find that the combination of beads to keep the hands occupied and repeated simple, scriptural prayers to quieten the surface of the mind allows them to concentrate more deeply on the basic Christian stories.

A Methodist minister has written about the hesitation that some may have in praying the 'Hail Mary': 'The first part of this prayer… is a way of bringing to mind our belief that the Incarnation of the Son of God is the most wonderful thing that has ever happened in history and, therefore, of restoring the mind to the joy which is at the foundation of the Christian life. It seems to me to be also particularly inspired in that our joy that God has revealed himself to us is associated with his favouring and blessing another human being, so that a basis is laid in our regular prayer for our training in that happiness at God's blessing of other people which is such an important part of loving.'[61] Perhaps this chapel, dedicated to Mary the paradigm Christian, can once again play an inspirational role in the prayers of pilgrims and visitors. Its garden imagery might still remind them of the Garden of Paradise, where 'the blessed will find themselves translated from the thorny world to …a place safe at last from the ravages of the anti-gardener Satan and from all earthly anxiety.'[62] And if Mary is the rose in the garden, her son is also a flower:

> Sprung from David's royal line,
> Jesse's fruitful stem foreshows
> Mary, maiden-mother blessed,
> and the flower her little child.
>
> Brimming with the seven-fold grace
> of the Holy Spirit's power,
> God entrusts to us this flower:
>
> by its beauty, scent and savour
> He delights us
> and invites us
> to be made anew in Him.[63]

The statue of Mary by David Wynne, together with the reredos and altar designed by John Maddison, display the significance of Mary in God's great scheme of redemption. She is 'the person who stands on the frontier between promise and fulfilment, between earth and heaven, between the two Testaments... That she can be represented in so many ways, thought

'My soul proclaims the greatness of the Lord'. 'And the Word became flesh and dwelt among us, full of grace and truth'

about and imagined in so many forms, is an indication of how deeply she speaks to us about the hope for the world's transfiguration through Jesus... After all, it is she who literally makes a home for the Creator of all things, the strangest reality we can conceive, in her own body and in her own house, she whom we meet again and again in the Gospels struggling with the strangeness of her son, from the finding in the Temple to the station at the cross.'[64]

CHAPTER 9

Monastery
I shall dwell in the House of the Lord for ever

Many religions have provided a way of life which, in its dedication and in its withdrawal from normal social and family responsibilities, is suited to those who feel called to concentrate on the life of the spirit. Christianity has provided this in the form of monasteries. Developed originally from groups of hermits who went out into the deserts of the Near East to find solitude with God, they became a major force in the spiritual life of medieval Christendom. Monks withdrew from society in order to attempt to live as angels in the world. They represented that world before God and held its needs and concerns in their prayers. 'In his social disengagement and his entry into a community created by free decisions the monk was proclaiming the existence here and now, not as a mere ideal possibility, of an alternative mode of social ordering, anticipating the life of the saints in the City of God...'[1]

A monastery is the home of a group of people, men or women, living together in a community. As with most communities, they follow an agreed pattern of life which enables each to know what is required and what discouraged. The pattern which the Ely monks followed was the Rule of St Benedict. This was written some time early in the sixth century and so wisely was it devised that it has proved suitable for many hundreds of communities right up to the present day.[2] Indeed, part of the cathedral's present ministry consists in showing how insights from the Benedictine Rule can help relations within modern business organizations.

For centuries the Rule of St Benedict was the major basis for monastic life in western Europe.[3] Its prologue states the purpose of the work, and the following seventy-three short chapters cover such matters as the duties of abbots and monks, the ordering of worship, the penalties to be imposed on faults, the internal running of the monastery, the reception of guests, the behaviour of the monks when travelling, and the conditions for admission to the community.

The abbot was the community's leader. St Benedict intended that an

abbot should be elected by the members of his own community; but by the twelfth century the abbot was more usually appointed by the king or the archbishop. He governed with complete authority. His was the final decision on any matter and he was to be considered as the representative of Christ. He was advised to ask the opinion of the monks before making important decisions, but was accountable for those decisions only to the judgment of God. This powerful status was moderated by Benedict's insistence that the abbot should live up to his name, which means 'father', by caring wisely and gently for his children.

Surviving monastery buildings, seen from the West Tower of the cathedral

Most monasteries were led by an abbot, with a prior as second in command. In cathedral monasteries such as Ely, the situation was slightly different. The bishop held the official title of abbot but, because of the bishop's wider responsibilities he was not simply elected by the monks. The king, the pope and other bishops would have a say in his election and the person chosen might not be at all to the liking of the monastic community. But since he was generally busy about the work of the diocese and in government, he in practice had only a minor part to play in the life of the monastery. Thus here at Ely, as in other cathedral monasteries, the prior ruled with an authority almost equal to that of an abbot.[4]

The monks took vows to remain celibate, to own no personal property, to stay in their monastery and to be obedient to the abbot. Celibacy, the renunciation of sexual activity, is the vow that is perhaps least understood today. Claims are frequently made that monastic celibacy represents a negative evaluation of the body on the part of Christians. In fact the monastic impulse was quite the reverse of this. 'To renounce marriage was not to reject the body; it was to take the whole, undivided self across that line which divides sin from holiness.'[5] Christianity values the body very highly; so highly indeed that it teaches the resurrection of the body to eternal life. Human beings are not souls which need to be detached from their bodies. After the death of the body the soul in heaven is incomplete until at the final resurrection both will be reunited. Dante shows the saints in heaven as radiant with joy in the presence of God, yet aware of incompleteness:

'And when we put completeness on afresh,
All the more gracious shall our person be,
Reclothèd in the holy and glorious flesh...'[6]

'The holy and glorious flesh' – this is the belief of the Church. How could a respect for the body be expressed more strongly? The image recurs in a hymn about the heavenly Jerusalem, written in the fifteenth-century and to be found in translation in modern hymn books:

O how glorious and resplendent
fragile body, shalt thou be,
when endued with so much beauty,
full of health and strong and free,
full of vigour, full of pleasure
that shall last eternally.[7]

But in this life both soul and body partake in the fallenness of human nature and both slip all too easily into sin. The story of Adam and Eve tells in the form of a myth something profound about us. We are creatures capable of much good, yet somehow so often go wrong. 'The web of our life is a mingled yarn, good and ill together.'[8]

The major focus of the community's life and work was the church. Here they prayed the daily 'offices' – services based on the psalms and other readings from the Bible. This was the primary work of the monks; indeed the word 'office' is derived from the Latin word *officium* meaning 'work'. They undertook that work as representatives of the entire society, praying on behalf of all who had not the opportunity to spend much time in prayer. Just as soldiers defend society and farmers grow food to feed it, so monks and nuns pray. Every human society needs some division of labour; those who must go out hunting cannot at the same time be looking after house and children; successful merchants will not have the time or opportunity to become physicists or composers. People vary in their interests and talents, and yet they can be united in a single community. St Paul explained this variety-in-unity by likening the members of the Church to the parts of a

opposite: the West Tower and the South Transept, seen from the monastery precinct

human body. Just as the body needs hands as well as eyes, feet as well as ears, so the Christian community needs people with different skills. Each does his or her own task for the good of the whole. So the monk or nun prays on behalf of others, thereby developing a spiritual life which spills out into the world and can enrich with a sense of transcendence, of a reality beyond and behind the material world, those who come as pilgrims or visitors.

Probable layout of cathedral and monastery

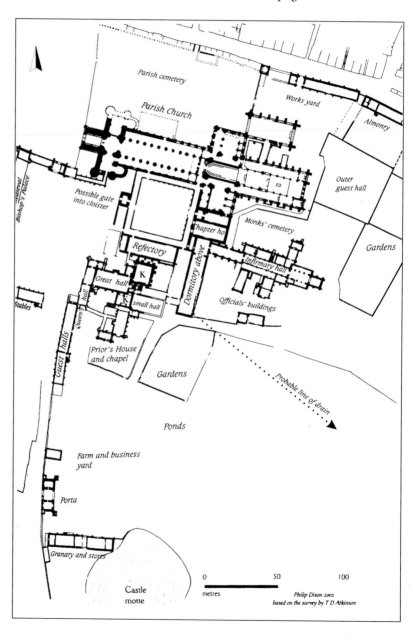

Parish cemetery

Works yard

Parish Church

Almonry

Medieval Bishop's Palace

Possible gate into cloister

Outer guest hall

Chapter ho

Monks' cemetery

Gardens

Refectory

Dormitory above

Infirmary hall

Great hall

K

Stables

Queen's hall

K

small hall

Officials' buildings

Guest halls

Prior's House and chapel

Gardens

Probable line of drain

Ponds

Farm and business yard

Porta

Granary and stores

Castle motte

0   50   100

metres

Philip Dixon 2002
based on the survey by T D Atkinson

The occupations of the monks, and the total time allotted to each on an average summer day, was intended to be roughly these: religious devotions (the night office of Matins, daily mass, and offices sung seven times between dawn and sunset), known as the 'Opus Dei' or God's Work and considered the most important aspect of monastic life, three and a half hours; solitary meditation, half an hour; reading, four hours; manual work, six and a half hours; sleep, eight and a half hours (divided into two parts by Matins); and meals, one hour. Benedict designed the life to contain a balance of manual work, study and prayer so that all aspects of human nature might be exercised and nourished. But this balance was not kept. By the later Middle Ages the requirements of the Office had increased, with the addition of further services and a greater elaboration of the way in which the services were celebrated. Most of the basic, practical tasks were taken over by laymen and women, servants of the monastery who lived apart from the monks and were paid for their work.

The Rule required that a monastery should contain all the buildings necessary for the various activities of the monks. Most of the monks' activities, other than those of worship, centred in the cloister. It was here that they had their school, studied, and copied manuscripts. Here also they meditated and were sometimes allowed to talk together informally.[9]

A cloister is a covered walk surrounding an approximately square garden or 'garth'. It joined the church with the main domestic buildings of the monastery, thus providing shelter for the monks as they went about their daily business. Little survives of the Ely cloister, just a short corner section

below left: cloister garth, Norwich cathedral

below right: cloister walk, Norwich Cathedral

Blocked-up tracery of
cloister walk

in the angle of the nave and south transept. The nearest, and very fine, surviving example of a monastic cloister is attached to the cathedral in Norwich. At either end of the nave of the cathedral are doors which gave access to and from the cloister. Here at Ely these are known as the Prior's Door and the Monks' Door. The function and decoration of these will be considered in the next chapter.

The cloisters of western European monasteries are approximately square in shape.[10] The four arms or walks of the cloister were used for various activities. The east walk housed the library books and the Chapter House, where the monks met to discuss the business of the monastery. The Chapter House at Ely has not survived. One of the recesses which may have contained a book cupboard can be seen just outside the Monks' Door. An inventory of 1093 recorded that the monastery owned two hundred and eighty seven books, of which seventy nine were service books. The latter were most probably kept in the church, but the others will have been stored in cupboards in the cloister wall. During the early years of the community's existence it is probable that many of the books were written and copied by the monks here in the cloister. The north walk – that which ran along the side of the cathedral – will have had carrels with desks, set under the windows looking onto the garth. Here the light would have been good for fine work and the sunlight will have given some warmth. By the fourteenth century, although some book-copying was probably still undertaken by the monks, most books may have been bought in from outside sources. Cambridge and (King's) Lynn are close and both had developed a trade in book production; Cambridge for its growing university and Lynn as part of its large and lively trading contacts both within Britain and across to the Continent.[11]

Some books were acquired by gift or bequest. One such gift, from William the priest of Stradsett asks: 'Let him who reads this remember him [William] with prayer'. On the other hand, some also may have been lost after being borrowed by secular priests living outside the monastery. The rector of Sudbury, in 1277, borrowed one for his lifetime. In 1320, after the death of the rector of Balsham, nine of the monastery's books had to be recovered from his executors.[12]

On the south side of the cloister, opposite the church, was the monks' refectory. In the west walk, just outside the refectory door, was the lavatorium where the monks washed their hands before meals. This was a symbolic as well as a physical task; it cleansed the body but also signified purity of heart. Eating was not simply a practical matter. At meals monks should meditate on the goodness of God in providing food for both body and soul. The communal meal was a reminder of the meals which Jesus shared with his disciples; many refectories had a painting of the Last Supper on one of the walls. There was no conversation; instead, one of the monks was deputed to read from a book during the meal.

East of the cloister the infirmary was situated. This was generally built in the same form as a parish church, with aisled nave and chancel. The nave was used as the ward, with beds set in the aisles. The chancel functioned as a chapel, so that even the sick could still feel that they were a part of the

The monastic infirmary

above: Prior Crauden's chapel and part of his lodging, with guest halls on the left

opposite top: the outer (west) wall of the monastery's guest halls

opposite bottom: the meadow and great barn

prayer life of the community. Here at Ely is the best preserved Norman infirmary building in England. The 'nave', with an arcade and clerestorey of nine bays was unroofed when the monastery was closed in the sixteenth century and the aisles were turned into houses for the cathedral canons. East of this is a chapel of four bays with a sanctuary of two vaulted bays, which now houses the Chapter Office.[13] Like the cathedral itself, the 'nave' of the infirmary had a wooden roof, but the more sacred space of the chapel was marked as such by its being vaulted in stone.

To the south west of the cloister was the prior's lodging and accommodation for important guests. Further west was the bishop's palace. This contained not just his household but also various of the diocesan administrative staff. South of the refectory was the kitchen, storerooms and workshops, the great barn and the 'home farm' on whose meadows domestic animals still graze. Originally monasteries would have grown their own food. But as they became larger and more complex, much of their food had to be brought from elsewhere, so large amounts of storage space were needed.

The monks were, of course, never fully cut off from the life led by

above: Great barn and 'Porta' gatehouse

opposite top: shops built into the outer wall of the monastery along the High Street

opposite bottom: exterior view of the 'Porta' gatehouse

ordinary people in the world outside the monastery. Indeed, many Benedictine monks were called out of their life of seclusion to serve the wider Church as bishops and other functionaries, for 'those who most successfully fled from the world and communed with God were also those most needed to pass on some of their insight and experience'.[14]

But those who remained in their monastery were nevertheless aware of the life and needs of ordinary people. Here in Ely even today it is evident how close the town is to the cathedral. The shops on the south side of the High Street are built into the outer wall of the precinct. The north and west sides of cathedral and monastery were open to lay men and women. Until the present Lady Chapel was built in the fourteenth century both men and women also had access to the south aisle of the Choir, where the previous Lady Chapel was situated, as well as to the nave. There was a school for young boys – the predecessor of the present King's School – where they were given a basic education. Those who excelled in their scholarship were encouraged to continue; those who were drawn to the monastic life were further educated in the Rule of St Benedict and might continue here as monks; those with fine voices would be drawn into the choir which sang in the Lady Chapel.

The great south-west gateway known as the Porta was in effect the tradesmen's entrance, giving direct access to the large barn in which the community's provisions were stored. There was constant coming and

going between monastery and outer world; '...lay servants, traders and administrators came and went, keeping the wheels of the monastic economy and administration turning; almonry boys were housed within the walls or came from nearby for their lessons and to sing in the Lady Chapel; illuminators on the monastic circuit stayed for a time to work up a few pages of a lavish manuscript; guests from great lords and their households downwards abounded alongside the poor; "poets, harpists, musicians and clowns" had to be warned off... and when it came to burying the great and the good, or the monastery's servants, no doubt their kin turned up in large numbers, as did the poor to receive their clothing and doles.'[15]

This reference to the poor is a reminder that Benedictine communities were expected to care for pilgrims and travellers, as also for the sick and the poverty-stricken. The Rule required that any visitor, rich or poor, should be received as Christ himself would be treated. 'Let special care be taken in the reception of the poor and of strangers, because in them Christ is more truly welcomed.'[16] Food and clothing were regularly doled out by the Almoner at the monastery gate; extra was provided on special feast days. The rich generally left instructions in their wills for money, food and/or clothing to be handed to a certain number of poor people on the day of their funeral, in return for prayer. The prayers of the grateful poor were considered to be particularly efficacious in benefitting the souls of the dead.

The religious ideal of Benedictine monasticism is to live a dedicated life of prayer for, and service to, the world. Like all high ideals it is fragile, incomplete and often betrayed. But it stands for the primacy of the things of the spirit and the possibility of living the life of heaven here on earth.

CHAPTER 10

The Romanesque Doorways
Go your way into his gates with thanksgiving

From their daily work in various parts of the monastic buildings the monks moved, at regular intervals, through the cloister into the church. Two doorways, one at the east and the other at the west end of the nave gave them access. Another doorway originally opened into the south transept. This doorway was altered when part of the transept was turned into a vestry, then it was blocked up when the Octagon was constructed.[1] Originally the covered cloister walk led from one to the other. All three doorways are thought to date from between 1120 and 1130.[2]

The most elaborate of these doorways is that at the west, known as the Prior's door. This doorway is covered in intricate carving.

Filling the arched head of the doorway is a stone tympanum carved with the figure of Christ in glory. He is shown within an almond-shaped halo, or mandorla, held by angels. The mandorla represents the clouds of heaven, in which the Lord will appear at the last day. These clouds signify the glory of the Lord, the impenetrable light in which the eternal essence of God is veiled.[3] The pose of the angels, moving away but looking back towards Christ, suggests that they are in the process of opening the clouds to reveal the Lord, in human form, seated on the rainbow throne. If that is so then what we have is an image of the moment of Christ's appearing at the end of this world. Christ who is God appears in the form of the man Jesus, God the Son.

One of the most striking and unusual features of the doorway is the pair of head corbels which

Early nineteenth-century view of the Prior's Door

above: Christ in glory on the tympanum of the Prior's Door

right: the two heads gaze down at all who enter

stare so enigmatically at all who approach. The doorway seems originally to have had some colouring, as was normal at the time of its making. At the very least these heads will have had pupils marked in the eyes so that instead of their present unfocussed gaze they would have been looking directly at everybody entering, commanding their attention. If the tympanum does indeed portray the final appearance of Christ as judge of the world, then the urgency of these faces is explained. Now is the time of choice. As you stand on the threshold of eternity which side are you on? This moment is the initial stage of what is generally known as 'The Last Judgment', when God finally ushers in the heavenly kingdom and goodness is at last vindicated. The Last Judgment scenes in later art generally show heaven and hell, with good people being ushered into heaven and the wicked falling or being dragged by demons into the jaws of hell. Here the imagery acts, rather, as a reminder that one's ultimate fate depends on one's own choice. As an eminent New Testament scholar puts it: 'All through the Gospel Jesus provokes self-judgment as men line up for or against him...'[4] This moment is also portrayed, albeit more explicitly, on the great thirteenth-century West Front of Wells cathedral.[5] There, the newly resurrected are shown either looking up towards Christ or down and away from him, thereby showing the choice that they have already made.

Here on the Prior's Door, Christ is shown as young and beardless. This is unusual for the twelfth-century but can be seen in early Christian images such as the mosaic of the baptism of Christ in the Arian Baptistery in Ravenna. He holds the cross, symbol of his victory over evil and death, and also a book. This is the book of the Gospels, in which the good news of Christ is told. It is also the Book of Life, in which are inscribed the names of all who are on the side of life, who will enter heaven at last.[6] The burgeoning leaves below Christ and the leafy spirals around the arch signify new growth and new life. They are a reference to St John's vision of the One sitting on the throne who says: 'Behold, I am making all things new.'[7] In contrast to the spiralling plants on the jambs below, these leaves are not inhabited by scenes of violence. The new world of Christ is a kingdom of peace.

The carving of the tympanum as a whole is meant to inspire the fear of God, but not as this phrase is now commonly understood. 'There is a biblical conception of fear or dread of God, which is in no wise fright of God or terror of punishment. ...This loving fear is rather reverence or respect. It is accompanied by confidence; it engenders peace; it is on a par with charity and with the desire for heaven. What the Bible calls "fear of God" is a way of referrring to charity under its somewhat negative aspect.'[8] Fear is the natural response to our recognition of how far we fall short of the beauty and attractiveness of God's perfect goodness. Those who have had no glimpse of this glory have likewise no sense of how puny are their own moral efforts; they can remain content with being 'good enough'. But the vision of God puts paid to such complacency. In the words of a modern prayer: 'O God, whose beauty is beyond our imagining and whose power we cannot comprehend: show us your glory as far as we can grasp it, and shield us from knowing more than we can bear until we may look on you without fear...'[9]

The jambs on each side of the door are also intricately carved. On either side is a colonnette carved with a series of roundels and another which has a scrolling vine spiralling up it. Some of the scenes seem to be more than merely ornamental. For instance the roundels on the west, on Christ's right, contain a selection of animals together with Signs of the Zodiac. The

two fishes of Pisces appear on the ninth roundel from the top. The eighth seems to be Aquarius, a man pouring water, and the third from the top can be plausibly interpreted as the ram of Aries. The bottom roundel shows a creature that might be either the scorpion of Scorpio or the crab of Cancer. Complete sets of these Signs were frequently portrayed in conjunction with the figure of Christ in Glory. They signified the cosmic Christ, creator, sustainer and ruler of the universe. The surviving twelfth-century painting on the chancel arch at Copford church in Essex is an example.

The medieval Church's attitude to astrology is frequently misunderstood. Theologians made a careful distinction between, on the one hand, considering the influence the stars might have on each individual's character and, on the other, the use of stellar configurations for the purpose of predicting the future. Since the stars and planets are part of God's creation it was considered that they might have

above: Pisces and Aquarius (?) on the left jamb of the Prior's Door

right: the cosmic Christ with Signs of the Zodiac, painted on the apse arch and vault in Copford church, Essex (twelfth-century heavily restored)

some influence on human life. There was no theological objection to studying this. But since humans were created with free-will the stars cannot *determine* how we behave. Thus, attempting to predict future behaviour is theologically unacceptable. This distinction was still understood in Shakespeare's day: 'The fated sky gives us free scope; only doth backward pull our slow designs when we ourselves are dull.'[10]

On the opposite jamb, on Christ's left hand, the roundels mostly show human figures engaged in various activities. These have generally been considered as merely decorative.[11] But there may be more to it than that. The figure, in the third roundel from the bottom, formed into a circle like an acrobat has rightly been likened to images of Salome. As we have seen, one of the choirstall misericords shows her thus, together with two more episodes from the story of the martyrdom of St John the Baptist. The figure of Salome was recognized as a figure of vice, for she had brought about

both: minstrels and acrobat on the Priest's Door

right: Salome dancing at Herod's feast on the misericord in the Choir

below: Scenes of Carousal

the death of the saint. This whole colonnette, being positioned on Christ's left, would be likely to portray those vices which render a person unapt for heaven. There is precedent for such an interpretation of most of the rest of these scenes.[12] The drinking and kissing couple at the top represent lust, which arises from carousing. Below them is a drinker, probably representing drunkenness. This behaviour is abetted, or even provoked, by the man on the third roundel from the top who is pouring wine from a barrel. Further down are musicians making, probably lewd, music and more acrobats. Taken together, these scenes suggest a riotous entertainment. It was at just such a feast that Salome danced in front of Herod and encompassed the death of St John.

Not all minstrels were considered vicious; but all the moral writers of the Middle Ages considered them as potential inciters to vice. 'Robert Mannyng of Brunne in *Handlyng Synne* was not alone in saying about minstrels that "Here doyng ys ful perylous" '('Their behaviour is very dangerous').[13] Moreover female jugglers and troubadours both had Salome as 'patron' and were identified with prostitutes.[14] Curiously enough, this identification was probably intensified by the fact that female dancers and acrobats, for the sake of decency, wore underpants. It was not until the nineteenth century that these were worn by respectable women.[15]

The lowest roundel shows two men rowing a boat. They are facing each other and rowing in opposite directions. It is a fine image of the counter-productiveness of vice, and one that would surely have been easily understood by those who lived and worked in the watery fens. It would also probably have brought to mind the different metaphor used in the Gospels to make a similar point: 'every house divided against itself cannot stand'.[16] Taking all these possible interpretations together, it may be that we have here a series related in meaning to the *psychomachia* (battle between virtues and vices) imagery. This shows personified virtues and vices in conflict and can be found on a number of church doorways of the twelfth century, such as that at Malmesbury Abbey.

The middle jamb on each side is carved with a leafy spiral, inhabited by scenes of attack and violence. On the right jamb, toward the bottom, a man beats a dog or bear with a large cudgel. Elsewhere pairs of beasts of various kinds are locked in combat – viciously biting or striking at each other. Scenes of violence were a conventional metaphor for spiritual struggle.

The monastic processions which moved around the cloister, blessing all the places in which the monks worked, prayed or rested, entered the

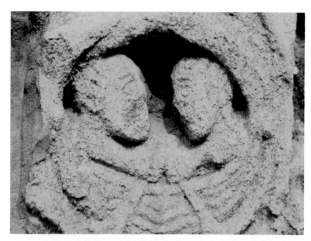

top: two men in a boat

bottom: man beating a bear or dog

western part of the church through this door. So, most likely, did secular visitors.

It seems likely that the abbey's more important and powerful guests were accommodated in the prior's lodgings.[17] These were the buildings to the immediate south west of the cloister.[18] From there they will have entered the church through this door. Its imagery reminded them forcibly of what the Church taught: that they should not spend their time, like Herod, on dangerous carousing. It was their task to use their riches to succour the poor and to ensure that the powerless obtained justice. Christ's judgment is not so much concerned with the condemnation of the wicked as with justice for the poor and oppressed.[19] Perhaps that is why the two heads look out so meaningfully, drawing attention to the figure of the just judge above them. Such figures have been said to be engaged in 'mute preaching'.[20] Indeed, St Hugh of Lincoln is reported to have used the sculpted Last Judgment over a

below: dog attacking hybrid beast

below right: The Prior's Door

church door as a warning and reproof to an erring nobleman.[21] As we have seen, medieval clerics were adept at explaining imagery. But perhaps with such guests it may have been deemed wiser to have the sculpture call attention to its own message.[22] The rich and powerful tend not to like being reminded of their responsibilities. Here, on the threshold of the heavenly Jerusalem, they were provoked into considering whether they were living a life fit for heaven.

Although the name 'Prior's Door' seems to be quite recent, this may have been the entrance for the Prior, whose lodgings were nearby and who governed the monastery. It may also have been the entrance for the bishop, but of this we cannot be sure since it is not known quite where the bishop resided in the twelfth century. As we have seen, the Rule of St Benedict gave full authority to the ruler of the community but reminded him that at the Day of Judgment he would be required to answer for all his decisions. So this doorway may also be a timely warn-

The blocked remnant of the Vestry Door, showing two arches of different dates

ing to any prior, abbot or bishop who might be tempted to misuse his position.

Two other Romanesque doors opened from the church into this, the north walk of the cloister. Unfortunately most of the cloister was pulled down at the dissolution of the monastery, so these doors are no longer reachable directly from the Prior's Door. Instead one needs to return to the church and approach all that remains of the cloister – the north east corner – from the east end of the south nave aisle. In this corner are the Monks' door and close to it, at right angles, the Vestry door. Of these two doors the latter was closed up when the Octagon was built; one of the massive Octagon buttresses encroaches upon its north side. But that was not its first alteration. It is clear from its two round-headed arches of different heights that the form of the doorway was changed from the original, but still in the Romanesque style. The lower and later of these two arches, contemporary with the other two doorways, is profusely carved with foliage. 'A beaded spiral band encircles the shaft and the arch, leading the eye from the bottom of the shaft upwards along an amazing variety of leaf motifs, up along the curve of the arch, finally to stop at the apex. There, from the foliage emerges a human head, giving a happy equilibrium to forms that seem to be in constant upward movement.'[23] This head may have performed a similar function to the two heads on the Prior's Door, reminding the monks of their obligations. Certainly it looks commandingly down on all who approach.

The Monk's Door was the usual entrance for the monastic procession at the beginning of the daytime offices. The monks would gather in order, two by two, in the east walk of the cloister a few minutes before the time of the service, then process in, cross the aisle and enter the Choir through the central doorway of the pulpitum screen. They were privileged to make their entry to the church through what has been described as 'one of the most outstanding and beautiful achievements of Romanesque art in England'.[24] Its lavish decoration is spread over four layers or 'orders', alternating flat and rounded forms and becoming more elaborate towards the inside. As with the Vestry door, there is a head at the top emerging from a spiral band; but this head is small and it sits above an elaborate composition sculpted in the trefoiled arch of the doorway.

In the cusps of the arch are two figures of monks, kneeling in prayer and

below: The Monk's Door

below right: decorated jambs of the Monk's Door

holding croziers. Above them are two intertwined dragons biting each other. This carving has generally been taken to be simply decorative; no very obvious meaning has been
found in it. But the doorway on which it is
placed was the major entrance for the monks
into their church, normally a place for significant imagery. At Norwich the correspon-
ding, later, doorway shows Christ and the
saints in a composition that is also related to
carved bosses in the vault of the cloister walk
leading to it. Here at Ely the cloister vault no
longer exists, nor is there any documentary
evidence of whether it contained further
imagery which would have provided a context for the doorways. So any attempt to
interpret the imagery can only be tentative.

It is very unusual for dragons – generally
symbols of evil when shown in conflict – to
be placed above human figures who are praying. Normally the higher place signifies
morally better. It is also unusual for *two*
crozier-bearing figures to be portrayed.[25] The

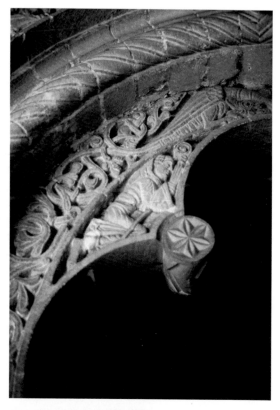

top: kneeling monk
with crozier

left: kneeling monks
with intertwined
dragons above them

crozier – a crook-headed staff -usually indicated a bishop or abbot, the sole leader of a community. The chain of authority would be muddled if more than one person held ultimate authority. If one of the figures wore a mitre, they might portray the division of responsibility in a cathedral monastery, where the prior took the abbot's role and the bishop was titular abbot but mainly concerned with the care of the diocese. Yet these two figures are identical; we need to look elsewhere for a possible explanation.

Croziers, although generally signifying the status of the holder, had a meaning in their own right. They were connected with the shepherd's crook with which David, before he became king, saved his sheep from a ravening lion. Thus the crook/crozier symbolized the overcoming of evil.[26] As we have seen when considering the Octagon imagery, just inside this door there are some later carvings which also remind the monks that their task is, by constant prayer, to overcome the devil. The size and dominance of the dragons on the doorway, placed as they are above the monks, is a reminder that evil is very powerful. It may be significant that the dragons are biting each other rather than attacking a human figure, as is the fiend on a gargoyle on the outside of the Choir. Here the violence of evil is turned on itself and is thus as ineffective as the two men on the Prior's Door, who row in opposite directions. The monks below are prostrate in prayer. They are sheltered, each under a curving line that closes him off from the dragons above. Perhaps evil is already being overcome by prayer and the help of God. Perhaps they are already obtaining the help for which they pray at Compline: 'Hide us under the shadow of thy wings'.

CHAPTER 11

Monuments
All these were honoured in their generation

Afine series of monuments[1] reminds the visitor that the cathedral has, for centuries, been home to a wide range of people. They have made many different contributions: to its spiritual life, its music, and its fabric, as also to the wider Church and the secular world. The monuments themselves display a range of religious imagery and symbolism, which has changed over the centuries and whose meaning has frequently been forgotten. It is not possible to discuss all of the monuments here, but some have imagery or symbolism which complements that of the cathedral as a whole.

The earliest monument is the pedestal in the south nave aisle, which supports a fragment of a stone cross. This was brought to the cathedral from Haddenham in 1770. On the pedestal is the Latin inscription, in Roman capitals, *Lucem tuam Ovino da Deus et requiem. Amen*: 'Grant, O God, to Ovin thy light and rest. Amen'. Owine (Ovin) was the name of Etheldreda's steward, and this stone has, since the eighteenth century, been considered to be his memorial. The stone and its inscription are certainly Anglo-Saxon in date but there is, alas, no good reason to connect it with the saint's steward.[2] It is not known whose monument it is.

The earliest post-Conquest monument is the Tournai marble slab, dating from the mid- to late-twelfth century[3], now to be found in the north choir aisle, against the choir enclosure wall. It is probably the monument of Bishop Nigel, who was bishop of Ely from 1133 to 1169. Nigel rose to prominence in the service of Henry I, and lived through the civil war between Stephen and Matilda. He survived to serve

Monument, probably of Bishop Nigel. The bishop's soul is shown, carried by the Archangel Michael, to the gate of Heaven.

under Henry II, and was present at Thomas Becket's consecration as Archbishop of Canterbury in 1162. The tombstone shows St Michael, wings folded above him, holding a small naked figure in a cloth. The figure is the soul of the bishop, his status indicated by his staff of office – or crozier – beside him. The Archangel stands under an arch, on which is inscribed in Latin *St Michael oret pro me*: 'May St Michael pray for me'. The image echoes the words used during the funeral service. In accordance with this, Nigel is shown, carried by angelic hands to the Bosom of Abraham. The Bosom of Abraham is a metaphor for heaven used by Jesus in the parable of Dives and Lazarus.[4] In medieval art it was sometimes portrayed by the figure of Abraham, holding tenderly in his lap just such a cloth containing the souls of the faithful. The Romanesque frieze on the west front of Lincoln cathedral has this image. But another way of understanding the metaphor is to take it as suggesting that the faithful soul will be reclining in the presence of Abraham at the heavenly banquet to which Jesus so frequently referred. So here Nigel is shown being taken up to heaven, where he will join that banquet. How would heaven be envisaged but as a Norman cathedral? And thus it is portrayed above the arch in which Michael stands, the arch which itself represents the gateway to heaven.

Bishop Hugh de Northwold's monument (c.1254) lies within one of the arches on the north side of the splendid presbytery, which he built. It is a sumptuous design in Purbeck marble. The bishop stands, crozier in hand, treading a dragon underfoot. The meaning of this, as we saw in Chapter 5, is explained by psalm 91. The bishop stands within an elaborate foliage canopy, echoing the foliage of the surrounding architecture. In the side

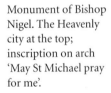

Monument of Bishop Nigel. The Heavenly city at the top; inscription on arch 'May St Michael pray for me'.

Monument of Bishop
Hugh de Northwold

St Etheldreda, carved
on the side of Hugh
de Northwold's
monument

shafts of the canopy are niches containing small figures of saints, males headed by St Edmund to his right and females headed by St Etheldreda to his left. 'Two of the female saints have on the outer frames of their canopies the head of a goat or ram, a symbol of lust vanquished; while Etheldreda, in reference perhaps to the idea that her staff was also a weapon in the struggle against vice, uses her fine flourishing crook to skewer a demon at her feet.'[5] The foot of the tomb is carved with scenes of the martyrdom of St Edmund. In the central scene the archers are shown firing at him. On one side of this scene is a wolf, on the other a soldier with raised sword is beheading the body. As we have seen, the pagan Danes took as trophies the heads of

The Martydom of St Edmund, carved on the base of Hugh de Northwold's monument

conquered enemies. But, unlike Byrthnoth's (see Chapter 5), St Edmund's head was recovered. A large wolf emerged from the forest, prevented the Danes from taking the king's head away and stood guard over it until his followers came to collect the body for burial. His relics became the pride of the great abbey of Bury St Edmunds. Northwold was abbot of that abbey before being made bishop of Ely. So he has the two saints with which his career was most closely connected, standing on either side of his effigy in token of their protection and patronage.

Northwold's successor, Bishop William of Kilkenny, is commemorated by another Purbeck monument which lies a couple of bays further west. 'The bishop stands, with his hands upraised to bless, in a niche whose sides are boldly decorated with foliage. The modelling of the whole design is simple, obedient to the quality of the stone from which it is made. But this restricted use of moulding and decoration has not robbed the artist of the power to express the texture and the majesty of the bishop's robes, or of the ability to model face and hands which are quick with life. Here is a master work of... assurance and serenity...'[6] At his head, flying down from either side of the arch above him, are two angels swinging censers. He tramples a dragon underfoot, piercing it with the crozier which, as we have seen, symbolises the power to overcome evil. The admiring mid-twentieth-century observer quoted above seems, however, to have been unaware of the restoration work that the figure has received, presumably some time in the previous century.[7] Parts of the face, nose, hands and beard have been replaced together with the upper parts of the angels. It is a tribute to the careful way in which this restoration was achieved, that an attentive observer should not have noticed it at all.

The late-thirteenth-century tomb of Bishop William de Luda can easily be overlooked because, in its present state, it seems to be simply an elaborate entrance to the Choir and presbytery. Its canopy forms an arch over the only entrance from the south Choir aisle to the presbytery. It is only on looking down within that canopy that one can see the marble tombstone of

opposite: the canopied monument of Bishop William de Luda

the bishop, with the outline of the memorial brass that it once held. This stone was originally placed at waist height, as is the slab on which the carved effigy of Bishop Redman reclines, just opposite. The tomb-chest was removed and the slab lowered, probably in the eighteenth century, to allow access to the Choir and altar when these were moved to the far east end of the church. Part of the tomb-chest was re-used in Bishop West's chapel (see below). The side sections of the canopy supports are enriched with figures of the Evangelists: St Mark and St Luke on the south side; St Matthew and St John, much restored in the nineteenth century, on the north. There are carvings also on the top of the canopy: Christ showing his wounds on the south and, in its restored state, Christ in Majesty on the north.[8]

It is particularly unfortunate that the monument of Bishop John Hotham, which stands between the south aisle and the High Altar, is so badly damaged, for it must also have been a sumptuous piece. Hotham was bishop at the time of the collapse of the Norman central tower in 1322, which necessitated the rebuilding of three bays of the Choir and the building of the Octagon. The responsibility for the rebuilding was divided. The

Details of Bishop William de Luda's monument.
below: St John with his eagle
below right: Christ showing his wounds

Bishop John
Hotham's monument

Sacrist, Alan of Walsingham, oversaw work on the Octagon. The bishop
was responsible for rebuilding the Choir bays. The style in which they were

rebuilt fits extraordinarily sympathetically with the thirteenth-century presbytery and the retro-Choir.[9] The rebuilding was probably not quite finished
when the bishop died in 1337. His monument has been separated from its original canopy and the niches along the
sides of the tomb-chest have been
denuded of most of the small figures
which they originally contained. Of
these, only one remains and that headless. Hotham was much involved in
matters of state, was for a time
Chancellor, and was probably the moti-
vating force behind King Edward II's
foundation of King's Hall in Cambridge,
later to become part of Trinity College.[10]

The elaborate stone screen at the east
end of the north Choir aisle belongs to
Bishop Alcock's chantry chapel. John
Alcock was bishop of Ely from 1486 to
1500.[11] He served Edward IV in a range
of important administrative and diplomatic roles and was made Chancellor by

Niche figure on John
Hotham's monument

Henry VII. As bishop of Ely he was *ex officio* visitor to Cambridge University, which he did much to assist. In 1496 he founded Jesus College, in the buildings of the dissolved nunnery of St Radegund. He also added a great new hall to the Bishop's Palace, just outside the west front of the cathedral. Alcock was generally liked and admired. 'Even the censorious protestant John Bale recalled him as one who had spent his life in vigils, study, abstinence, and in the subjugation of the temptations of the flesh'[12]. Bale describes him when bishop of Ely as '... a father distinguished for his piety and virtue...' noting that, after his death, he was by some venerated as a saint.[13] He was buried in his chapel.

Half concealed behind the arched opening on the north side of the chapel is what may be the bishop's effigy. Carved in stone, it is so badly worn that its original form can hardly be discerned. The head is loose and seems not to have originally belonged to this figure. But the effigy may have been a cadaver, a carving of a corpse. Such figures were fashionable in the fifteenth century; they can be found in other great churches[10] and in some parish churches.[14] To most modern eyes such an image is more suited to a horror film than to a church. But this type of image is intimately connected with moral teaching about the shortness of life and the need to make wise use of our time. A graffito in Gamlingay church makes a similar point: *Mors comparatur umbre que semper sequitur corpus* – Death is like a shadow that always follows the body.[15] It is a reminder of what we all must eventually come to. One of the psalms asks: 'So teach us to number our days: that we may apply our hearts unto wisdom.'[16] As one commentator on this psalm has written: 'With God's blessing, there is something solid, lasting, well-founded in human endeavor. Each of our lives is fleeting... but the works we perform, out of a proper awareness of our vulnerable mortality, can have substance, are our human means of continuity and renewal from one generation to another.'[17] These shocking images were meant to bring onlookers to their senses so that they might take stock and seek that which is lasting.[18]

We saw in Chapter 2 that the West Front of the cathedral may have been used in the twelfth and thirteenth centuries for the ceremony of the Maries' visit to Christ's sepulchre. By the later Middle Ages the Easter Sepulchre and its associated ceremonies had, in most churches, been transferred to the east end, generally to the north side of the chancel.[19] On the north side of Bishop Alcock's chapel, which is itself to the north of the presbytery, there is a stone shelf with above it twelve corbels – possibly for statues of the Apostles – and above that the cadaver. Could the shelf have been used for the Easter Sepulchre? In the parish church of Fulbourn, near Cambridge, a fifteenth-century monument on the north side of the chancel has a cadaver with a flat shelf above it. If these two cadaver monuments

opposite: the entrance screen of Bishop Alcock's chapel

Arched alcove with bishop's effigy at the top, behind the canopy

were indeed used for the Easter Sepulchre, the imagery has profound implications. The reminder of mortality would have been connected with both the death and the resurrection of Christ. These monuments, although insisting on the inevitability of death, thus hold the promise of resurrection for those whom they commemorate and for all those who, in viewing them, meditated upon their range of meaning.

This chapel now also contains a series of panels, painted by John Maddison, representing the Instruments of the Passion. These are the physical objects associated with Christ's sufferings: the cross, crown of thorns, nails, scourge, dice, spear and sponge were generally portrayed; others could be added. They were a late-medieval shorthand reminder of Christ's sufferings, used for meditation. Angels were sometimes shown holding the instruments, to underline the spiritual importance of Christ's death.

The instruments were also sometimes emblazoned on shields to indicate, not the coats of arms of earthly families but the heraldry of Christ. Some of the earliest blazons on shields are said to have represented objects related to a courageous act of the knight in battle; these were known as his 'achievements' or 'arms'. Thus the Instruments of the Passion are also known as the *Arma Christi*.

Throughout the Middle Ages, as indeed later, there was much interest in

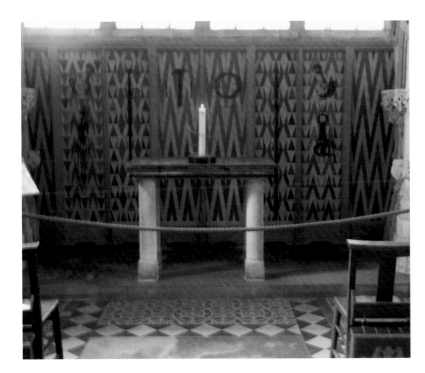

The east wall of Bishop Alcock's chapel with painted Instruments of the Passion by John Maddison

chivalry. Stories of heroic deeds were very popular among all classes of society. Since Christ's redemption of humankind was the greatest of all deeds, it came to be sung in similar style to the popular chivalric romances. Christ was portrayed as a lover-knight who battled against Satan to save the human soul. One of these Romances addresses Christ thus: 'As a valiant warrior You robbed hell and led out Your dear love, that is to say: man's soul, to your bright bower, full of all bliss, to live in Your embrace always without end.'[20] Those objects that were instrumental in his suffering and death became, to use the technical term from heraldry, his 'achievements'. They were frequently shown on shields and were used as a focus for meditation upon his Passion. In this way what could have been a morbid preoccupation with pain and death became instead a recollection of the cost of that great redemptive victory over sin and death won for all humanity by Christ. A book of prayers associated with Ely in the thirteenth century recommends looking at the *Arma Christi* while reciting prayers referring to the Passion of Christ.[21]

On the north side of the chancel is the sumptuous monument to Richard Redman, bishop of Ely from 1501 to 1505. Redman was a monk/canon of the Premonstratensian order, abbot of Shap in Westmoreland from 1458 and head of the order since 1468. He took these positions seriously. Together with his administrative responsibilities for the Crown they left him little

time for his diocesan duties. But he chose to be buried here and left 100 marks to the fabric of the cathedral.[22] This monument was altered at the same time as the de Luda monument. The tomb-chest was cut back to allow space for access to the Choir. The monument is embellished along the cornice of the canopy with carved Instruments of the Passion and also with another image related to the sufferings of Christ.

Associated with the Instruments of the Passion was devotion to the Five Wounds of Christ.[23] These were frequently shown, rather strangely to modern eyes, as the detached wounded hands, feet and heart of Jesus. These can be seen painted on the corbel-shelf on the east wall of the Redman monument and also on the canopy, where they are on a shield as another of the 'achievements' of Christ. The shields of these memorials of the Passion were not simply a reference to heraldry but also a reminder of the practical function of a shield. A shield is for protection and the psalms refer to God as a shield.[24] The wounds of Christ, sustained in the great fight against Satan, which was his Passion, are thus seen to provide protection for his people against the assaults of the devil.

Bishop Redman's monument

There survives a poignant late-fourteenth-century poem, an extended meditation upon the wounded Christ, which gives an insight into these strange images. A wounded man (Christ) is seen sitting upon a hill, speaking of how he has suffered out of love for the human soul. The poem has as a refrain a phrase from the Bible – from that great poem of love, the Song of Solomon: *'Quia amore langueo'* (Because I languish for love). As we saw in Chapter 8, that book of the Bible has traditionally been taken as a song of the love between Christ and the human soul.

Carvings on the
canopy of Bishop
Redman's monument
far left: Instruments
of the Passion
left: the Five Wounds

Marvel not, man, though I sit still:
See, love hath shod me wonder strait,
Buckled my feet (as was her will)
With a sharp nail: well mayest thou wait!
In my love was never deceit;
All my members I have opened her-to;
My body I made her heart's bait,
   Quia amore langueo.

In my side I have made her nest;
Look in! How wet a wound is here!
This is her chamber, here shall she rest
That she and I may sleep in-fere,[25]
Here may she wash, if any filth were;
Here is seat for all her woe:
Come when she will, she shall have cheer,
   Quia amore langueo.[26]

In the seventeenth century Thomas Traherne's meditation upon the wounds leads him to marvel at the immensity of Christ's eternal love for humankind:

Holy Jesus I Admire thy Lov…O that I could see it through all those
Wounds!…These Wounds are in themselves Orifices too small to let in my
sight, to the vast comprehension of thine Eternal Lov. These Wounds
Engraven in thy Hands but Shady Impressions; unless I see the Glory of thy
Soul, in which the fullness of the GODHEAD Dwelleth Bodily.[27]

At the east end of the south choir aisle, is the beautiful chapel of Bishop Nicholas West. In the mid-nineteenth-century a most appreciative observer thought its style far superior to that of Bishop Alcock:

> 'Here is very little of pinnacle-work; but the niches are far more numerous, and the canopies and corbels are of endless variety, in workmanship, size, shape, and decoration. There are places for considerably more than two hundred statues, great and small. Yet no part seems heavy and overloaded... The lining of the canopies is of such exquisitely fine tracery, that it looks like lace. And there are, here and there, some small heads in relief, of a medal size, executed with all the softness and nicety of wax... Over the door in the inside is this inscription in delicate tracery, "Gracia Dei sum id quod sum Anno Dei 1534"...'[28]

'By the Grace of God I am what I am, in the Year of God 1534'. This inscription incorporates a quotation from one of St Paul's letters.[29] It expresses the belief that whatever position, power or influence the bishop had was derived, not from his own efforts, but from the work of God within him.

In this exquisite chapel the seven Anglo-Saxon benefactors found their latest resting place. When the Choir was removed from beneath the Octagon in 1771 their remains were placed in the south wall of the chapel under seven niches, inscribed with their names. These niches are recycled parts of the monument of Bishop de Luda.[30] 'Every pious and benevolent spectator will surely and sincerely join in the full meaning of the emphatic word inscribed over them – *Requiescant*. Here may they rest without further migration...'[31] From the vault of the chapel hang two stone pendants, each formed of the figures of three angels, holding the arms of the bishop and those of Henry VIII, the king who was shortly to put an end to the monastic life in England and to begin the Reformation which destroyed or mutilated so much medieval imagery. In his last years Bishop West became caught up in the controversy over Henry's divorce proceedings. He suffered a brief period of imprisonment for his support of Katherine of Aragon, died at Downham and was buried here in his chapel.[32]

This chapel has also been beautified with an ensemble of east window and altar fittings designed

Bishop West's chapel

opposite top: the entrance screen

opposite bottom: canopied niche and inscription above the doorway

below: the vault

The niches with the names of the seven Anglo-Saxon benefactors – in the south wall of Bishop West's chapel

by Sir Ninian Comper. These were inserted in stages between 1934 and 1945.[33] In the window a young, beardless Christ is shown seated in glory, arms held wide in a gesture of welcome which also echoes the shape of a cross. He is flanked by standing saints. Over him hovers the dove of the Holy Spirit and above that are the symbols of the Evangelists. Below is shown the Virgin and Child, also flanked by saints.

In the floor of the south choir aisle are set two brasses. That to the east commemorates Bishop Thomas Goodrich, who presided over the diocese during the first part of the Reformation. It is probably Goodrich who was responsible for the destruction of much of the medieval imagery through-out the cathedral and Lady Chapel.[34] He was Lord Chancellor under Edward VI. To him is attributed the account of the Christian's duty towards God and towards other people which is part of the Catechism in the *Book of Common Prayer*. This is an explanation of the meaning of the Ten Commandments as requirements for daily behaviour:

> My duty towards God, is to believe in him, to fear him, and to love him with all my heart, with all my mind, with all my soul, and with all my strength; to worship him, to give him thanks, to put my whole trust in him, to call upon him, to honour his Holy Name and his Word, and to serve him truly all the days of my life.
>
> My duty towards my Neighbour, is to love him as myself, and to do to all men, as I would they should do unto me: to love, honour, and succour my father and mother; to honour and obey the Queen, and all that are put in

authority under her; to submit myself to all my governors, teachers, spiritual pastors and masters; to order myself lowly and reverently to all my betters: to hurt nobody by word nor deed: to be true and just in all my dealing: to bear no malice nor hatred in my heart: to keep my hands from picking and stealing, and my tongue from evil-speaking, lying, and slandering: to keep my body in temperance, soberness, and chastity: not to covet nor desire other men's goods; but to learn and labour truly to get mine own living, and to do my duty in that state of life, unto which it shall please God to call me.

The Catechism was to be taught to all children and contained the basics of the Christian faith that all must know. Its foundation was the teaching of the Apostles' Creed, the Ten Commandments and the Lord's Prayer, which everyone was required to learn by heart. The Catechism helps them to understand the meaning of their baptism and the way in which a Christian should try to live in this world. Interestingly, the Reformers held to the same basic requirements as the medieval Church; that everyone should know by heart the Creed, the Ten Commandments and the Lord's Prayer.

Bishop Martin Heaton's monument

Only the *Ave Maria* was repudiated. Despite his reforming proclivities Goodrich conformed and retained his position under the Roman Catholic Queen Mary, during whose reign he died.[35] His memorial brass shows him dressed in the full set of medieval liturgical vestments but carrying a book, probably the Bible, and the Great Seal of England, which he held as Chancellor.

The other brass is to a Dean of the cathedral, Humphrey Tyndall, who was Master of Queens' College Cambridge before becoming Dean. He died in 1614, and is portrayed in full academic robes. The inscription, 'The body of the worthy and reverende prelate, Umphry Tyndall, doth here expect the coming of our Saviour' is highly appropriate to a cleric known as a 'moderate puritan'.[36]

The alabaster effigy of Bishop Heton, who died in 1609, is set into a niche on the outer wall of the south choir aisle. He is shown recumbent, with his hands held together in prayer, wearing a mitre and a splendidly embroidered cope. This latter was a vestment generally worn for solemn services, during the reign of James 1st. It is embroidered

down each side of the front with figures of Apostles standing under canopies. In this it looks back to the style of late medieval vestments, an interesting example of a more general early-seventeenth-century trend of reviving medieval forms. Heton was a successful and popular bishop, esteemed for his tact and for his scholarship. King James admired his preaching and is said to have commented that his sermons were 'larded with much good learning'.[37]

After the Reformation a range of symbols, different from those we have studied on the late-medieval monuments, was used to signify mortality and eternal life. On the monument to Bishop Simon Patrick there are obelisks and cherubs. These, like pyramids and spires, were well-known symbols of eternity; they point to the stars, as the poet Milton recognised in his epitaph on Shakespeare:

> What needs my Shakespeare for his honoured bones
> The labor of an age in pilèd stones,
> Or that his hallowed relics should be hid
> Under a star-y-pointing pyramid?[38]

Seventeenth- and early eighteenth-century monuments frequently also display skulls, urns and cherubs. Skulls are an obvious symbol of mortality. The urn was used in antiquity for burial of cremated ashes and hence also functions as a symbol of mortality. But flames issuing from the top of the urn, shooting so irrepressibly upwards, signify new life arising from death,

Bishop Simon
Patrick's monument,
with obelisks, cherubs
and a flaming urn

as the phoenix arises from its fiery death. Cherubs are spirits, reminders of
the eternal life of heaven.

Bishop Peter Gunning's monument is on the south wall of the Choir, to
the east of Bishop Heton's. He is shown reclining, propped on his left arm,

Bishop Peter
Gunning's
monument

wearing mitre and robes. Gunning, who died in 1684, is said to have con-
tributed to the 1662 *Book of Common Prayer* a 'Prayer for all Conditions of
men'.

> O God, the Creator and Preserver of all mankind, we humbly beseech thee
> for all sorts and conditions of men; that thou wouldest be pleased to make
> thy ways known unto them, thy saving health unto all nations. More
> especially, we pray for the good estate of the Catholick Church; that it may
> be so guided and governed by thy good Spirit, that all who profess and call
> themselves Christians may be led into the way of truth, and hold the faith in
> unity of spirit, in the bond of peace, and in righteousness of life. Finally, we
> commend to thy fatherly goodness all those, who are any ways afflicted, or
> distressed, in mind, body, or estate; that it may please thee to comfort and
> relieve them, according to their several necessities, giving them patience
> under their sufferings, and a happy issue out of all their afflictions. And this
> we beg for Jesus Christ his sake. Amen.

It is a fine prayer for all the needs of the world and its people but especially notable for its recognition that those who call themselves Christians need
God's help in attempting to live up to the ideals which they profess. For, as
we have seen, the light of Christ is still dawning; the darkness is not yet fully
dispelled.

Nineteenth-century monuments, like nineteenth-century architecture,
show a return to medieval imagery and Ely cathedral has some fine examples of these.

At the west end of the north nave aisle, just outside the entrance to the
cathedral shop, is the monument to Canon Hodge Mill, who died in
1853. In this we see the creative way in which mid nineteenth-century artists
used medieval motifs and styles. It is a tomb-chest with a copper effigy

recumbent on top. The sides of
the chest have alternating IHC
and Chi-Rho symbols – the initials of the name Jesus Christ, as
we saw on the west transept ceiling. These initials are gorgeously
carved in white marble roundels.
The spaces between them are
filled with multi-coloured stone
inlays, reminiscent of twelfth-
century Cosmati work, such as
can also be seen on the spiral
columns of the High Altar retable.
At the feet of the effigy are two figures kneeling in prayer, a fairly
common late-medieval conceit.
But these two figures represent
students, one English and the
other Indian, because the canon
taught in India before returning to
become Professor of Hebrew at
Cambridge.

Just to the east of Canon Hodge
Mill's monument is that to Bishop
John Woodford[39] who died in
1885. Here is another fine example

Bishop's John Woodford's monument

of Victorian medievalism, designed by G. F. Bodley. The bishop's effigy, carved in white marble, lies recumbent on a grey marble tomb chest. His crozier skewers a very fierce and lively dragon, which seems to be attempting to chew through it. On the back wall of the monument is carved a crucifixion group; Christ on the cross, flanked by the Virgin and St John. The whole ensemble is contained within a richly decorated, canopied niche and surrounded by an elaborate iron railing.

Perhaps the most controversial monuments are the War Memorials. In the north transept, next to the chapel of St Edmund, is the memorial chapel for those who died in the First World War. The north Choir aisle contains a window commemorating airmen from local bases who were killed in action during the Second World War and plaques in the south nave aisle are dedicated to the memory of cathedral choristers who died in the two World Wars. Some people believe that such monuments glorify warfare and violence and thus are inappropriate for a church. But this is surely a misunderstanding. It is hard to believe that anyone standing in the north

above: St George's chapel – First World War memorial

left: plaque commemorating cathedral choristers killed in World War II

St George's chapel –
lists of men killed in
World War I

transept chapel, reading the hundreds of names of young men who died all too early, could feel anything but sadness and compassion at the terrible waste and suffering that accompanies war. What these memorials do is to bring that suffering into the Christian meaning provided by the suffering of Jesus the Son of God, whose resurrection promises eternal life to all who follow his way of courage and loyalty.

All these monuments, scattered around the cathedral inside and out, are reminders of the continued companionship which we enjoy with those who have gone before us into the light and joy of the heavenly Jerusalem. 'In this city dwell our parents and dearest friends ready to call upon God on our behalf; they await our coming. ...'[40]

CHAPTER 12

On the Margins
The Lord shall rejoice in his works

Humans are not the only inhabitants that can be found here. In many places throughout the cathedral one can unexpectedly encounter creatures of various kinds. Some of these we have already come across on the Choirstalls. But there are others worth our attention. One beast frequently encountered in churches is the eagle, used to support a lectern. A fine, large modern brass eagle lectern stands under the Octagon. Such lecterns are designed in imitation of the late-medieval eagle lecterns, some of which survive in parish churches. As we saw

The Eagle Lectern

when considering the font, the eagle is one of the symbols of the Evangelists. The eagle was thought proper to St John because his Gospel sees most clearly into the divinity of Christ, as the eagle was supposed to be able to look directly at the sun. When it became old and decrepit it was believed that the bird flew straight towards the sun, which would burn away the deposit of age and renew its youth. This is a biblical idea; Psalm 103 likens God's restoring care for those who love him, to the eagle's renewed youth. From the lectern the gospel of the divinity of Christ is publicly proclaimed as the source of renewed life for all.

Most of the other creatures to be found in the building, like so many of the misericord carvings, have tended to be written off. They are considered simply the jokes and doodles of the carvers, worked into inconspicuous corners. No doubt the carvers did enjoy their work and approached it with humour. But there is more to it than that. We have already seen how the devil and lion on the south west arch of the Octagon served as reminders to the monks, as they moved in and out of the church about their daily business, that the devil prowls around looking for prey.

In Bishop Alcock's Chapel, on the corbels and elsewhere, are some symbolic beasts. The most obvious is the oft-repeated *rebus* of the bishop. A *rebus* is a visual pun on a name. Happy the late-medieval man whose name lent itself to such punning. Here we see the cockerel standing on a globe. The cock is self-explanatory. The globe represents the world, all that exists. Christ is frequently shown, as Saviour of the World, holding a globe in his hand ('He's got the whole world in His hand'). It may be some such image that Julian of Norwich had at the back of her mind when she experienced the vision of Christ holding a small round thing on the palm of his hand. She was told that it is 'all that is' and that it is kept in being by the love of God.[1] Here in Bishop Alcock's chapel the globe simply represents the 'All' in the bishop's name. Jesus College which, as we have seen, was founded by Alcock, has his rebus scattered profusely around the buildings. Wilburton church, whose nave roof was largely paid for by Alcock, has a single cock-on-a-globe suspended in the middle.

Bishop's Alcock's cockerels, with mitre and globe

One corbel in his chapel has three rabbit heads set together in a triangle

right: two snails on a corbel in Bishop Alcock's chapel

far right: Christ as Saviour of the World, holding the globe: carving on the choirstalls in Blythburgh church, Suffolk

in such a way that they share ears – there are in fact only three ears between them. This three-in-oneness is a humorous reminder of the Trinity. It survives also in the stained glass of Long Melford church not so far away in Suffolk. Another corbel shows two snails, creatures of mud who need to be cleansed. Humans likewise, who also are of the earth, need to be cleansed by baptism and repentance in order to take their place in the fellowship of Christ.[2]

Just to the west of Bishop Alcock's chapel the piers of the retrochoir have on their bases spurs, most of which are carved as stiff-leaf foliage. But some of them form grotesque heads. It is probably no coincidence that all of these leering faces are on the north side for this, the dark side which faces away from the sunlight, was the side of Satan.[3] If the Octagon devil is armed ready for open battle, these heads seem poised to snap at the ankles of the unwary. This may well have brought to mind God's curse upon the serpent-devil who tempted Eve and provoked the Fall: 'I will put enmity between you and the woman, and between your offspring and hers; he will strike your head, and you will strike his heel.'[4] Here is another reminder of the need for vigilance in those whose vocation it is to fight evil, on behalf of the people outside the monastery who are caught up in the business of everyday life. The position of these heads, at the base of the piers, mimicking the stiff-leaf on other pier bases, gives them a character similar to that of the 'Green Man'.

As in many other medieval churches and cathedrals, carvings of the Green Man lurk in odd corners of the building. They grimace from the corbels in Choir and presbytery, lurk under the Choir-stalls, and peer down from the Lady Chapel vault. In the Lady Chapel they are also to be found on the small corbels with standing saints under the wall arcading. It is this position beneath the feet of the saints that indicates their significance. Unfortunately a great deal of misinformation has been published about this figure. It is not a sign of continuing pagan beliefs, nor is it an emblem of our oneness with nature. The reference is once again devilish.[5] 'The Green Man's place in the scheme of things may [be] understood from the imagery of the joyous Incarnation group in Exeter Cathedral. The Virgin

top: foliated base of the retro-choir arcade

middle: devilish face on base of north arcade in the retro-choir

bottom: Green Man capital

Green Man boss on
the vault of the Lady
Chapel

treads on the Green Man as she might tread on the
head of the old serpent, the tempter himself, lurking
in the Tree of Life. ...[This] represents the darkness
of unredeemed nature as opposed to the shimmering
light of Christian revelation.'[6] The green men in the
Ely Lady Chapel are particularly sinister looking.[7]

The Lady Chapel is especially blessed with small
creatures, some but not all grotesque. Most of the
cleric saints standing under the canopies are placed
on corbels carved with grotesques; some of these are
Green Men. The meaning of this we have already considered; the saints are
trampling evil underfoot. But not all of the grotesques are devilish. Many
seem to have been created out of a joy in devising new and often humorous combinations. They are hybrid creatures, formed out of parts of two or
more animals. By doing this the sculptor could join, in a small and deriva-
tive but nevertheless real way, in the boundless creative joy with which God
made and sustains the universe. Such imagery was considered important

Two grotesque Green
Men corbels, beneath
standing saints, in the
Lady Chapel

for catching and holding the attention of those trying to meditate, as the people moving around this chapel were meant to be doing. It was held that what is marvellous and unusual strikes us and is retained in memory more than what is ordinary. Its forceful impression on us causes us to remark it, and that engenders both inquiry and reminiscence. Likewise, funny images were recommended to catch and hold the attention, as they still do.[8] Unfortunately, now that the statues and the scenes in the spandrels have been so comprehensively smashed we no longer know precisely what they were meant to direct our attention towards.

Snail with goat's head

But the hybrid creatures were not merely eye-catching curiosities. They pointed to a much more serious and amazing fact. Christ himself was a hybrid, a combination of God and Man. The greatest theologians marvelled at this. *Cur deus homo?* – 'Why the God/Man?' asked St Anselm, late eleventh-century Archbishop of Canterbury, in a treatise in which he discusses how the death and resurrection of Jesus gained salvation for humankind. So, while the more naïve visitors might simply marvel at the carvings, their attention drawn to saints whom they could recognise, more

Marginal beasts in the Lady Chapel

Lion on corbel

below: mother and baby dragon

below right: father dragon

theologically sophisticated observers could be led to meditate on the most profound fact of the Christian faith.

In the Lady Chapel, as on the Choirstalls, there are also recognizable animals; lions and dogs, goats and deer, rabbits and dogs, and many more. They will have brought to mind the beast fables which were so well known. Beast fables, some of which are still known, were used as texts for elementary reading. They were seen as ideal school texts; their simplicity made them easy to follow and they combined pleasure with instruction. Because of their moral value they were used by preachers.[9] The edification provided by such tales need not have been explicitly didactic. But people of all classes were used to finding morals in beast stories, and were used to casting their messages in stories about animals.[10]

A family of dragons gazes out from one arch at the north end of the west wall of the Lady Chapel. In the cusp on one side is the mother with a baby dragon curled up beside her. On the opposite side is the larger and rather fiercer-looking father dragon keeping guard over his family. In the fourteenth century when these were carved less was known about the range of creatures to be found in the world than is now known. There were stories about dragons, the largest of creatures, and no good reason to think that

they did not exist. A griffin is shown in the illustration of the creation of the animals, in the Genesis section of the Queen Mary Psalter; a dragon is shown flying from the ark in the Disembarkation illustration of the Egerton Genesis.[11] So here they are also, beautifully imagined by one of the Lady Chapel sculptors, as part of God's amazingly varied creation. 'Praise the Lord' as one psalm so delightedly recommends, 'ye dragons'.[12] They might cause us to meditate on the fact that, although we now know that dragons do not exist, far stranger creatures unknown in the Middle Ages have been discovered. The carvings of such a profusion of creatures real and imaginary, so appropriate in this chapel which is also a garden, were designed to catch our attention. They were meant to delight, and to help us move in contemplation through the manifold creatures of this physical world to love of the God who made them. This attitude is expressed by many writers, as in

left: curled-up dragon

below: a beast on the Lady Chapel arcading

this example from *The Mirror of Holy Church* by the early thirteenth-century Archbishop of Canterbury, St Edmund Rich:

> How many things there are which delight our earthly eyes by their beauty and our taste by their sweetness and our touch by their smoothness and so all our other senses! …[If] there is so much beauty, sweetness and goodness in every created thing, how much beauty must there be in its Creator, Who made all this and every thing, and out of nothing!... Therefore say to Him in your heart: 'Because Thou art beautiful they are beautiful, because Thou art good they are good.'[13]

Many of the psalms echo this thought, but there is one psalm in particular which dwells at length upon the wonders of God's creation. The author of Psalm 104 sings the praise of God for all his marvellous works. 'The works

Beasts on the Lady Chapel arcading

of creation of which the psalm speaks bring joy to the one who recounts them. Delight in them unites God with man and man with God, and praise of God gives voice to this joy. Saying 'yes' to God, or greeting Him, is one with rejoicing in His creation.'[14] Such rejoicing in the variety of God's creatures is particularly appropriate here in the Lady Chapel which celebrates the woman whose 'Yes' to God brought the Saviour into the world.

Conclusion
And I saw a new heaven and a new earth

E ly cathedral is a gateway to heaven. It is, of course, not the only gate way. Mountains and stars, butterflies and crystals; all the wonders of this manifold universe are capable of opening to the receptive and enquiring soul a glimpse of something beyond. But a church building spells out more clearly the nature of that something; it places the glimpse within the Christian understanding of the purpose of human life.

The pilgrims who came, and still come, to this place are on a journey. Arriving here, they have finished one stage of that journey. Here they can obtain refreshment for soul and body; here they may obtain a fresh view of the purpose of their lives and a sense of dimensions beyond the everyday material world.

> Holy places are places where our vision is transfigured – not so much in simply seeing God afresh, but (as always follows from that seeing of God) seeing the world afresh – and ourselves in it. New frontiers have been crossed, not from one bit of the world's territory to another, but from one level of being in the world to another, a deeper belonging with God and creation.[1]

This experience of holiness is not the end of journeying, nor an end in itself. Those who come must go again, back to daily life in all its humdrum practicality. Daily life is itself a journey, even for those who stay at home. Nothing in this life is unchangeable, nothing enduring. But perhaps those who have travelled attentively through a great cathedral with its beautiful and eye-catching imagery will have caught a glimpse of what is truly unchanging. A glimpse of the 'beauty so ancient and so new' can beckon the traveller on, encouraging joyful perseverance in the way of Christ.

St Augustine captured very neatly the meaning of pilgrimage as well as the need for persistence in continuing the journey to its proper end: 'So, my dear friends, let us sing 'Alleluia', albeit not yet in the enjoyment of our heavenly rest, but in order to sweeten our toil in this life. Let us sing as travellers sing on a journey in order to help them keep on walking. ...And what do I mean by walking? I mean press on from good to better in this life. ...Advance in virtue, in true faith and in right conduct. Sing up – and keep on walking!'[2]

Notes

Preface

1 Maddison 2000.
2 Meadows and Ramsey 2003.
3 *Liber Eliensis* 2005.

Introduction

1 Palmer 1993, pp. 2–3.
2 Her name is variously spelt, Aethelthryth is closest to the original spelling; by the later Middle Ages it had become Audrey, but Etheldreda is the most widely used.
3 Also spelt Seaxburh.
4 Also spelt Wihtburh.
5 The earliest account of the lives of Etheldreda and Sexburga is in Bede's *Ecclesiastical History*, Chs. XIX & XX. See also Goscelin 2004 and *Liber* I, 1–35, pp. 12–69.
6 I am grateful to Christopher Brooke for drawing my attention to this.
7 See Cobb 1980, pp. 74–91, Cocke 2003, Lehmberg 1996.
8 I Kings 8:13, 27–29.
9 Rev. 21:2.
10 John of Fecamp, *Confessio Theologica*, quoted in Feiss 2000, p. 76.
11 See, for instance, Mark Stibbe, *A Kingdom of Priests: Deeper into God in Prayer*, London, 1994.
12 Williams 2002, p.xiv.
13 *Golden Legend* 1991, p. 778.
14 Mathews 1993, p. 142.
1⁵ Ward 1992, p. xiv.

16 See David Wallace, 'Dante in English', in *The Cambridge Companion to Dante*, ed. Rachel Jacoff, Cambridge, 1993, pp. 237–241.
17 A useful introduction to these is Krochalis and Peters 1975.
18 See Hiscock 2000.
19 This delightfully apt phrase was suggested by Janet Fairweather.
20 *Liber* II, 148, pp. 282–3.
21 *Liber* III, 121, p. 458.
22 Carruthers 1990 and 1998.
23 This, at least, was the ideal and intention. There is evidence that by the later Middle Ages the ideal was somewhat diluted, but even then most of the psalms were chanted weekly.
24 Miles 1985, p. 67.
25 Ward 1999, p. 32.
26 Broughton 1996.
27 Dorothy L. Sayers; speech by the Archangel Michael at the end of *The Zeal of thy House*: in Sayers 1948, p. 103.

Chapter 1

1 Birt 1949, p.1.
2 *Liber* III:35, p. 331. I am grateful to Janet Fairweather for drawing my attention to this passage.
3 For a detailed discussion of this with reference to St Albans, see Binski 2004, pp. 172–174.
4 Cambridge Trinity College Ms. R. 16.2, fol. 25v and fol. 26r; Bodleian Library, Ms. Douce 180, fol. 57v. These are illustrated in Schiller 1991,

plates 772, 774a and 779. I am grateful to John Maddison for suggesting this comparison.

5　See, for just one example of many, Gildea 1991, p. 126.

6　Furnivall and Pollard 1904, pp. 75–186.

7　*Myroure* 1873, p. 72.

8　See Hearn and Willis 1996; Marks 2004, p. 193ff.

9　Luke 1:26–38.

10　There are no surviving examples of this way of representing the Virgin, being crowned by the members of the Trinity dating before the beginning of the fifteenth century; the Lady Chapel is generally dated to the 1320s–40s. However, one scholar has argued that the upper part of the structure, in particular the vault, was built later than the lower parts (see Woodman 1984). My suggestion concerning the possible contents of the west gable niches could be taken as further evidence for the later date.

11　Fitzwilliam Museum Cat. no. M.2–1923.

12　John 14:2.

13　Ephesians 2:19b–22.

14　See Introduction p. 9

15　For further details see Carrasco 2000.

16　'Sic insensibiles lapides mysteria claudunt/ Vivorum lapidum, manualis spiritualem/ Fabrica designat fabricam...' Garton 1986, pp. 58–9.

17　*Piers Plowman*, Passus XIX, ll.321–328; quoted from Donaldson 1990, pp. 224–225.

18　Matt. 25: 31–40.

19　Krochalis and Peters 1975, p. 195; my modernisation.

20　For the history of the replacement of these windows see Maddison 2003, pp. 135–139.

21　Hilton 1957, p. 140.

22　Chaucer 1957, ll.147–161, pp. 566–7. My modernisation.

23　'The Parson's Tale' ll . 710–17; Chaucer 1957, pp. 250–1.

24　*Liber* II:131. My thanks to Janet Fairweather for this reference.

25　Zarnecki 1958, p. 38.

26　Thurlby 1999, pp. 51–67; see also Weir and Jerman 1986. Camille 1992 has a different

interpretation of some of such 'images on the edge', see particularly pp. 77–93.

27　Ps 48:12.

Chapter 2

1　For the details of the building sequence and its dating see Maddison 2003, pp. 113–116.

2　See, for instance, Taylor 2003, p. 214: '...almost everyone [in the Roman Empire] understood the basic visual vocabulary of imperial ideology...'.

3　2 Cor. 2:14.

4　Seidel 1981, pp. 32–3. For evidence of admiration for Roman triumphal arches in the twelfth century see Ross 1938.

5　*Liber* III:122, p. 461. I am grateful to Janet Fairweather for drawing this to my attention.

6　This is reviewed in Mathews 1993.

7　Matt. 21:1–11; Mark 11:1–11; Luke 19:28–40; John 12:12–19.

8　Zechariah 9:9–10.

9　Mathews 1993, p. 43.

10　*Liber* III:44, p. 346.

11　or whatever local substitute was available – in England generally willow branches. In Palestine olive branches, a proverbial sign of peace, would have been used, as well as palms.

12　See Wright 2000, p. 345.

13　'In at least two uses – at Christ Church Canterbury and at Hereford – the procession actually went outside the city walls and the second station (at which *Gloria laus* was sung) was at one of the city gates, the third station being at the church door.' Rastall 1996, p.266.

14　See Wright 2000, pp. 354–356.

15　Details of this procession, taken from the surviving Consuetudinal of Peterborough abbey, can be found in Bristan 2006.

16　'...pueri in altum supra ostium ecclesie canant versum, "Gloria, laus" etc.' Quoted from the York Missal in Rock 1853, vol. III, part II, p. 233.

17　Peterborough and Salisbury also have what seems to be such provision. The lower screen across the front at Exeter was probably used for this purpose; see Tudor-Craig 1991.

18 Written by Theodulph of Orleans who died in 821.

19 *Hymns Ancient and Modern: New Standard,* 1985, no. 328.

20 'The origin of the term is conjectural. Some derive it from the Latin *galeria,* a long porticus or porch. Others suppose that the verse in S. Mark xvi, 7: "He goeth before you into Galilee: there shall ye see him," suggests a meeting-place, and hence the name.' Sir Banister Fletcher, *A history of Architecture on the Comparative Method,* eighth ed., New York and London, 1929.

21 See Bristan 2006, pp. 43–4.

22 Maddison 2000, pp.36–7 and ill. 29.

23 The antiphon 'Ingrediente Domino in sanctam civitatem', see Rastall 1996 p. 266; Rock 1853 vol. III, pt II, p. 232.

24 Sampson 1998, p. 176

25 ibid. pp. 173–4.

26 Honorius Augustudonensis, *Gemma animae,* I.cl, PL 152, col. 590.

27 For a detailed description of the consecration rite and of the uses of porches see Spatz 2001.

28 Statuary was also a feature of the west fronts of French cathedrals – witness Chartres – but the French fronts do not extend beyond the side walls of the nave, as do the English screen fronts.

29 I am grateful to Pamela Tudor-Craig for this suggestion.

30 Maddison 2000, p. 27

31 Kühnel 1987, p. 130.

32 Mark 16: 1–8.

33 Ogden 2002, pp. 19–67.

Chapter 3

1 Clement of Alexandria, from a treatise entitled *The Teacher,* 1,12; PG8, cols 367–70, quoted in Atwell 1999, p. 370

2 *Liber* III, 42, pp. 340–342.

3 See Ward 2001 for a sympathetic account of the range of pilgrims' motivations.

4 Rudy 2000, p. 263. For a broader discussion of late medieval views on pilgrimage see Botvinick 1992.

5 Matt 11:28.

6 Alter 1985, p. 116.

7 Jer. 6:16.

8 'A Wreath' in Herbert 1991, pp. 174–5.

9 Taken from the Shaker website: http://www.pbs.org/wnet/ihas/icon/shakers.html, accessed 4 April 2006.

10 Nilson 1998, pp. 131–2.

11 Donovan 1991, p. 47.

12 They seem to have been sung on the final stages of the journey to Jerusalem and also, as we shall see in Chapter 8, when ascending the steps of the Temple in Jerusalem.

13 Donovan 1991, p. 115.

14 See Clanchy 2004, p. 107; Duffy 2006.

15 Hilton 1957, p. 236.

16 Heslop 1994, p. 38: 'The combination of foliage detailing superimposed on a spiral clearly conveys the notion of burgeoning increase because of its association with the natural unfurling of a plant.'

17 Rev. 4:7; see also Ezekiel 1:5–11.

18 *Liber* II: 148, p. 282. My thanks to Janet Fairweather for this reference.

19 John 4:14.

20 Miller 2002, p. 65.

21 Eastern Orthodox practice traces the arms of the cross from right to left.

22 Quoted from the Life of St Oswald, in Hiscock 2000, p. 162.

23 John 14:6.

24 Middleton 1995, p. 9.

25 Rom. 8: 38–39.

26 For an in-depth discussion of this see Ward 1976, p.42.

27 Blakesley 1998, p.140.

28 Colossians 2:15.

29 Traherne 1966, p. 190.

30 *Golden Legend* 1991, p.271.

31 See Thiede and d'Ancona 2000, esp. pp. 123–148. Examples of this symbol can be dated back to the second century. Early fourth-century English examples of the Chi-Rho symbol, now in the British Museum, were found by archaeologists at Water Newton in Huntingdonshire.

32 William Langland, 'Piers Plowman' Passus

XVIII, ll.427–9; quoted from Donaldson 1990, p. 214.

33 'The Crosse', Donne 1969, pp. 302–303; my modernisation.

34 *Liber* II, 136, p. 263.

35 See St Paul's Letter to the Romans 6:3–4.

36 In the church of S Paolo fuori le mura; see the discussion in Kessler and Zacharias 2000, pp. 179–182.

37 Psalm 78 vv13–15. For the full story see Exodus 14:15–15:1.

38 *Myroure* 1873, p. 82.

39 Ibid. p. 173.

40 Gen. 1:1–2.

41 *Handbook* 1862, pp. 178–9.

42 Rev. 4: 11.

Chapter 4

1 Birt 1949, p. 10.

2 Birt 1949, p. 11.

3 Here there is an untranslatable pun on 'lumen' = light and 'lumen' = eye.

4 'Aspectu digne graciles pulchreque columpne/ Respondent aliis formaque situque columpnis/ Lumina nec saturant licet ipse lumine pascant./ Fulget opus clarum, decus et décor ecclesiarum,/ Artificis donis ueluti templum Salomonis./ Aula decora foris, sed et intus plena decoris,/ Artificis cura similem non est habitura.' Gregory of Ely, *Verse Life and Miracles of St Aethelthryth*, ll. 361–367, quoted from Thompson and Stevens 1988. P. 362.

5 Fernie 1979, p. 4.

6 For a discussion of the reasons for the size of the naves of Norman cathedrals see Brooke 1999 pp. 185–187 and Brooke 1995 pp. 42–3.

7 Prose translation of *Paradiso* xiv, 33–8 in Boyde 2000, p. 72.

8 Is. 6:3.

9 *Liber* III:132. I am grateful to Janet Fairweather for this reference.

10 Thiede and d'Ancona 2000, pp. 119–122.

11 Binski 2003, p. 45, points out that many major Benedictine churches were being redecorated at this time.

12 Matthew 1:1–17; Luke 3:23–38.

13 *Handbook* 1862, p. 183.

14 *Handbook* 1862, p. 184.

15 Gen. 1:26–28.

16 Gen. 3:1–24.

17 Gen. 6:5 – 8:19.

18 Gen. 22:1–13.

19 Gen. 28:11–17.

20 Bath Abbey has on its west front sculpted angels climbing ladders, an explicit example of this imagery.

21 Precisely this text was inscribed over the Apsidal arch of the pilgrimage church of St Martin at Tours.

22 The Book of Ruth.

23 *Moralia in Job*, bk. 2, Ch. 1. PL 75, cols 553–555.

24 Luke 1:26–38.

25 Luke 2:1–7.

26 Luke 2:8–20; Matt. 2:1–12.

27 Rev. 21:1–6.

28 'The Church Floor' in Herbert 1991, p. 60.

29 See Foster 2003.

30 See the reconstruction drawing of the pulpitum in Meadows and Ramsey 2003, plate 3(c) between pages 258 & 259.

31 Maddison 2000, p.82

32 For a useful account of how these screens functioned see Russo 1994, esp. pp. 257–263.

33 See Draper 2003, pp. 79–84.

34 See Murray and Addiss 1990, pp. 44 ff for a description of a similar effect at Amiens.

35 For the Prior's Door see Chapter 10.

36 Murray and Addiss 1990, p. 52.

37 Luke 1:78.

38 von Allmen 1965, pp. 265–7.

39 Heb. 7:25.

40 John 20: 11–18.

41 Lancelot Andrewes, Easter Sermon 1620, quoted from Dorman 1993, p.155.

42 Matt. 16:19

Chapter 5

1 Birt 1949, p.19.

2 Eccl. 1:14.

3 Rev. 21:4

4 Brown 1966, p. 106.

5 Duby 1981, p. 23.

6 See Brooke and Brooke 1984, pp. 104–5. For archaeological analysis of the Lateran Baptistery see Brandenburg 2005, pp.37–54; for the symbolism of the octagonal shape see esp. p. 48.

7 Bony 1979, p. 40. The major details of my discussion of the Octagon imagery are taken from Lindley 1986.

8 Thus the *Liber Eliensis* I:12: 'And although she did not endure martyrdom, as it was a time of peace, nevertheless she is adorned with the glory of martyrdom, since, being in conflict with vices and desires, she continually carried the cross of the Lord in her bodily condition.'

9 Verses 19–20.

10 Verses 11–12.

11 Wood 1997, p. 122.

12 Grant 2000, p. 53.

13 Hiscock 2000, p. 127.

14 *Liber* I:41, p. 75.

15 This meaning of the shape was still well-known in the C17 when, for instance, the church of Santa Maria della Salute in Venice was built as an octagon explicitly to evoke it: '...like an early Christian baptismal font, the octagon was to evoke the 'eighth day' of creation, presented as a geometrical configuration of the number of the new beginning through resurrection.' Concina 1998, p. 242.

16 Ps 119 is the longest of the acrostic psalms; Pss 25, 34, 111, 145 are also acrostics.

17 Cardinal Bellarmine, as quoted in Neale and Littledale 1874, p.3.

18 Matt. 5:3–10.

19 Rev. 22:13. Alpha and omega are the first and last letters in the Greek alphabet, Greek being the language in which the New Testament was written.

20 1 Cor. 1:23–4.

21 In what follows I am particularly indebted to Lindley 1986.

22 These were first brought together in Ely by Prior Alexander in the 1150s; see Crook 2000 pp. 210–211.

23 Trans. Gavin Bone, *Anglo-Saxon Poetry*, Oxford, 1943, p. 32.

24 The common claim that the king and queen represent King Edward III and Queen Philippa cannot be correct. These carvings will have been put in place in 1324–5 (see Lindley 1995, p.116) when Edward II was still alive and his son still a youth. The bearded king's head could be claimed as a portrait of Edward II but this also is unlikely. Although it bears some resemblance to the effigy of Edward II in Gloucester, this effigy is itself held to show no sign of any attempt at genuine portraiture (Lindley 1995, p. 110, quoting Stone 1972, p.161). The most likely conclusion is that the Ely heads are generalised images.

25 1 Peter 5:8–9.

26 Ps. 91:2, 4, 13.

27 *Myroure* 1873, p. 167.

28 Maddison 2000, p. 32.

29 Maddison 2000, p. 66; but the evidence is ambiguous.

30 The illustrations of two of the corbels in Meadows and Ramsey 2003, B&W plates 10 (c) and (d), are misdescribed. 10 (c) is described as 'Etheldreda made Abbess' but is in fact the Miracle of St Abb's Head. 10 (d) is described as 'the death and burial of Etheldreda' but John Maddison is surely correct in suggesting that it shows her death and translation (see text and note 36 below).

31 Also spelt Tondberht.

32 My interpretation of this corbel follows Maddison 2000, p. 66, rather than Lindley 1995.

33 See Lindley 1995, p. 119 and Maddison 2000, p. 66.

34 See Lindley 1995, pp.118–120.

35 These two corbels reverse the story as told in the *Liber Eliensis*. This may simply be due to a mistake in placement of the stones. On the other hand, it may reflect another account of Etheldreda's life which placed the events in a slightly different order from that in the *Liber*. It was normal to have available various versions of the saint's story, as is witnessed by the two surviving accounts of the life of St Hugh of Lincoln, one in prose and one in verse.

36 In this also I follow Maddison's interpretation.

37 See Thompson 1996.

38 For the story see *Golden Legend* 1991, pp. 689–695.

39 Two of the Evangelists, Matthew and John, were also Apostles; so they are duplicated. This is because each series represents, not just the individuals but also their function.

40 From the fourteenth-century treatise 'How men that ben in hele sholde visite sike folk...' Krochalis and Peters 1975, p. 195; my modernisation.

41 Taken from 'Burnt Norton', the first of the *Four Quartets*, in *Eliot* 1963, p. 191.

42 It was only later that architects re-learnt what the ancient Roman builders had been able to achieve: how to cover such a large space with a circular dome.

43 Dante's final vision of God in the highest heaven; *Paradiso* Canto XXXIII 144–5.

44 As Dante's was in that final vision in heaven; *Paradiso* Canto XXXIII 143.

45 Matt 24:30

46 Kessler and Zacharias 2000, p. 123.

47 Inscription in the church of Sts Cosmas and Damian; translation taken from Kessler and Zacharias 2000, pp. 98–9.

48 Frisch 1987, p. 7.

49 2 Cor. 4:6.

50 St Cyril, bishop of Jerusalem 348–386, *Catechetical Lectures* (quoted from Atwell 1999, p. 283).

51 Kitzinger 1989, p. 148

52 Kitzinger 1989, pp. 147–150.

53 *Paradiso* Canto XXXI, ll. 25–27; quoted in Longfellow's translation from Royal 1999, p. 238.

54 Twelfth-century *Kyrie*-trope, quoted from Blakesley 1998, p. 140.

55 Rabanus Maurus, *De Laudibus Sanctae Crucis*, PL 108, 158 (MT); quoted from Flint 1991, p. 178.

56 Eaton 1984, p. 71, commenting on Psalm 150.

57 Gregory the Great, quoted from Gardner 1911, p. 256.

58 Middleton 1995, p36.

Chapter 6

1   Dearmer 1933, p.170.

2   There is some debate as to whether the entire Book of Psalms was prayed in the early Church, but no doubt that many of them were regularly so used. See Bradshaw 1990.

3   *Myroure* 1873, pp. 36–7.

4   Luke 1:39–55.

5   For further discussion of this see Robertson 2000, pp. 302–303.

6   Meredith 1997, pp. 80 and 82. The play is embedded in the so-called 'N-Town' cycle. The editor makes a strong case that this play was written for an East Anglian audience.

7   Commentary on St Luke's Gospel, Bk 2:26; Ambrose 2001, p. 36.

8   For the dates of this work see Meadows 2003, pp. 312–313.

9   Fearn 1997. Tracy 1987 Ch. VI also gives details of the history of the stalls, together with an analysis of their structure.

10 *Handbook* 1862, p. 204.

11 This is how a twelfth-century bestiary described the bird: 'The Pelican is excessively devoted to its children. But when these have been born and begin to grow up, they flap their parents in the face with their wings, and the parents, striking back, kill them. Three days afterward the mother pierces her breast, opens her side, and lays herself across her young, pouring out her blood over the dead bodies. This brings them to life again. In the same way, Our Lord Jesus Christ, who is the originator and maker of all created things, begets us and calls us into being out of nothing. We, on the contrary... have struck him in the face by devoting ourselves to the creation rather than the creator. That was why he ascended into the height of the cross, and, his side having been pierced, there came from it blood and water for our salvation and eternal life.' White 1984, pp. 132–3.

12 *Paradiso* XXV.113.

13 So it seems to me, despite Malcolm Jones's claim (Jones 2000, p. 159) that 'It is too readily assumed that all imagery to be found in a medieval context when not overtly religious in

subject matter must be 'symbolic'…'
Characteristically, Jones considers only the
misericords on the Beverley choirstalls, in
isolation from the rest of the structure. He cites
documentary evidence concerning the early
sixteenth-century stalls in Amiens cathedral
which suggests that the choice of subject
matter was left to the whim of the carver. No
reference is given for this. In fact the Amiens
stalls exhibit a detailed and comprehensive
programme of biblical scenes from both Old
and New Testaments, together with the
apocryphal life of the Virgin Mary (personal
observation). The documentation cited, if it is
indeed for these stalls, can only refer to a small
number of very marginal images.

14 Sandler 1997, p. 43.

15 For instance Bond 1910 is divided into two
volumes, one discussing the misericords, the
other covering the rest of the structures.
Grössinger 1997 and Wood 1999 also treat
misericords in isolation from their context.
Remnant 1998 provides an exhaustive
catalogue of misericords in Great Britain.
None of these authors is entirely reliable in
their description and identification of the
subjects of the carvings.

16 These technical terms are given in the
Glossary in Tracy 1987; when one looks at the
stalls, the terms are self-explanatory.

17 From Peter of Waltham's *Remediarum
Conversorum*, a late-twelfth century
abridgement of St Gregory the Great's *Moralia
in Job*. Both of these works were widely
available and much read, especially in
monastic circles, throughout the Middle Ages.
Translation quoted from Gildea 1991, p. 23. For
the influence of the *Moralia* see Rudolph 1997.

18 Sandler 2000, p. 75.

19 Grössinger 1997, p. 129.

20 Gen. 3:1 – 4:2.

21 Gen. 2:25.

22 Gen. 6:5 – 8:22.

23 This point has been very aptly made in
Maddison 2000, pp. 70–72, where the
misericord is illustrated.

24 Lewis 1995, p. 321.

25 Judges 14:5–6.

26 Barber 1992, pp. 36–7; Cummins 1988 pp.
154–5 has more detail about the symbolism of
the unicorn.

27 See the anecdote quoted in *Myroure* 1873, p. 59.

28 See Hassig 1999, p. 32, referring to Oxford,
Bodl., Ms. Douce 88, f. 69v.

29 The central section is illustrated in Wood
1999, p. 116.

30 See Wood 1999, p. 29.

31 *Liber Eliensis* III:34. My thanks to Janet
Fairweather for drawing this passage to my
attention.

32 I am grateful to Jessica Finch for drawing my
attention to this reference.

33 Barber 1992, p. 52.

34 For further examples of this image see Sandler
2000, p. 81 and fn. 46.

35 See Dressler 2004, pp. 98–101.

36 Camille 1992, pp. 93–97 makes far too much of
this aspect of such carvings, but the
scatological implications are nevertheless
present. Compare with Wentersdorf 1984.

37 Maddison 2000, p. 72; ill. 61 shows this
misericord.

38 Some of these are nineteenth-century
carvings.

39 Verzar 1992, pp. 130–3; Janson 1952, p. 46

40 See below, Ch. 10, pp. 170–171 for medieval
attitudes to minstrels.

41 Veronica Sekules' comment on the Bristol
corbels in Alexander and Binski 1987, p. 419.

42 See *Dialogue of Miracles* 1929, IV.XXXII, p. 230.

43 See Varty 1967, p. 54; Jones and Tracy 1991, p.
110. The latter misdescribes the fox as wearing a
cowled robe; in fact he is dressed as a bishop,
wearing a chasuble, with a mitre on his head
and a crozier in his hand. Because of this
misdescription they wrongly suggest that the
earliest woodcarvings of the fox as bishop 'date
from about 1400'. Haddon Hall in Derbyshire
posses a late medieval bench end showing the
fox preaching, with 'pax vobiscum' carved on
a scroll.

44 A fine set of benches in Brent Knoll church in
Somerset shows various scenes of the fox,
including his preaching.

45 For a succinct account of these difficulties see Greatrex 1997.

46 Barber 1992, p. 65.

47 See Baxter 1998.

48 'To see only the human and profane side of the work is to be ignorant of its deep seriousness, whereas to see only the spiritual, moralizing implications is to miss its essential *joie de vivre*.' Forsyth 1978, p. 282.

49 The beast being hunted is generally described as a hare, but I can see no clear evidence in the carving that it is not a rabbit. Illustration in Grössinger 1997, p. 165.

50 '...for non other wilde best in Engelond is called *ryot* sauf the conynge alonly.' Quoted from a medieval manual of hunting in Cummins 1988, p. 237. My modernisation.

51 Luke 10:2.

52 See Boynton 2002, p. 60.

53 *Liber Eliensis* II:6, p. 302. I am grateful to Janet Fairweather for bringing this entry to my attention.

54 Westermann 1989, p. 34.

55 See Greatrex 2003 for the musical observance of the monks at Ely. Unfortuately there seems to be as yet no detailed study of the polyphonic music sung here before the Reformation.

56 Page 1992, p. 76.

57 'The Thanksgiving': Herbert 1991, p. 32.

58 'Hymn to God My God, in My Sicknesse' Donne 1969, p. 336.

59 *Myroure*, quoted in Notes pp. 55–6.

Chapter 7

1 For the account of the 'translation' of the relics of St Withburga, see *Liber* II, 53, pp. 145–148.

2 Heb. 12:1.

3 Wegman 1990, p. 225.

4 Ward 1999, pp. 57–8.

5 For a detailed account of the sophisticated complex of architecture, shrine and Northwold's monument see Binski 2004, pp. 84–101.

6 Morgan 2001.

7 Of the Ely work Peter Draper comments: 'the astonishingly rich ornamentation of all the architectural elements at Ely gives it a distinct character quite unlike the comparatively austere treatment of the Lincoln nave. It is as if the architect at Ely had employed the architectural vocabulary of the Lincoln nave in the decorative spirit of St. Hugh's Choir.' Draper 1976, p.9.

8 That is, from St Hugh's Choir to the west end; the Angel Choir was built last, as an extension to the east end.

9 Draper 1996 p. 28; see also Brown 1999, p. 13.

10 Maddison 2000, p. 50. This point has been elaborated upon in Binski 2004.

11 Thurlby 1994, p. 181.

12 'Hic conditus est sanctae memoriae Martinus episcopus
Cuius anima in manu dei est, sed hic totus est Praesens manifestus omni gratia virtutum' quoted from Brown 1981, p. 4.

13 Henderson 1999 drew the analogy with St Martin, p. 158.

14 When Etheldreda's shrine was dismantled at the Reformation – probably in 1539 – much was made of the fact that she was enclosed, not in marble but in 'common stone'. This was claimed as disproof of the stories of her life and death. (See Atherton 2003, p. 172.) But the original marble coffin was hardly likely to have been carried with the remnant of the community who fled to escape the Danes in 870 or thereabouts. (See Keynes 2003, pp. 14–15.) The likelihood is that the relics were at that time moved into a more portable casket and that the antique marble coffin was destroyed by the marauders.

15 Bede (673–735): *Ecclesiastical History of the English Nation*, Book IV, taken from Medieval Sourcebook; http://www.fordham.edu/halsall/basis/bede-book4.html; accessed 14/6/07.

16 See Crook 2000, p. 167. 'Stolen by the monks of Ely' according to the inscription on St Withburga's holy well, to the west of the church at Dereham.

17 From *The Portiforium of St Wulfstan*, translation from Dales 2001, p. 113.

18 Ward 1991, p. 2.

19 His name is also spelt Byhrtstan.

20 The story is given in detail in *Liber* III, 33, pp. 320–325.

21 Draper 2003, p. 77.

22 St Basil the Great, Treatise on the Holy Spirit, Ch 9, 23 (quoted in Attwell 1999, p. 286).

23 Gregory the Great, *Moralia in Job*, 29, 3; PL 76, col 479; translation from Attwell 1999, p. 481.

24 Quoted from the end of Part One.

25 Boase 2004

26 For these see below, Ch. 11.

27 'St John the Divine' is another way of referrring to St John the Evangelist, author of the fourth Gospel and, so it was thought, the Book of Revelation.

28 *Handbook* 1862, pp. 205–6.

29 See Draper 2003, p. 80.

30 See Maddison 2003, p. 124.

31 Lady chapels were also built on the north side of the Choir of two other nearby Benedictine abbeys whose domestic quarters were situated on the south side of the church: Bury St Edmunds and Peterborough.

32 This is implied by the Sacrist's roll for the late 1350s. I am grateful to John Maddison for this information.

Chapter 8

1 Ps. 141:2.

2 Rev. 8:4.

3 2 Cor. 2:14.

4 *Notes* pp, 264–266.

5 *Summa Theologiae*, trans. Thomas Gilby O. P., London and New York, n.d., LIX, 169 (3a.83.5.2).

6 Atchley 1909, p. 130, quoting a gloss by William Lindewode on a constitution of Thomas Arundel.

7 Tudor-Craig 2002, p. 118. This interpretation, which refers to Chapter Houses with the Annunciation on the doorway, is surely also appropriate here.

8 *Paradiso* canto 32, ll. 94–114.

9 Millers 1807, p.96.

10 For medieval gardens see: Harvey 1981; Landsberg 1995; McLean 1981.

11 Song of Solomon (also known as the Song of Songs or the Canticle of Canticles), 4:12.

12 For the history of devotion to Mary see Graef 1994, especially Chapters 5 and 6.

13 'Forsoth, Marye, thowe ert gardin of alle swettenesse.' *The Mirour of Mans Saluacioun*, ed. Avril Henry, p. 53, l. 577.

14 For a discussion of the manifold meanings of the Paradise garden see J. T. Rhodes and Clifford Davidson, 'The Garden of Paradise', in Davidson 1994, pp. 69–109.

15 Cave 1948, p. 40.

16 *Myroure* 1873, p. 78.

17 See Morgan 1991, who quotes the Latin and Middle English texts of one of these, p. 91 and p. 100 respectively.

18 In the Sarum Masses for the feast of the Assumption and its Octave: 'Area uirga prime matris eve florens rosa processit maria.' '...et ex eva formans ave eue uerso nomine.' Legg 1916, pp. 479, 481.

19 Luke 1:26–42.

20 During the fifteenth and sixteenth centuries a further, non-biblical, element came to be added: 'Holy Mary, Mother of God, pray for us sinners now and at the hour of our death.' This extended form has been the standard Roman Catholic version of the prayer since that time. Members of other denominations tend to be more comfortable using only the scriptural sections. For the history of the 'Hail Mary' see Thurston 1953, pp. 90–114.

21 '...the evidence proves overwhelmingly that the combination of the words of St Gabriel with those of St Elizabeth, the practice of addressing a long series of salutations to Our Lady's image or altar, and finally the preference shown for the exact number of the psalms of David, had all become features of popular devotion before the latter part of the twelfth century.' Thurston 1953, p. 108. The addition of biblical scenes to be meditated while repeating the salutation came later.

22 For a brief, lucid account of the anchorite life, see Ward 1991, pp. 2–4.

23 *Ancrene Wisse*, in Savage and Watson 1991, pp. 61–2.

24 For the history of the Rosary see Miller 2002, Wilkins 1969 and Winston-Allen 1999.

25 'Glory be to the Father, and to the Son, and to the Holy Spirit; as it was in the beginning, is now and ever shall be, world without end. Amen'.

26 *The Commonplace Book of Robert Reynes*, ed. Cameron Louis, New York,1980, pp. 287–288:
'Man, in the chirche not idyll thow stande,
But take thy bedys in thyn hande.
And yf thow have here none of thyne,
I praye the, take these for the tyme, …
And whanne thow wylt no lenger stonde,
Leve the bedys ther thow them fonde.'

27 'O marie, flour of virgines, as the rose or the lilie, make preiers to thi sone, for the helpe of alle cristen men.' Quoted in Morgan 1991, p. 103.

28 For the complete poem see Grey, 1988, pp 162–163.

29 Winston-Allen p. 9.

30 The major reference for the whole sequence of scenes is James 1892, pp.345–362.

31 The story is told in *The Golden Legend* entry for the feast of the Nativity of Mary, though this account does not include her recital of the gradual psalms. See Ryan and Ripperger 1941, pp. 519–530.

32 Pss. 120–134.

33 According to the prophet Ezekiel (40:22, 26, 31, 37) seven steps to the outer court and eight to the inner court but generally shown, as in our carving, as one flight. See also Eaton 1984, p. 64.

34 Neale and Littledale 1874, p.164.

35 Meredith, 1997, p. 43. My modernization.

36 They were so well known that they continued to be quoted in Latin, as prefaces to the English translation of the psalms, in the post-Reformation Book of Common Prayer.

37 This is suggested by Gibson 1989, p. 133, with reference to the monks of Bury St Edmunds.

38 See Lindley 1995, pp. 80–82 for a discussion of the surviving fragments of this imagery.

39 The feet of one of these survives in the north east bay.

40 *Myroure* 1873, p. 36.

41 Solomon is shown thus on a boss of the fifteenth-century nave vault in Norwich cathedral; for an illustration see Rose and Hedgecoe 1997, p. 80.

42 1 Kings 3:16–28.

43 I Chron. 17:12

44 See Luke 1:31–33

45 The most thorough discussion of the Lady Chapel sculptures available in print is still James 1892. A more recent detailed discussion of the imagery can be found in P. G. Lindley, 'The Monastic Cathedral at Ely, circa 1320 to circa 1350: Art and Patronage in Medieval East Anglia' (Unpublished PhD Thesis, University of Cambridge 1985).

46 Oxford, Bodl. Lib., Douce 79, f.3, reproduced as pl. 147 in Sandler 1986, vol. 1.

47 Rev. 11:19– 12:2.

48 Tronzo, in Tronzo 1989, p. 182.

49 Gibson 1989, p. 174.

50 Folda 1999, p. 17.

51 Doyle 1990, p. 4.

52 Wordsworth and Littlehales 1904, p. 134, and see also p. 139.

53 Keen 1979, pp. 47–57.

54 Millers 1807, p. 97.

55 *Handbook* 1862, p. 46.

56 See Lindley 1986, repr. 1995, p. 145.

57 Winston-Allen, p. 129.

58 Quoted from John Geiler of Keisersberg, in Douglass, pp. 191–2.

59 See Blackburn 1967, pp. 53–76.

60 ibid. p. 76.

61 Ward 1971, pp. xi and xii.

62 Davidson 1994, p. 95.

63 A twelfth-century mass sequence, trans. Blakesley 1998, p. 15.

64 Williams 2002, pp. xv–xvi.

Chapter 9

1 Markus 1990, p. 82.

2 The major references are Knowles 1963 and 1948–59; Burton 1994, especially Chs 2 and 7–11 is a good introduction to medieval monastic life in England, as is Lawrence 1989, Ch. 7.

3 There are various editions of the *Rule* both in English and in the original Latin. An easily accessible translation with commentary is in de Waal 1995.

4 For details of the monastic community at Ely see Owen 2003; for the monastic buildings see Holton-Krayenbuhl 1998. See also Greatrex 1997 for insights into the specific tasks of a cathedral monastery; Greatrex 2003 considers the liturgical and spiritual life of the monks at Ely.

5 Markus 1990, p.82

6 *Paradiso*, Canto xiv 43–45.

7 From the hymn 'Light's abode, celestial Salem' ascribed to Thomas a' Kempis, trans. J. M. Neale, *Hymns Ancient and Modern: New Standard*, 1983, no. 185.

8 William Shakespeare, *All's Well That Ends Well*, Act 4, scene 3.

9 A succinct account of the function of a cloister can be found in Greene 1992, pp. 6–11.

10 See Braunfels 1972; *Gesta*, 1972; cf Brooke 1987.

11 But see Bell 1999, p.236 for the suggestion that 'it seems clear that there was more monastic book production in the fifteenth and early sixteenth centuries than has hitherto been supposed'.

12 Owen 1973, pp. 1–3.

13 See Fernie 2000, p. 206.

14 Thompson 1999, p. 24.

15 Thompson 1999, p. 23.

16 *Rule* Ch. LIII; but cf. Rubin 1987 for evidence of the less than ideal way in which such charitable obligations were carried out in medieval Cambridge.

Chapter 10

1 For a succinct account of the history of these doors see Zarnecki 1958, pp.17–37.

2 Zarnecki 1958, p. 22.

3 Brendel 1944, pp. 5–24.

4 Brown 1996, p. cxvii.

5 See Sampson 1998.

6 Rev. 20:12.

7 Rev. 21:5.

8 Lerclercq 1985, p. 76.

9 Post-Communion prayer for the Third Sunday after Trinity, *Common Worship* 2000, p. 481.

10 *All's Well That Ends Well*, Act 1, Scene 2.

11 Zarnecki 1958 p. 35: '[the sculptor's] aim was to produce a splendid, decorative whole rather than a comprehensive religious narrative.'

12 See for instance the discussion of similar scenes on the corbels of Kilpeck church, in Thurlby 1999.

13 Quoted in Davidson 1991, p. 108. For a discussion of both positive and negative attitudes to minstrels, see Baldwin 1997.

14 See Rieger 1991, pp. 229–242.

15 Hollander 1978, pp. 132–3.

16 Matt. 12:25.

17 Important visitors would normally have been guests of the abbot or prior of a monastery. See Gilchrist 2005, pp. 156–7 for details of how this worked at Norwich.

18 That is, in the complex of buildings near the prior's hall. See Maddison p. 88 and the plan of the monastery p. 85.

19 Isaiah 11:4.

20 Lewis p. 285. On p. 250 Lewis also refers to the Getty Apocalypse in which marginal figures mimic the phrase 'I saw'.

21 Douie and Farmer 1985, 2, 137.

22 Harvey 1993, p.4 comments that '[Westminster] Abbey's Customary, compiled about 1270, permits the sacrist to speak in a natural voice when showing visitors of the highest status around the church, but requires him to drop his voice for lesser visitors. Behind that rule, we may suspect, lay a long experience of minimizing the disturbance caused by talkative visitors of noble rank.'.

23 Zarnecki 1958, p. 19.

24 Zarnecki 1958, p. 21.

25 Except in a group of bishop or abbot saints, who would be standing or sitting, not kneeling as here.

26 See Norman 1988, pp. 160–1.

Chapter 11

1 For more detail see Edmund Esdaile 1973.
2 See Keynes 2003, p. 11 and n. 40.
3 For a discussion and dating see Schwartzbaum 1981, who agrees with Zarnecki 1958, p. 40, in suggesting the date of 1169 for this tomb slab.
4 Luke 16:19–31.
5 Binski 2004, p. 98.
6 Birt 1949, p. 16.
7 I am grateful to John Maddison for drawing this to my attention.
8 For a detailed discussion of the tomb see Lindley 1984; repr. 1995, pp. 85–96.
9 See Maddison 2003, pp. 132–7 for details of this work.
10 For the suggestion about the founding of King's Hall I am grateful to Professor Christopher Brooke.
11 Schoek 2004.
12 Heal 2004.
13 Bale 1971, pp. 631, 632. 'Qui tandem Elygensis episcopus factus… pater sanctimonia & virtute clarus…' '…in ecclesia Elygensi tandem post fata sepultus, ac pro Papistico veneratus.' I am grateful to Richard Rex for drawing my attention to this passage.
14 For instance, Lincoln and Tewkesbury.
15 Grey 1972, p.178.
16 Ps 90: 12.
17 Alter 1985, p. 129.
18 For the early history and development of cadaver monuments see King 2002.
19 For a detailed description of these ceremonies see Duffy 1992, pp. 29–37.
20 Westra, pp. 34–35.
21 Kamerick 2002, p. 186.
22 Rose 2004.
23 See Rubin 1991, pp. 302–6, Duffy 1992, pp. 238–48.
24 See for example Ps. 91:4.
25 'in-fere' = together.
26 *Quia amore* 1995, p. 12.
27 Traherne 1966, p. 193.
28 Millers 1807, pp. 93–4.
29 1 Corinthians 15:10.
30 See Lindley 1984, pp. 91–94.
31 Millers 1807, p. 95.

32 Neale 2004.
33 Symondson and Bucknall 2006, p. 259.
34 See Cobb 1980, p. 74; Owen 1970.
35 Neale 2004.
36 See Atherton 2003, p. 177.
37 Usher 2004.
38 'On Shakespeare, 1630', in Milton 1966, p. 82.
39 Strictly speaking, this is a cenotaph, since the bishop is not buried here.
40 Leclercq 1961, repr. 1985, p. 66 quoting John of Fécamp on the Heavenly Jerusalem.

Chapter 12

1 Julian 1986, p. 5.
2 For much more detail on this sort of punning in books designed for meditation see Carruthers 1998, pp. 161–165.
3 It is probably also not coincidental that at Westminster Abbey the spurs on the bases of the crossing piers are decorated with leaves, but the 'north-west pier has monkeys' or dragons' heads, and the north-east a lion attacking a horse.' Tudor-Craig 1986, p. 94. The meaning of these images on the north is also devilish.
4 Gen. 3:15.
5 This is clearly demonstrated in Basford 1978, which is by far the most reliable and seriously researched book on the subject.
6 Basford 1978, p. 20.
7 See Basford 1978, plates 56–60.
8 See Cameron 1991, pp. 136–141.
9 Ziolkowski 1993, pp. 22–4.
10 Ziolkowski 1993, p. 237.
11 Both are reproduced in Kaufmann 2003, pp. 219 and 222.
12 Ps. 148.
13 Translation taken from Colledge 1961, pp. 138–9, 131.
14 Westermann 1989, p. 248.

Conclusion

1 Williams 2002, p. 73.
2 Augustine, Sermon 256, 3 quoted from Atwell 1999, p. 499.

Glossary

Aisle: the side sections of the church, open to the main body of the church through an **arcade**.

Almoner: the monastic official charged with the duty of distributing alms to the poor and needy; **almonry** the premises from which the almoner operated; **almonry boys**: boys from poor families housed and educated in the monastery precinct.

Antiphon: A short chant, normally sung before and after the psalms of the **Divine Office** or during processions.

Apse: semicircular or polygonal end of a church or chapel, generally vaulted.

Arcade: a series of arches supported on columns or piers, either free-standing or used as decoration when set against a wall (**blank arcading**).

Bays: internal compartments of a church; each is divided from its neighbour not by solid walls but by divisions marked in the side walls (such as columns) or the ceiling (beams).

Boss: a knob or projection usually placed at the intersection of vaulting ribs.

Chancel: the part of the church to the east of the crossing, including the **Choir**, **Presbytery** and **Sanctuary**.

Chantry: endowment for the saying of Masses and other prayers for the soul of the founder(s). So **chantry chapel** – area set aside for such prayers.

Chapel: screened area within a church, providing space for small congregations or for private prayer.

Choir: that part of the church building in which seats – **choir stalls** – are provided for the choir and in which divine service is sung.

Clerestorey: the upper storey of the nave walls of a church, with windows letting light into the centre of the nave.

Cloister: a covered passage joining the various buildings of a monastery, normally built around the four sides of an oblong garden – the **cloister garth**.

Communion (Holy Communion): also known as the **Mass** or **Eucharist**; the central Christian service, in which bread and wine are prayed over by a priest (consecrated) and consumed by the faithful as the body and blood of Christ.

Corbel: a stone shelf projecting from a wall to support something on its top surface.

Corbel table: a series of corbels placed just below the roof; often found on Norman buildings and frequently carved with heads and/or grotesque figures.

Cosmati: an Italian family of craftsmen in the twelfth century who specialised in complex, multi-coloured decorative stonework.

Crocket: a projecting piece of stone, carved with foliage, decorating the edges of spires and canopies.

Cruciform: cross-shaped.

Divine Office: this consists of the regular daily prayer services of the **Hours**.

Eucharist: *see* **Communion**.

Finial: the pointed top of a canopy; a pinnacle.

Foliated: carved with leaf shapes.

Galilee: a porch-like vestibule, usually at the west end of a church.

Gallery: the upper storey above an aisle, opening to the nave through arches, sometimes called a **Triforium**.

Gargoyle: grotesquely carved projecting water-spout to throw water off the roof.

Host: the consecrated bread of the **Communion**. This is generally a round, white wafer.

Hours: the rota of seven daily prayer services appointed to be recited throughout each day by monks, nuns and other clergy.

Jambs: the straight, vertical sides of doors and windows.

Lady Chapel: chapel set aside for prayer services in honour of the Virgin Mary, mother of Jesus, frequently referred to as 'Our Lady'.

Lintel: the horizontal timber or stone that spans an opening (such as a doorway) and supports the weight of the wall above.

Liturgy: The formal public worship services of the Church; the written forms of such services.

Mass: see **Communion**. The text of the Mass consists of two parts – the Canon, which is invariable, and the Proper, which is variable. Hence the word Mass is also used to denote the text proper to the Mass for a particular occasion, as in 'Lady Mass' = the form of words for Masses in honour of the Virgin Mary.

Misericord: a small, shelf-like projection beneath the hinged seat of a **choir stall**; when the seat is upright, the misericord provides support while the occupant of the seat is standing.

Narthex: enclosed vestibule at the main entrance to a church.

Nave: that part of a church west of the **Screen** and **Choir**; also the central section of this, as contrasted with the side **Aisles**.

Niche: a recess in a wall, hollowed like a shell to hold a statue.

Presbytery: the part of the church to the east of the **Choir**, where the High Altar is placed; see also **chancel**.

Psalter: the Book of Psalms – part of the Bible, prayed as the major ingredient of the daily **Offices**.

Pulpitum: stone screen in a large church, dividing the **Choir** from the **nave**.

Purbeck marble: a grey stone from Dorset; not a true marble but so-called because it can be highly polished.

Relief (carving): Shallow carving in which the image does not stand free of its background.

Reservation: Storage of the consecrated **Host** between services. The Host was generally kept in a secure cupboard near the **High Altar**. In more recent times it tends to be kept, similarly securely, in a side chapel.

Rood: crucifix; usually the major crucifix in a church, set over the **Rood Screen** which is placed to the west of the **Choir** and, where one exists, of the **pulpitum**.

Sanctuary: the area around the **High** (main) **Altar**.

Spandrel: the approximately triangular space between an arch and a rectangular surround or between adjacent arches.

Stalls: see **choir stalls**.

Tabernacle work: elaborately carved niches with canopies, often used as a small-scale decorative feature.

Tracery: slender intersecting stone rib patterns in the top of a window.

Transept: the transverse portion of a church with a **cruciform** ground plan.

Tree of Jesse: the family tree of Jesus, shown as the reclining figure of his ancestor Jesse, from whose side grows a tree in which are Jesse's descendants with Mary and/or Jesus at the top.

Triforium: *see* **Gallery**.

Triumphal Arch: free-standing single or triple arch built to celebrate the victory of a Roman emperor; the form of such an arch used in church architecture as an implicit reference to the triumph of Christ over sin and death.

Tympanum: the, roughly triangular, space enclosed between the **lintel** and the arch of a doorway.

Bibliography

Alexander, Jonathan and Paul Binski, eds. *Age of Chivalry: Art in Plantagenet England 1200–1400*, London, 1987

Alexander, J. Neil, *Time and Community, Essays in Honor of Thomas Julian Talley*, Washington, D. C., 1990

Altenburg, Detlef, *Feste und Feiern im Mittelalter*, Jörg Jarnut and Hans-Hugo Steinhoff, eds, Sigmaringen, 1991

Alter, Robert, *The Art of Biblical Poetry*, Edinburgh, 1985

Atchley, E. G. Cuthbert F., *A History of the Use of Incense in Divine Worship*, London, 1909

Atherton, Ian, 'The Dean and Chapter: Reformation to Restoration', in Meadows and Ramsay 2003, pp. 167–192

Atwell, Robert, *Celebrating the Seasons: Daily Spiritual Readings for the Christian Year*, Norwich, 1999

Backhouse, Janet, *The Medieval English Cathedral: Papers in Honour of Pamela Tudor-Craig, Proceedings of the 1998 Harlaxton Symposium*, Donington, 2003

Baldwin, John, 'The Image of the Jongleur', *Speculum 72*, 1997, pp. 635–663

Bale, John, *Scriptorum Illustrium maioris Brytannie, quam nunc Angliam & Scotiam vocant: Catologus...*, Basle, 1557, 1559, facsimile reprint Farnborough, 1971

Barash, Moshe, *Imago Hominis: Studies in the Language of Art*, Vienna, 1991

Barber, Richard, *Bestiary: Being an English Version of the Bodleian Library, Oxford M. S. Bodley 746*, London, 1992

Baring-Gould, S., *The Lives of the Saints*, vol. 16, Edinburgh, 1914

Barron, Caroline M. and Jenny Stratford, *The Church and Learning in Later Medieval Society: Essays in Honour of R. B. Dobson, Proceedings of the 1999 Harlaxton Symposium*, Donington, 2002

Basford, Kathleen, *The Green Man*, Woodbridge, 1978, repr. 1996

Baxter, Ron, *Bestiaries and their Users in the Middle Ages*, Stroud, 1998

Bede, the Venerable, *Bede's Ecclesiastical History of the English People*, ed. B Colgrave and R. A. B. Mynors, Oxford, 1969

Bell, David N., 'Monastic Libraries: 1400–1557', in Hellinger and Trapp 1999, pp. 229–254

Binski, Paul, *Becket's Crown: Art and Imagination in Gothic England*, New Haven and London, 2004

Binski, Paul, 'The Painted Nave Ceiling of Peterborough Abbey', in Backhouse 2003, pp. 41–62

Binski, Paul and David Park, ' A Ducciesque Episode at Ely: The Mural Decorations of Prior Crauden's Chapel', in Ormrod 1986, pp. 28–41

Birt, Raymond, *The Glories of Ely Cathedral*, London, 1949

Blackburn, Bonnie J., '*Te Matrem Dei Laudamus*; A Study in the Musical Veneration of Mary', in *The Musical Quarterly*, Vol. LIII, no.1, 1967, pp. 53–76

Blakesley, John, *A Garland of Faith: Medieval Prayers and Poems newly translated and arranged for the three year Lectionary*, Leominster, 1998

Blanton-Whetsell, Virginia, '*Imagines Aetheldreda*: Mapping Hagiographic Representations of Abbatial Power and Religious Patronage', in Emmerson and Sheingorn 2002, pp. 55–107

Boase, G. C., 'Rattee, James (1820–1855)', rev. Christopher Marsden, *Oxford Dictionary of National Biography*, Oxford University Press, 2004 [http://www.oxforddnb.com/view/article/23164, accessed 4 April 2006]

Bond, Francis, *Wood Carvings in English Churches: Misericords*, London, 1910

Bond, Francis, *Wood Carvings in English Churches: Stalls and Tabernacle Work*, London, 1910

Bony, Jean, *The English Decorated Style: Gothic Architecture Transformed 1250–1350*, Oxford, 1979

Botvinick, M., 'The Painting as Pilgrimage', *Art History*, vol. 15, No. 1, March 1992, pp. 1–8

Boyde, Patrick, *Human Vices and Human Worth in Dante's 'Comedy'*, Cambridge, 2000

Boynton, Susan, 'Work and Play in Sacred Music and its Social Context, c. 1050 – 1250', in Swanson 2002, pp. 57–79

Bradshaw, Paul, 'Cathedral vs. Monastery: The Only Alternatives for the Liturgy of the Hours?', in Alexander 1990, pp. 123–136

Brandenburg, Hugo, *Ancient Churches of Rome from the Fourth to the Seventh Century: The Dawn of Christian Architecture in the West*, Turnhout, 2005

Braunfels, Wolfgang, *Monasteries of Western Europe: The Architecture of the Orders*, London, 1972

Brendel, Otto, 'The origin and meaning of the Mandorla', *Gazette des Beaux Arts*, 1944, pp 5–24

Bristan, Margaret, 'Peterborough Consuetudinal – Part 2', in *The Friends of Peterborough Cathedral Journal*, 2006, 41–44

Brooke, C. N. L., *Churches and Churchmen in Medieval Europe*, London, 1999

Brooke, C. N. L., *Medieval Church and Society* London, 1971

Brooke, C. N. L.,'English Episcopal "Acta" of the Twelfth and Thirteenth Centuries', in *Medieval Ecclesiastical Studies in honour of Dorothy Owen*, ed M. J. Franklin and Christopher Harper-Bill, Woodbridge, 1995

Brooke, Rosalind and C. N. L. Brooke, *Popular Religion in the Middle Ages: Western Europe 1000–1300*, London, 1984

Broughton, Lynne, *Interpreting Lincoln Cathedral: The Medieval Imagery*, Lincoln, 1996

Brown, Peter, *The Cult of the Saints*, Chicago and London, 1981

Brown, Raymond E., Intro., trans. and notes, *The Gospel According to John*, 2 vols, *The Anchor Bible*, New York, 1966

Brown, Sarah, *Sumptuous and Richly Adorned: The Decoration of Salisbury Cathedral*, London, 1999

Buckton, David and T. A. Heslop, eds., *Studies in Medieval Art and Architecture*, Stroud, 1994

Burton, Janet, *Monastic and Religious Orders in Britain, 1000–1300*, Cambridge, 1994

Cameron, Averil, *Christianity and the Rhetoric of Empire*, Berkeley, 1991

Camille, Michael, *Image on the Edge: The Margins of Medieval Art*, London, 1992

Carrasco, Magdalena Elizabeth, 'The Construction of Sanctity: Pictorial Hagiography and Monastic Reform in the First Illustrated *Life of St Cuthbert* (Oxford, University College MS 165)', in Emmerson and Sheingorn 2000

Carruthers, Mary J., *The Book of Memory: A Study of Memory in Medieval Culture*, Cambridge, 1990

Carruthers, Mary J., *The Craft of Thought: Meditation, Rhetoric, and the making of images, 400–1200*, Cambridge, 1998

Cate, James Lea and Eugene N. Anderson, eds, *Medieval and Historiographical Essays in Honour of James Westfall Thompson*, Chicago, 1938

Cave, C. J. P., *Roof Bosses in Medieval Churches: An Aspect of Gothic Sculpture*, Cambridge, 1948

Chaucer, Geoffrey, *The Complete Works of Geoffrey Chaucer*, 2nd edn, ed. F. N. Robinson, Oxford, 1957

Clanchy, Michael, 'Images of Ladies with Prayer Books: What do they signify?', in Swanson 2004, pp. 106–122

Clark, James G., 'Monastic Education in Late Medieval England', in *The Church and Learning in Later Medieval Society: Essays in Honour of R. B, Dobson, Proceedings of the 1999 Harlaxton Symposium*, ed. Caroline M. Barron and Jenny Stratford, Donington, 2002, pp. 25–40

Clark, James G., *The Religious Orders in Pre–Reformation England, Studies in the History of Medieval Religion 18*, Woodbridge, 2002

Clarke, Georgia and Paul Crossley eds, *Architecture and Language: Constructing Identity in European Architecture c. 100 – c. 1650*, Cambridge, 2000

Cobb, Gerald, *English Cathedrals: The Forgotten Centuries*, London, 1980

Cocke, Thomas, 'The history of the fabric from 1541 to 1836', in Meadows and Ramsey 2003, pp. 213–224

Coldstream, Nicola and Peter Draper, eds, *Medieval Art and Architecture at Ely Cathedral: The British Archaeological Society's Conference Transactions 1976*, Leeds, 1979

Colledge, Eric, ed and intro., *The Medieval Mystics of England*, New York, 1961

Collinson, Patrick, Nigel Ramsay and Margaret Sparks, eds, *A History of Canterbury Cathedral*, Oxford, 1995

Colvin, Howard, *Architecture and the After-Life*, New Haven and London, 1991

Common Worship: Services and Prayers for the Church of England, London, 2000

Concina, Ennio, *A History of Venetian Architecture*, trans. Judith Landry, Cambridge, 1998

Crook, John, *The Architectural Setting of the Cult of the Saints in the Early Christian West c. 300–1200*, Oxford, 2000

Cummins, John, *The Hound and the Hawk: The Art of Medieval Hunting*, London, 1988

Dales, Douglas, *Christ the Golden Blossom: A Treasury of Anglo-Saxon Prayer*, Norwich, 2001

d'Avray, D. L., *The Preaching of the Friars: Sermons diffused from Paris before 1300*, Oxford, 1985

Davidson, Clifford, ed. *The Iconography of Heaven*, Kalamazoo, 1994

Davidson, Clifford, ed., *Word, Picture and Spectacle*, Kalamazoo, 1984

Dearmer, Percy, *The Story of the Prayer Book in the Old and New World and throughout the Anglican Church*, Oxford, 1933

de Waal, *A Life-Giving Way: A Commentary on the Rule of St Benedict*, London, 1995, repr. 2000

Dodwell, C. R., *Anglo-Saxon Art: A New Perspective*, Ithaca New York, 1982

Donaldson, E. Talbot, *William Langland: Will's Vision of Piers Plowman: An Alliterative Verse Translation*, New York, 1990

Donne, John, *The Poems of John Donne*, ed. Sir Herbert Grierson, London, 1969

Donovan, Claire, *The de Brailes Hours: Shaping the Book of Hours in Thirteenth-Century Oxford*, London, 1991

Dorman, Marianne, ed., *The Liturgical Sermons of Lancelot Andrewes*, vol 2, *The Paschal and Pentecostal Sermons*, Durham, 1993

Douglass, E. Jane Dempsey, *Justification in Late Medieval Preaching: A Study of John Geiler of Keisersberg*, Leiden, 1966

Doyle, A. I., The Shaping of the Vernon and Simeon Manuscript' in Pearsall 1990

Draper, Peter, 'Bishop Northwold and the Cult of St. Etheldreda', in Coldstream and Draper, 1976, pp. 8–27

Draper, Peter, 'Enclosures and Entrances in Medieval Cathedrals: Access and Security' in Backhouse 2003, pp. 76–88

Draper, Peter, 'Salisbury Cathedral: Paradigm or Maverick?', in Keen and Cocke 1996, pp. 21–31

Dressler, Rachel Ann, *Of Armour and Men in Medieval England: The Chivalric Rhetoric of Three English Knights' Effigies*, London, 2004

Duby, Georges, ed., *A History of Private Life*, vol. II, *Revelations of the Medieval World*, trans. Arthur Goldhammer, Cambridge MA, 1988

Duby, Georges, *The Age of the Cathedrals: Art and Society, 980–1420*, trans. Eleanor Levieux and Barbara Thompson, London, 1981

Duffy, Eamon, *Marking the Hours: English People and their Prayers 1240–1570*, New Haven and London, 2006

Duffy, Eamon, *The Stripping of the Altars: Traditional Religion in England 1400–1580*, New Haven and London, 1992

Eaton, John, *The Psalms Come Alive*, Oxford, 1984

Eliot, T. S., *Collected Poems 1909–1962*, London, 1963

Ellington, Donna Spivey, *From Sacred Body to Angelic Soul: Understanding Mary in Late Medieval and Early Modern Europe*, Washington D. C., 2001

Emerson, Jan Swango, and Hugh Feiss, eds. *Imagining Heaven in the Middle Ages*, New York, 2000

Emmerson, Richard K. and Pamela Sheingorn, *Studies in Iconography*, vol. 18, 1997, Kalamazoo, 1997

Emmerson, Richard K. and Pamela Sheingorn, *Studies in Iconography*, vol. 21, 2000, Kalamazoo, 2000

Emmerson, Richard K. and Pamela Sheingorn, *Studies in Iconography*, vol. 23, 2002, Kalamazoo, 2002

Esdaile, Edmund, *The Monuments in Ely Cathedral*, Ely, 1973

Douie, Decima L. and David Hugh Farmer, eds, *Magna Vita Sancti Hugonis*, corr. repr. Oxford Medieval Texts, 1985

Fassler, Margot E. and Rebecca A. Baltzer, *The Divine Office in the Latin Middle Ages: Methodology and Source Studies, Regional Developments, Hagiography*, Oxford, 2000

Fearn, Kate, 'Medieval and later Woodwork from the Choir in Ely Cathedral',
  Journal of the British Archaeological Association, vol. CL, 1997, pp. 59–75

Feiss, Hugh, 'John of Fecamp's longing for Heaven' in Emerson and Feiss, New
  York, 2000, pp. 65–81

Fernie, Eric and Paul Crossley, eds, *Medieval Architecture in its Intellectual Context:*
  Studies in Honour of Peter Kidson, London, 1990

Fernie, Eric, 'Observations on the Norman Plan of Ely Cathedral', in Coldstream
  and Draper, 1979, pp. 1–7

Fernie, Eric, *The Architecture of Norman England*, Oxford, 2000

Flint, Valerie I. J., *The Rise of Magic in Early Medieval Europe*, Oxford, 1991

Flynn, William T., *Medieval Music as Medieval Exegesis*, Lanham, Maryland and
  London, 1999

Folda, Jaroslav, 'Problems in the Iconography of the Art of the Crusaders in the
  Holy Land: 1098–1291/1917–1997', in Hourihane 1999, pp. 11–24

Forsyth, Ilene H. 'The Theme of Cockfighting in Burgundian Romanesque
  Sculpture', *Speculum*, 53, 1978, pp. 252–82

Foster, Richard, 'Feet on the Ground, Eyes on the Heavens: Some Aspects of
  Porphyry Opus Sectile Pavements in England' in Backhouse 2003, pp. 63–75

Frisch, Teresa G., *Gothic Art 1140 – c.1450: Sources and Documents*, Toronto, 1987

Gardner, Edmund, ed, *The Dialogues of Gregory the Great*, trans P. W., London,
  1911

Garton, Charles, *The Metrical Life of St Hugh of Lincoln: The Latin Text with*
  Introduction, Translation, and Notes, Lincoln, 1986

Gibson, Gail McMurray, *The Theatre of Devotion: East Anglian Drama and Society*
  in the Late Middle Ages, Chicago, 1989

Gilchrist, Roberta, *Norwich Cathedral Close: The Evolution of the English Cathedral*
  Landscape, Woodbridge, 2005

Gildea, Joseph, O.S.A., *Source Book of Self-Discipline: A Synthesis of 'Moralia in Job'*
  by Gregory the Great, A Translation of Peter of Waltham's 'Remediarium
  Conversorum', New York, 1991

Glasscoe, Marion, *The English Medieval Mystics*, London, 1993

Glasscoe, Marion, ed., *Julian of Norwich: A Revelation of Love*, Exeter, 1986

Golden Legend of Jacobus de Voragine, The, trans. Granger Ryan and Helmut
  Ripperger, Salem, New Hampshire, 1941, repr. 1969 and 1991

Goldman, Bernard, *The Sacred Portal*, Detroit, 1966

Goscelin of Saint-Bertin, *The Hagiography of the Female Saints of Ely*, ed. and trans.
  Rosalind C. Love, Oxford, 2004

Graef, Hilda, *Mary: A History of Doctrine and Devotion*, 2 vols, London, 1963 &
  1965, combined edition 1985, fourth impression 1994

Grant, Lindy, 'Naming of Parts: Describing Architecture in the High Middle Ages',
  in Clarke and Crossley 2000, pp. 46–57

Greatrex, Joan, 'The Cathedral Monasteries in the Later Middle Ages', in Rees 1997,
  pp. 118–134

Greatrex, Joan, 'Benedictine Observance at Ely: The Intellectual, Liturgical and
  Spiritual Evidence Considered', in Meadows and Ramsey 2003, pp. 77–93

Greene, J. Patrick, *Medieval Monasteries*, London and New York, 1992

Greenway, Diana, 'A Miracle of St Etheldreda: Bricstan's Shackles', *Friends of Ely*
  Cathedral Year Book, 1997, pp. 18–20

Grey, Douglas, ed., *The Oxford Book of Late Medieval Verse and Prose*, Oxford, 1988

Grey, Douglas, *Themes and Images in the Medieval English Lyric*, London, 1972

Grillo, Michael, *Symbolic Structures: The Role of Composition in Signaling Meaning in Italian Medieval Art*, New York, 1997

Grössinger, Christa, *The World Upside-Down: English Misericords*, London, 1997

Gurevich, Aron, *Medieval Popular Culture*, trans. Janos M. Bak and Paul A. Hollingsworth, Cambridge and Paris, 1988

Handbook to the Cathedrals of England: Eastern Division, London, 1862

Harper-Bill, Christopher et al., *Studies in Medieval History*, Woodbridge, 1989

Harvey, Barbara, *Living and Dying in England 1100–1540*, Oxford, 1993

Harvey, John, *Mediaeval Gardens*, London, 1981

Hassig, Debra, 'The Iconography of Rejection: Jews and Other Monstrous Races', in Hourihane 1999, pp. 25–37

Heal, Felicity, 'Goodrich , Thomas (1494–1554)', *Oxford Dictionary of National Biography*, Oxford University Press, Sept 2004; online edn, Oct 2005 [http://www.oxforddnb.com/view/article/10980, accessed 2 April 2006]

Heal, Felicity, 'West, Nicholas (*d.* 1533)', *Oxford Dictionary of National Biography*, Oxford University Press, 2004 [http://www.oxforddnb.com/view/article/29091, accessed 2 April 2006]

Hearn, M. F., and Lee Willis, 'The Iconography of the Lady Chapel of Salisbury Cathedral', in Keen and Cocke 1996, pp. 40–45

Heffernan, Thomas J. and E. Ann Matter, *The Liturgy of the Medieval Church*, Kalamazoo, 2001

Hellinger, Lotte and J. B. Trapp, eds, *The Cambridge History of the Book in Britain: Volume III 1400–1557*, Cambridge, 1999

Henderson, George, *Vision and Image in Early Christian England*, Cambridge, 1999

Herbert, Christopher, 'Permanent Easter Sepulchres: a Victorian Re-creation?', *Church Archaeology*, vols 7, 8 and 9, 2003–05, pp.7–19

Herbert, George, *The Complete English Poems*, ed. John Tobin, 1991

Heslop, T. A., 'Towards an Iconology of Croziers' in Buckton and Heslop 1994, pp. 36–45

Heslop, T.A. 'Brief in Words but Heavy in the Weight of its Meaning', *Art History*, 1986. pp. 1–11

Hilton, Walter, *The Ladder of Perfection*, trans. Leo Shirley-Price, Harmondsworth, 1957

Hiscock, Nigel, *The Wise Master Builder: Platonic Geometry in Plans of Medieval Abbeys and Cathedrals*, Aldershot, 2000

Hollander, Anne, *Seeing Through Clothes*, Berkeley, 1978

Holton-Krayenbuhl, Anne, *The Benedictine Monastery of Medieval Ely*, Ely, 1998

Horbury, W., ed., *Templum Amicitiae*, Sheffield, 1991

Horrox, Rosemary, *Beverley Minster: An Illustrated History*, Beverley, 2000

Hourihane, Colum, *Image and Belief: Studies in Celebration of the Eightieth Anniversary of the Index of Christian Art, Index of Christain Art, Occasional Papers III*, Princeton, 1999

Inge, John, *A Christian Theology of Place*, Aldershot, 2003

James, M. R. 'The Sculptures of the Lady Chapel at Ely, *The Archaeological Journal*, XLIX, 1892, pp. 345–362

Janson, H. W. *Apes and Ape Lore*, London, 1952

Jones, Malcolm and Charles Tracy, 'A Medieval Choirstall Desk-end at Haddon Hall: The Fox-Bishop and the Geese-Hangmen', *Journal of the British Archaeological Association*, vol. CXLIV, 1991, pp. 107–115

Jones, Malcolm, 'The Misericords', in Horrox, 2000, pp. 157–174

Julian of Norwich, *A Revelation of Love*, ed. Marion Glasscoe, Exeter, 1986

Kahn, Deborah, ed., *The Romanesqe Frieze and its Spectator*, London, 1992

Kamerick, Kathleen, *Popular Piety and Art in the Late Middle Ages: Image Worship and Idolatry in England 1350–1500*, New York, 2002

Kaufmann, C. M., *Biblical Imagery in Medieval England 700–1550*, London/Turnhout, 2003

Keen, Laurence, 'The Fourteenth-Century Tile Pavements in Prior Crauden's Chapel and in the South Transept', in Coldstream and Draper 1979, pp. 47–57

Keen, Laurence, and Thomas Cocke, *Medieval Art and Architecture at Salisbury Cathedral, The British Archaeological Association Conference Transactions XVII*, Leeds, 1996

Kessler, Herbert L., and Johanna Zacharias, *Rome 1300: on the Path of the Pilgrim*, New Haven and London, 2000

Keynes, Simon, 'Ely Abbey 672–1109', in Meadows and Ramsey 2003, pp. 3–58

King, Pamela M., 'The Treasurer's Cadaver in York Minster Reconsidered', in Barron and Stratford 2002, pp. 196–209

Kitzinger, Ernst , 'Mosaic Decoration in Sicily under Roger II and the Classical Byzantine System of Church Decoration', in Tronzo 1989, pp. 147–165

Klingender, Francis, *Animals in Art and Thought to the End of the Middle Ages*, Cambridge MA, 1971

Knighton, Tess, and David Fallows, *Companion to Medieval and Renaissance Music*, London, 1992

Knowles, D., *The Monastic Order in England: A History of its Development from the Times of St Dunstan to the Fourth Lateran Council, 940–1216*, 2nd edn Cambridge, 1963

Knowles, D., *The Religious Orders in England*, 3 vols., Cambridge, 1948–59

Krochalis, Jeanne and Edward Peters, ed. and trans., *The World of 'Piers Plowman'*, University of Pennsylvania, 1975

Kühnel, Bianca, *From the Earthly to the Heavenly Jerusalem: Representations of the Holy City in Christian Art of the First Millenium*, Rome, Freiburg, Vienna, 1987

Labarge, Margaret Wade, *Medieval Travellers*, London, 1983

Landsberg, Sylvia, *The Medieval Garden*, New York, n.d

Lawrence, C., H., *Medieval Monasticism: Forms of Religious Life in Western Europe in the Middle Ages*, 2nd edn. London, 1989

le Goff, Jacques, *Time, Work and Culture in the Middle Ages*, Chicago, 1980

Leclercq Jean, *The Love of Learning and the Desire for God*, New York 1961, repr.1985

Legg, J. Wickham, ed., *The Sarum Missal edited from Three Early Manuscripts*, Oxford, 1916

Lehmberg, Stanford E., *Cathedrals under Siege: Cathedrals in English Society, 1600–1700*, Exeter, 1996

Lewis, Suzanne, *Reading Images: Narrative Discourse and Reception in the Thirteenth-Century Illuminated Apocalypse*, Cambridge, 1995

Liber Eliensis: A History of the Isle of Ely from the Seventh Century to the Twelfth, trans. Janet Fairweather, Woodbridge, 2005

Lindley, Phillip, '"Carpenter's Gothic" and Gothic Carpentry', *Architectural History*, 1987, pp. 83–112

Lindley, Phillip, 'The Fourteenth Century Architectural Programme at Ely Cathedral', in Ormrod 1986, pp. 119–129

Lindley, Phillip, 'The Imagery of the Octagon at Ely', in *Journal of the British Archaeological Association*, 1986, pp. 75–99, repr. in Lindley 1995, pp. 113–146

Lindley, Phillip, 'The Tomb of Bishop William de Luda: an Architectural Model at Ely Cathedral', *Proceedings of the Cambridge Antiquarian Society*, 73, 1984, pp. 75–87, repr. in Lindley 1995, pp. 85–96

Lindley, Phillip, *Gothic to Renaissance: Essays on Sculpture in England*, Stamford, 1995

Maddison, John, 'The Gothic Cathedral: new building in a historic context', in Meadows and Ramsay 2003, pp. 113–141

Maddison, John, *Ely Cathedral: Design and Meaning*, Ely, 2000

Marks, Richard, *Image and Devotion in Late Medieval England*, Stroud, 2004

Markus, R. A., *The End of Ancient Christianity*, Cambridge, 1990

Mathews, Thomas F., *The Clash of Gods: A Reinterpretation of Early Christian Art*, Princeton, 1993

McLean, Teresa, *Medieval English Gardens*, London, 1981

Meadows, Peter and Nigel Ramsay, *A History of Ely Cathedral*, Woodbridge, 2003

Meadows, Peter, 'Cathedral Restoration: Fabric and Furnishings 1836–1980', in Meadows and Ramsay, 2003, pp. 305–332

Meredith, Peter, ed., *The Mary Play from the N. Town Manuscript*, Exeter, 1997

Middleton, Arthur, *Towards a Renewed Priesthood*, Leominster, 1995

Miles, Margaret R., *Image as Insight: Visual Understanding in Western Christianity and Secular Culture*, Boston MA, 1985

Miller, John D, *Beads and Prayers: The Rosary in History and Devotion*, London, 2002

Millers, George, *A Description of the Cathedral Church of Ely*, 1807

Milton, John, *Milton Poetical Works*, ed. Douglas Bush, London, 1966

Morgan, Nigel, 'Marian Liturgy in Salisbury Cathedral', in Backhouse 2003, pp. 89–111

Morgan, Nigel, 'Texts and Images of Marian Devotion in English Twelfth-Century Monasticism, and Their Influence on the Secular Church', in Thompson 1999, pp. 117– 136

Morgan, Nigel, 'Texts and Images of Marian Devotion in Thirteenth-Century England', in Ormrod 1991, pp. 69–104, pp. 44–66

Murray, Stephen and James Addiss, 'Plan and Space at Amiens Cathedral' *Journal of the Society of Architectural Historians*, XLIX, 1990

Myroure of oure Ladye, The, ed. John Henry Blunt, Early English Text Society, London, 1873

Neale, J. M., and R. F. Littledale, *A Commentary on the Psalms: from Primitive and Mediaeval Writers*, London, 1874

Nilson, Ben, *Cathedral Shrines of Medieval England*, Woodbridge, 1998

Norman, Joanne S., *Metamorphoses of an Allegory: The Iconography of the Psychomachia in Medieval Art*, American University Studies IX, Peter Lang, New York, 1988

Notes on the Divine Office, London, c.1878

Ogden, Dunbar H., *The Staging of Drama in the Medieval Church*, Newark and London, 2002

Ong, Walter, 'Wit and Mystery: A Revaluation of Mediaeval Latin Hymnody', *Speculum* 22, 1947, pp. 310–341

Ormrod, W.M., ed., *England in the Fourteenth Century: Proceedings of the 1985 Harlaxton Symposium*, Woodbridge, 1986

Ormrod, W. M., ed., *England in the Thirteenth Century: Proceedings of the 1989 Harlaxton Symposium*, Stamford, 1991

Owen, D. M., 'The Enforcement of the Reformation in the Diocese of Ely', *Miscellenea Historiae Ecclesiasticae*, III, Colloque de Cambridge 1968, Louvain, 1970, pp. 167–174

Owen, Dorothy, 'Ely 1109–1539: Priory, Community and Town', in Meadows and Ramsey 2003, pp. 59–75

Page, Christopher, 'Musicus and cantor', in Knighton and Fallows 1992, pp. 74–78

Palmer, Martin, *Living Christianity*, Shaftsbury, 1993

Pearsall, Derek, ed., *Studies in the Vernon Manuscript*, Cambridge, 1990

Pilkington, Evan, *Learning to Pray*, London, 1986

PL. *Patrologiae Cursus Completus, series latina*, ed. J. P. Migne, 221 vols, Paris, 1857–66

Plank, Steven, *The Way to Heaven's Doore: An Introduction to Liturgical Process and Musical Style*, Metuchen and London, 1994

Platt, Colin, *King Death: The Black Death and its aftermath in late-medieval England*, London, 1996

Porter, Stanley E., Michael A. Hayes and David Tombs, *Images of Christ Ancient and Modern*, Sheffield, 1997

'*Quia amore langueo*': *A translation close to the Original Middle English*, trans. Oliver Bernard, with illustrations by Eric Gill, n.p., 1995

Rastall, Richard, *The Heaven Singing: Music in Early English Religious Drama*: I, Woodbridge, 1996

Rees, Daniel, ed., *Monks of England*, London, 1997

Remnant, L., *Catalogue of Misericords in Great Britain*, Oxford, 1969, repr. 1998

Rieger, Angelica, 'Beruf: *Joglaressa* – Die Spielfrau im okzitanischen Mittelalter', in Altenburg et al. 1991, pp 229–242

Roberts, Lawrence D., *Approaches to Nature in the Middle Ages*, New York, 1982

Robertson, Anne Walters, 'From Office to Mass: The Antiphons of Vespers and Lauds and the Antiphons before the Gospel in Northern France', in Fassler and Baltzer 2000, pp. 300–323

Rock, Daniel, *The Church of our Fathers*, 4 vols, London, 1853

Rollason, D., M. Harvey and M. Prestwich, eds, *Anglo-Norman Durham*, 1994

Roper, Sally, *Medieval English Benedictine Liturgy: Studies in the Formation, Structure and Content of the Monastic Votive Office c. 950–1540*, New York and London, 1992

Rose, Martial and Julia Hedgecoe, *Stories in Stone: The Medieval Roof carvings of Norwich Cathedral*, London, 1997

Rose, Richard K., 'Redman, Richard (*d.* 1505)', *Oxford Dictionary of National Biography*, Oxford University Press, 2004 [http://www.oxforddnb.com/view/article/23260, accessed 4 April 2006]

Rosenberg, Charles M., *Art and Politics in Late Medieval and Early Renaissance Italy: 1250–1500*, Notre Dame and London, 1990

Ross, James Bruce, 'A Study of Twelfth Century interest in the Antiquities of Rome' in Cate and Anderson 1938, pp. 302–321

Royal, Robert, *Dante Alighieri: Divine Comedy, Divine Sprituality*, New York, 1999

Rudolph, Conrad, *Violence and Daily Life: Reading, Art, and Polemics in the Citeaux, 'Moralia in Job'*, Princeton NJ, 1997

Rudy, Kathryn M., 'A Pilgrim's Book of Hours: Stockholm Royal Library A233', in Emmerson and Sheingorn 2000, pp. 237–279

Russo, Thomas E., 'The Romanesque Rood Screen of Durham Cathedral: Context and Form', in Rollason, Harvey and Prestwich 1994, pp. 251–268

Salisbury, Joyce E., ed. *The Medieval World of Nature*, New York and London, 1993

Sampson, Jerry, *Wells Cathedral West Front: Construction, Sculpture and Conservation*, Stroud, 1998

Sandler, Lucy Freeman, *Gothic Manuscripts 1285–1385*, 2 vols, London and Oxford, 1986

Sandler, Lucy Freeman, 'The Study of Marginal Imagery: Past, Present, and Future', in Emmerson and Sheingorn 1997, pp. 1–49

Sandler, Lucy Freeman, 'The Images of Words in English Gothic Psalters', in *Studies in the Illustration of the Psalter*, ed. Brendan Cassidy and Rosemary Muir Wright, Stamford, 2000, pp. 67–86

Saul, Nigel, ed., *The Age of Chivalry: Art and Society in Late Medieval England*, London, 1992

Savage, Anne and Nicholas Watson, trans. and intro. *Anchoritic Spirituality: Ancrene Wisse and Associated Works*, New York, 1991

Sayers, Dorothy L., *Four Sacred Plays*, London, 1948

Schiller, Gertrud, *Ikonographie der christlichen Kunst*, Band 5, *Die Apokalypse des Johannes*, Bildteil, Gütersloh, 1991

Schoeck, R. J., 'Alcock, John (1430–1500)', *Oxford Dictionary of National Biography*, Oxford University Press, 2004 [http://www.oxforddnb.com/view/article/289, accessed 2 April 2006]

Schwartzbaum, E., 'Three Tournai Tombslabs in England', *Gesta*, Vol.XX, 1981, pp. 89–97

Seidel, Linda, *Songs of Glory: The Romanesque Facades of Aquitaine*, Chicago and London, 1981

Southworth, John, *The English Medieval Minstrel*, Woodbridge, 1989

Spatz, Nancy, 'Church porches and the Liturgy in twelfth-century Rome', in Heffernan and Matter 2001, pp. 327–367

Stevens, Martin, *Four Middle English Mystery Cycles*, Princeton, 1987

Stone, Lawrence, *Sculpture in Britain: The Middle Ages*, Harmondsworth, 1972

Stookey, Laurence Hull, 'The Gothic Cathedral as the Heavenly Jerusalem: Liturgical and Theological Sources', *Gesta*, VIII, 1969, pp. 35–41

Swanson, R. N., ed., *The Church and the Book, Studies in Church History* vol. 38, Woodbridge, 2004

Swanson, R. N., ed., *The Church Retrospective, Studies in Church History* vol. 33, Woodbridge, 1997

Swanson, R. N., ed., *The Use and Abuse of Time in Christian History, Studies in Church History* 37, Woodbridge, 2002

Swanton, M., ed., *Exeter Cathedral: A Celebration*, Exeter, 1991

Symondson, Anthony and Stephen Arthur Bucknall, *Sir Ninian Comper: An Introduction to his Life and Work 'with complete gazetteer'*, Reading, 2006

Szarmach, Paul, ed, *An Introduction to the Medieval Mystics of Europe*, NY, 1984

Taylor, Rabun, *Roman Builders: A Study in Architectural Process*, Cambridge, 2003

Thiede, Carsten Peter, and Matthew d'Ancona, *The Quest for the True Cross*, London, 2000

Thompson, Benjamin, 'Introduction: Monasteries and Medieval Society', in Thompson 1999, pp. 1–33

Thompson, Benjamin, ed., *Monasteries and Society in Medieval Britain: Proceedings of the 1994 Harlaxton Symposium*, Stamford, 1999

Thompson, Pauline A., 'St Aethelthryth: The Making of History from Hagiography', in *Studies in English Language and Literature: Papers in honour of*

E. G. Stanley, ed. M. J. Toswell and E. M. Tyler, London and New York, 1996, pp. 475–492

Thompson, Pauline A. and Elizabeth Stevens, 'Gregory of Ely's Verse Life and Miracles of St Aethelthryth', in *Analecta Bollandiana*, 106, 1988, pp. 333–390

Thurlby, Malcolm, *The Herefordshire School of Romanesque Sculpture*, Logaston Herefs., 1999

Thurlby, Malcolm, 'The Romanesque Apse Vault at Peterborough Cathedral' in Buckton and Heslop 1994, pp. 171–186

Thurston, Herbert, *Familiar Prayers: Their Origin and History*, London, 1953

Tracy, Charles, *English Gothic Choir Stalls 1200-1400*, Woodbridge, 1987

Traherne, Thomas, *Poems, Centuries and Three Thanksgivings*, ed. Anne Ridler, Oxford, 1966

Tronzo, William, ed., *Italian Church Decoration of the Early Middle Ages and Early Renaissance*, Bologna, 1989

Tronzo, William, 'Apse Decoration, the Liturgy and the Perception of Art in Medieval Rome: S. Maria in Trastevere and S. Maria Maggiore', in Tronzo 1989, pp. 168–193

Tudor-Craig, Pamela, 'Bishop Grandisson's Provision for Music and Ceremony', in Swanton 1991, pp. 137–144

Tudor-Craig, Pamela, 'The Embellishments and Furnishings of the Medieval Church', in *Westminster Abbey*, New Bell's Cathedral Guides, London, 1986, pp. 115–140

Tudor-Craig, Pamela, 'The Iconography of Corpus Christi', in Porter, Hayes and Tombs 1997, pp. 315–337

Tudor-Craig, Pamela, 'The Iconography of Wisdom and the Frontispiece to the *BIBLE HISTORIALE*, British Library Additional Manuscript 18856', in Barron and Stratford 2002, pp. 110–127

Usher, Brett, 'Heton, Martin (1554–1609)', *Oxford Dictionary of National Biography*, Oxford university Press, 2004 [http://www.oxforddnb.com/view/article13138, accessed 15 Dec 2007]

van Os, Henk, with Eugène Honée, Hans Nieuwdorp, Bernhard Ridderbos, trans. Michael Hoyle, *The Art of Devotion*, London, 1994

Varty, Kenneth, *Reynard the Fox: A Study of the Fox in English Medieval Art*, Leicester, 1967

Verzar, Christine B., 'Text and Image in North Italian Romanesque Sculpture', in Kahn 1992, pp. 121–40

Visser, Margaret, *The Geometry of Love: Space, Time, Mystery and Meaning in an Ordinary Church*, London, 2000

von Allmen, J.-J., *Worship: Its Theology and Practice*, London, 1965

Ward, Benedicta, *High King of Heaven: Aspects of Early English Spirituality*, Mowbray, London, 1999

Ward, Benedicta, *Pilgrimage of the Heart*, Oxford, 2001

Ward, Benedicta, 'Preface', in Savage and Watson 1991, pp. 1–5

Ward, Benedicta, *Signs and Wonders*, Variorum Press, 1992

Ward, J. Neville, *Five for Sorrow, Ten for Joy: A Consideration of the Rosary*, London, 1971

Ward, J. Neville, *Friday Afternoon*, London, 1976

Webb, Diana, *Pilgrims and Pilgrimage in the Medieval West*, London, 1999

Webster, Leslie and Michelle Brown, eds, *The Transformation of the Roman World AD 400–900*, London, 1997

Wegman, Herman, 'Successio sanctorum', trans. Gordon Lathrop, in Alexander 1990, pp. 219–241

Wentersdorf, Karl P., 'The Symbolic Significance of *Figurae Scatalogicae* in Gothic Manuscripts', in Davidson 1984, pp. 1–9

Westermann, Claus, *The Living Psalms*, trans. J. R. Porter, Edinburgh, 1989

Westra, M. Salvina, ed., *A Talking of the Love of God*, The Hague, 1950

White, T. H., trans. and ed., *The Book of Beasts*, New York, 1954, repr. 1984

Wieck, Roger S., *Time Sanctified*, New York, 1988

Weir, Anthony and James Jerman, *Images of Lust: Sexual Carvings on Medieval Churches*, London, 1986

Wilkins, Eithne, *The Rose-Garden Game: The Symbolic Background to the European Prayer-Beads*, London, 1969

Williams, Jane Welch, *Bread, Wine and Money: The Windows of the Trades at Chartres Cathedral*, Chicago, 1993

Williams, Rowan, *Ponder These Things,: Praying with Icons of the Virgin*, Norwich, 2002

Wills, Garry, *Saint Augustine*, London, 2000

Wilson, Christopher, 'The Medieval Monuments', in Collinson, Ramsay and Sparks 1995, pp. 451–510

Winston-Allen, Anne, *Stories of the Rose: The Making of the Rosary in the Middle Ages*, University Park, Pennsylvania, 1997

Wood, Ian, 'The Transmission of Ideas', in Webster and Brown, 1997, pp. 111–127

Wood, Juanita, *Wooden Images: Misericords and Medieval England*, Madison NJ, 1999

Woodman, Francis, 'The Vault of the Ely Lady Chapel: Fourteenth or Fifteenth Century?', *Gesta*, 23, 1984, pp. 137–41

Wordsworth, Christopher and Henry Littlehales, *The Old Service Books of the English Church*, London, 1904

Wright, Craig, 'The Palm Sunday Procession in Medieval Chartres', in Fassler and Baltzer 2000, pp. 344–371

Zarnecki, George, 'Some Observations Concerning the Romanesque Doorways of Ely Cathedral', in *Studies in Medieval History Presented to R. Allen Brown*, ed. Christopher Harper-Bill, Woodbridge, 1989, pp. 345–352

Zarnecki, George, *The Early Sculpture of Ely Cathedral*, London, 1958

Zarnecki, George, *Later English Romanesque Sculpture 1140–1210*, London, 1953

Index